Arduino Experiments

Beginner to Pro

A Complete Guide to Use, Understand and Build Amazing Projects with Arduino Sensors

---

Author
Ekansh Mann

Edition
First Edition
Published 2026

About the Author

Ekansh Mann

Ekansh Mann is 8 years old and is currently studying in Class 3.

This project started simply - Ekansh received a 37-sensor Arduino kit and wanted to learn what every single sensor did. Rather than just experimenting for himself, he decided to write down everything he learned so that other beginners could benefit too. The result is this book: 101 experiments, written to be understood by anyone, at any age.

Ekansh believes that electronics and coding should not be scary or complicated. He has designed every experiment in this book to be clear, simple, and fun - the same way he would explain it to a friend in his class.

If an 8-year-old can understand it, anyone can.

First book **at age 8**

101 experiments completed

37 sensors explored

Class 3 Student

> *"I want every kid to know that electronics is not difficult. You just need to try."*
> - **Ekansh Mann**

Table of Contents

Level 2 - Sensor + Output Projects (56–90)

Introduction

Welcome to Arduino

If you have never written a line of code or connected a wire in your life, this book was written for you. Arduino is a small, affordable circuit board with a brain - it can read signals from the world around it (sensors) and respond with actions (lights, sounds, motors). Millions of students, hobbyists, and engineers use it every day to build real things.

This book gives you 101 hands-on experiments using a 37-sensor kit. You will start with something as simple as pressing a button, and by the end you will have built a multi-sensor smart home monitoring system. Every step is explained in plain English. No electronics background required.

What is the Arduino Uno?

The Arduino Uno is the board you will use throughout this book. It is about the size of a credit card and has two rows of metal pins along its edges - these are how you connect sensors and other components. On one side are digital pins (numbered 0–13) that read or send simple ON/OFF signals. On the other side are analog pins (A0–A5) that can read a range of values, like how bright a light is or how loud a sound is.

In the centre of the board is a small black chip - this is the microcontroller, the brain that runs your code. The board connects to your computer with a USB cable, which also powers it during development. You do not need batteries to get started.

Installing the Arduino IDE

The Arduino IDE (Integrated Development Environment) is the free software you use to write and upload code to your board. Here is how to install it:

1. Open your web browser and go to arduino.cc/en/software
2. Click the download button for your operating system (Windows, Mac, or Linux)
3. Run the downloaded installer and follow the on-screen steps
4. Once installed, open the Arduino IDE - you will see a white editing area where you write code

Next, connect your Arduino Uno to your computer with the USB cable. In the IDE, go to Tools → Board and select "Arduino Uno". Then go to Tools → Port and select the port that shows your Arduino (on Windows it looks like COM3, on Mac like /dev/cu.usbmodem).

You are now ready to upload your first program.

Installing Libraries

Some sensors in this book need extra software called libraries - think of them as instruction packs that teach Arduino how to talk to a specific sensor. Here is how to install them:

1. In the Arduino IDE, go to Sketch → Include Library → Manage Libraries
2. A search box will appear - type the name of the library you need
3. Find the correct library in the list and click Install
4. Wait for the installation to finish, then close the window

Libraries you will need for this book:

- DHT sensor library by Adafruit - for the DHT11 temperature and humidity sensor
- OneWire by Paul Stoffregen - for the DS18B20 temperature sensor
- DallasTemperature by Miles Burton - also for the DS18B20
- IRremote by z3t0 - for the IR receiver and emitter modules

Install all four before you begin the experiments that use them. If a library is already installed, the button will say Update instead of Install.

Understanding the Serial Monitor

The Serial Monitor is a window that lets your Arduino send text messages to your computer screen. It is how you will see sensor readings, check if your code is working, and observe results in real time.

To open it, click the magnifying glass icon in the top-right corner of the Arduino IDE, or go to Tools → Serial Monitor. Make sure the baud rate at the bottom of the window matches what is in your code - most experiments in this book use 9600.

When your Arduino sends Serial.println("Hello"), the word Hello appears in the Serial Monitor window. When it sends a number like Serial.println(lightValue), you will see the actual reading from your sensor. You will use this constantly throughout the book.

How to Read This Book

Each experiment follows the same layout so you always know where to look:

Sensor - tells you which sensor from the kit is used

Difficulty - one star (★) means beginner, two stars (★★) means intermediate, three stars (★★★) means pro

Objective - one sentence explaining what you will achieve

How It Works - a plain English explanation of how the sensor or concept works

Concepts Learned - the coding and electronics ideas introduced

Components Required - everything you need from your kit

Wiring - a table showing which pin connects where, plus a connection diagram

Arduino Code - the complete code to copy into your IDE

How the Code Works - a plain English walkthrough of what the code does

Real-World Applications - where this technology is used in the real world

Understanding Your Sensor Kit

Your 37-sensor kit contains a variety of input and output modules. Input modules (sensors) detect something from the world - light, sound, heat, movement. Output modules produce something - a buzzer makes sound, an LED makes light, a relay switches a device on or off.

Every module in the kit has three or four pins. Most have three:

- S (Signal) - the data pin, connects to an Arduino digital or analog pin
- + (VCC) - power, connects to Arduino 5V
- – (GND) - ground, connects to Arduino GND

A few modules have four pins and add a separate analog output (A0) or digital output (D0). The wiring table in every experiment tells you exactly where each pin goes, so you never need to guess.

Use jumper wires to make all connections. The female end plugs into the sensor module, and the male end plugs into the Arduino. Keep your wiring neat - it makes finding mistakes much easier.

Your First Upload - Blink Test

Before starting any experiment, test that your Arduino and IDE are working with this simple built-in example:

1. In the Arduino IDE go to File → Examples → 01.Basics → Blink
2. Click the Upload button (the right-arrow icon)
3. Wait a few seconds - you will see "Done uploading" at the bottom
4. The small orange LED on your Arduino board should now be blinking on and off every second

If it blinks, everything is working. If you see an error, double-check that the correct Board and Port are selected under the Tools menu.

Kit & Equipments used

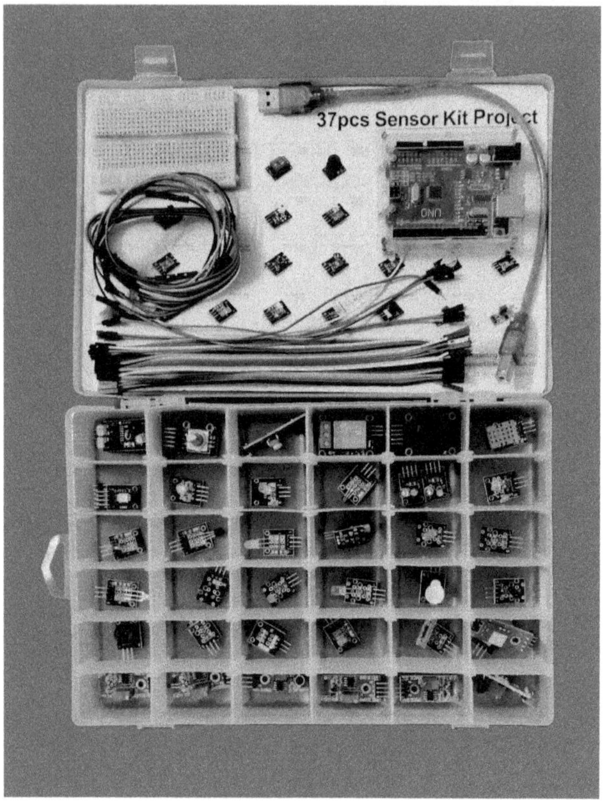

Kit Specifications

Everything you need to complete all 101 experiments in this book.

Kit	37-in-1 Sensor Kit
Board	Arduino Uno R3 (ATmega328P, 16MHz)
IDE	Arduino IDE 2.x or later
USB Cable	Type-A to Type-B (included in kit)
Jumper Wires	-
Breadboard	2
Power	USB from computer (5V, up to 500mA)
OS Support	Windows 11

> Every experiment in this book uses only components included in this kit plus the Arduino Uno board.

Sensor Reference Guide

A quick reference for all 37 sensors included in this kit.

#	Name	Image	Function	Description
1	**Avoidance**		Obstacle detection using infrared reflection	Detects nearby objects without contact. Commonly used in line-following and obstacle-avoiding robots.
2	**Rotary Encoder**		Measures rotational movement and direction	Produces pulses when rotated, allowing precise position or speed measurement.
3	**Tracking Sensor**		Line tracking	Uses infrared light to detect black/white surfaces, commonly used in line-following robots.
4	**Relay**		Switches higher-voltage devices using a low-voltage signal	Allows Arduino to control lamps, motors, pumps, and other AC/DC loads.

#	Name	Image	Function	Description
5	**Joystick Module**		2-axis position input	Provides X and Y analog outputs plus a push-button function.
6	**DHT11 Temp & Humidity**		Measures temperature and humidity	Low-cost digital sensor used in weather stations and environmental monitoring.
7	**7 Color Flash LED**		Automatic color-changing LED	Cycles through multiple colors without needing external control.
8	**RGB LED**		Multi-color light output	Contains red, green, and blue LEDs that can be mixed to create various colors.
9	**SMD RGB LED Module**		RGB light generation	Surface-mount RGB LED used for color indication and lighting projects.
10	**Analog Hall Sensor**		Magnetic field measurement	Produces an analog voltage proportional to magnetic field strength.
11	**Magic Light Cup**		Interactive LED effect	Works with tilt detection to create alternating light effects.
12	**Heartbeat Sensor**		Pulse detection	Detects blood flow changes through a fingertip and estimates heart rate.
13	**Mercury Switch**		Tilt detection	Uses a mercury droplet to open or close a circuit when tilted.
14	**DS18B20 Temp Sensor**		Digital temperature measurement	Accurate waterproof-compatible temperature sensor using OneWire communication.
15	**Dual Color LED**		Two-color indication	Displays different colors depending on current direction or control signals.

#	Name	Image	Function	Description
16	**Laser Module**		Laser light generation	Emits a focused laser beam for alignment, communication, and optical experiments.
17	**Tilt Switch**		Orientation detection	Detects when the module is tilted beyond a certain angle.
18	**Analog Temperature**		Temperature measurement	Outputs an analog voltage corresponding to ambient temperature.
19	**Mini Two-Color LED**		Status indication	Compact dual-color LED module for visual feedback.
20	**Button Switch Module**		User input	Simple momentary push-button for triggering actions.
21	**Photo-Resistor (LDR)**		Light intensity measurement	Resistance changes based on ambient light levels.
22	**IR Emission Module**		Infrared signal transmission	Emits IR light for remote-control and communication applications.
23	**Buzzer Module (Active)**		Sound generation	Produces a tone when power is applied.
24	**Shock Switch Module**		Vibration and impact detection	Detects sudden movement, tapping, or shocks.
25	**Passive Buzzer**		Programmable sound generation	Requires PWM signals from Arduino to generate different tones and melodies.
26	**Mini Reed Switch**		Magnetic switch detection	Activates when a magnet comes close.

#	Name	Image	Function	Description
27	**Analog Hall Sensor Module**		Magnetic field sensing	Another Hall-effect sensor version providing analog output.
28	**IR Receiver Module**		Infrared signal reception	Receives signals from TV remotes and IR transmitters.
29	**Knock Sensor**		Knock and vibration detection	Detects taps on surfaces for interactive projects.
30	**Photo Interrupter**		Object interruption detection	Detects when an object blocks the optical path between emitter and receiver.
31	**Reed Switch Module**		Magnetic proximity detection	Switches state in the presence of a magnetic field.
32	**Digital Temperature**		Digital temperature measurement	Provides temperature status through digital output.
33	**Small Sound Sensor**		Sound level detection	Detects claps, speech, and other sound events.
34	**Metal Touch Sensor**		Touch detection	Senses touch through conductive metal surfaces.
35	**High-Sensitivity Voice**		Enhanced sound detection	More sensitive than standard sound sensors, useful for voice-triggered projects.
36	**Linear Hall Sensor**		Linear magnetic field measurement	Outputs a varying voltage proportional to magnetic field strength.
37	**Flame Sensor Module**		Flame detection	Detects infrared light emitted by flames, useful for fire alarm projects.

Level 1 - Single Sensor Experiments

Experiment 1 | Read Button State

Sensor: Button Switch Module
Difficulty: ★ Beginner
Objective: Learn how Arduino reads a digital input from a sensor/module.

Concepts Learned

- What a sensor input is
- HIGH and LOW signals
- Digital pins
- pinMode() - sets a pin as INPUT or OUTPUT
- digitalRead() - reads HIGH or LOW from a digital pin
- Serial Monitor - displays values on your computer

Components Required

Component	Qty
Arduino Uno	1
Button Switch Module	1
Jumper Wires	3
USB Cable	1

How It Works

The Button Module contains a simple momentary switch. When you press it, two metal contacts inside touch each other and complete an electrical circuit, pulling the signal pin to the same voltage as GND. When you release it, a spring pushes the contacts apart and the pin floats back up - the Arduino reads this as LOW when pressed and HIGH when released. This experiment is the foundation for every input experiment in this book.

Wiring

Button Module Pin	Arduino Pin
S	D2
+	5V
-	GND

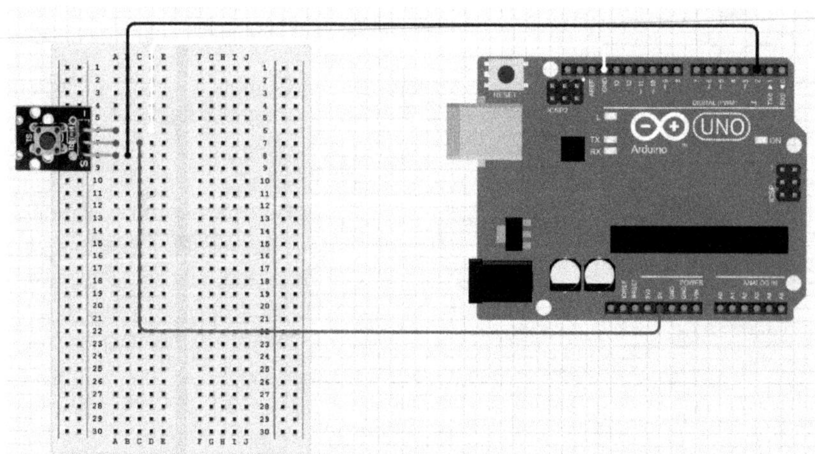

Arduino Code & Serial Monitor Output

```
int buttonPin = 2;

void setup() {
  pinMode(buttonPin, INPUT);
  Serial.begin(9600);
}

void loop() {
  int buttonState = digitalRead(buttonPin);
  if (buttonState == LOW) {
    Serial.println("Button Pressed");
  } else {
    Serial.println("Button Released");
  }
  delay(100);
}
```

How the Code Works

int buttonPin = 2 declares which Arduino pin is connected to the button. In setup(), pinMode(buttonPin, INPUT) tells the Arduino that pin 2 is for reading - not writing. Serial.begin(9600) opens communication with your computer at 9600 baud. In loop(), digitalRead(buttonPin) reads the current state of the pin every 100 milliseconds. The if-else checks whether that state is LOW (pressed) or HIGH (released) and prints the appropriate message. The delay(100) at the end means the loop runs about 10 times per second.

Real-World Applications

- Keyboard keys and TV remote controls
- Elevator call buttons
- Doorbell systems
- Game controllers and joysticks
- Emergency stop buttons in machinery

Experiment 2 | Button Counter

Sensor: Button Switch Module
Difficulty: ★ Beginner
Objective: Count how many times the button has been pressed.

How It Works

To count button presses accurately we need to detect the exact moment the button transitions from released to pressed - called the falling edge. If we simply checked whether the button was pressed on every loop iteration, we would count hundreds of times during a single press. Instead, we compare the current state to the previous state and only count when a change from HIGH to LOW occurs.

Concepts Learned

- Digital Input
- Variables - storing and updating values
- Edge Detection - detecting the moment a button changes state
- Counting Events
- Serial Monitor

Components Required

Component	Qty
Arduino Uno	1

Component	Qty
Button Module	1
Jumper Wires	3

Wiring

Button Module Pin	Arduino Pin
S	D2
+	5V
-	GND

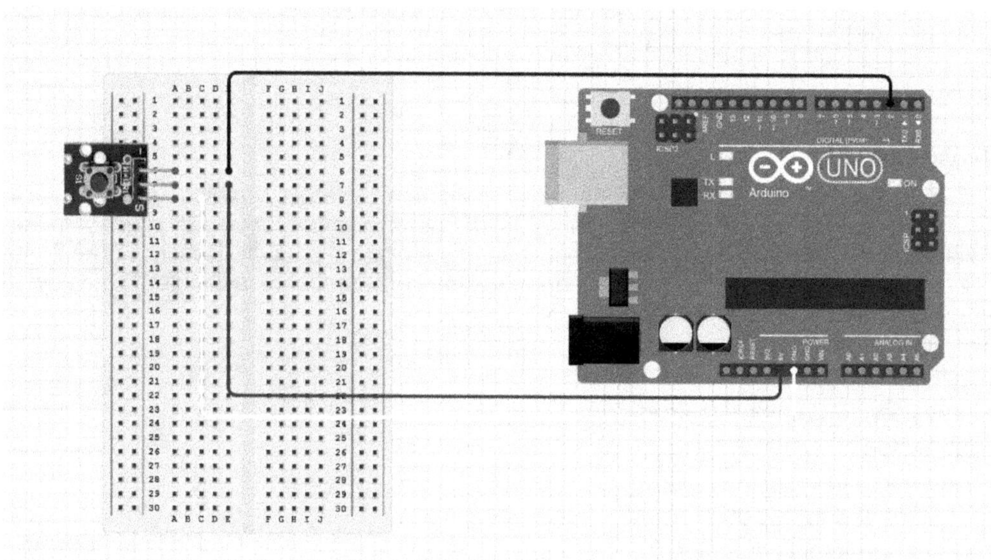

Arduino Code & Serial Monitor Output

```
int buttonPin = 2;
int buttonState = HIGH;
int lastButtonState = HIGH;
int count = 0;

void setup() {
  pinMode(buttonPin, INPUT);
  Serial.begin(9600);
}

void loop() {
  buttonState = digitalRead(buttonPin);
  // Active LOW - detect press on falling edge
  if (buttonState == LOW && lastButtonState ==
HIGH) {
    count++;
    Serial.print("Button Count: ");
    Serial.println(count);
    delay(200); // debounce
  }
  lastButtonState = buttonState;
}
```

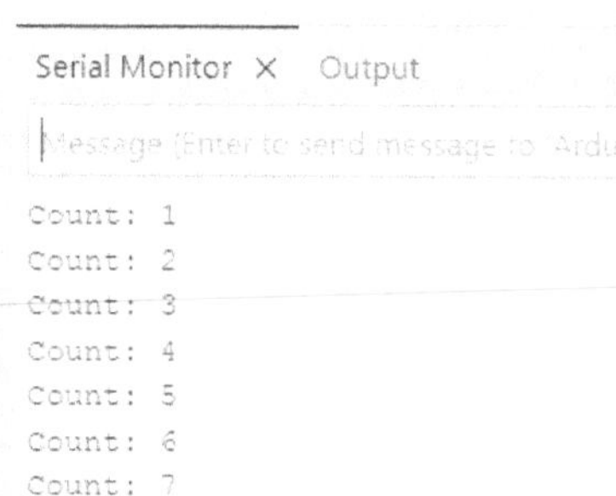

How the Code Works

Four variables are declared at the top: buttonPin stores the pin number, buttonState and lastButtonState track current and previous readings, and count holds the running total. In loop(), the current state is read and compared to lastButtonState. The condition buttonState == LOW && lastButtonState == HIGH is only true for one single loop iteration - the exact moment of press. When true, count is incremented, printed, and a 200ms debounce delay prevents a single physical press from being counted twice due to contact bounce. At the end of loop(), lastButtonState = buttonState updates the memory for next time.

Real-World Applications

- Visitor counters at entry points
- Score counters in games and sports
- Production line unit counters
- Inventory click-counters
- Vote counting machines

Experiment 3 | Long Press Detector

Sensor: Button Switch Module

Difficulty: ★ Beginner

Objective: Detect whether a button press is short or long.

How It Works

To measure how long a button is held, we record the time when pressing starts and compare it to the time when it ends. Arduino's millis() function returns the number of milliseconds since the board was powered on - a constantly growing counter. By saving this value at press-start and subtracting it from the value at press-release, we get the exact hold duration in milliseconds. 2000 milliseconds equals 2 seconds.

Concepts Learned

- millis() - reads elapsed time in milliseconds
- Measuring elapsed time between events
- Press and release events
- Real-world button behaviour

Components Required

Component	Qty
Arduino Uno	1
Button Module	1
Jumper Wires	3

Wiring

Button Module Pin	Arduino Pin
S	D2
+	5V
-	GND

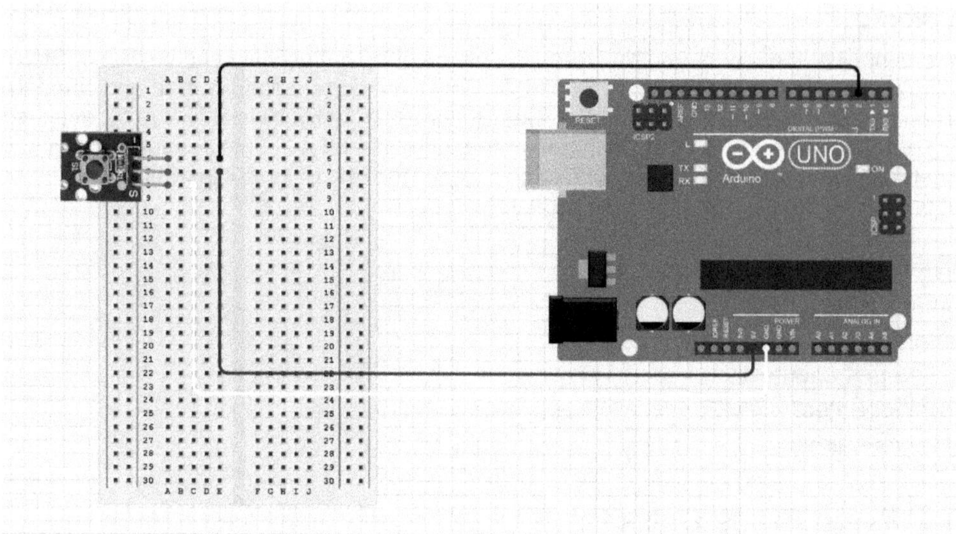

Arduino Code & Serial Monitor Output

```
const int buttonPin = 2;
unsigned long pressTime = 0;
bool buttonPressed = false;

void setup() {
  pinMode(buttonPin, INPUT_PULLUP);
  Serial.begin(9600);
}

void loop() {
  int buttonState = digitalRead(buttonPin);

  // Button pressed (falling edge)
  if (buttonState == LOW && !buttonPressed) {
    pressTime = millis();
    buttonPressed = true;
  }

  // Button released (rising edge)
  if (buttonState == HIGH && buttonPressed) {
    unsigned long holdTime = millis() - pressTime;
    if (holdTime >= 2000) {
      Serial.println("Long Press Detected");
    } else {
      Serial.println("Short Press");
    }
    buttonPressed = false;
  }
}
```

Output Serial Monitor ×

```
Short Press
Short Press
Short Press
Short Press
Short Press
Short Press
Long Press Detected
Long Press Detected
Long Press Detected
Long Press Detected
```

How the Code Works

pressTime is an unsigned long - a large integer that can hold the millisecond counter without overflowing. buttonPressed is a boolean flag that prevents the press-start time from being overwritten while the button is still held. When the button goes LOW and buttonPressed is false, we record millis() into pressTime and set the flag true. When the button goes HIGH again (release), we calculate holdTime = millis() - pressTime. If holdTime is 2000 or more, it was a long press; otherwise a short press. Finally, buttonPressed resets to false ready for the next interaction.

Real-World Applications

- Phone power buttons (short = wake, long = power off)
- Smart bulbs (short = toggle on/off, long = change colour)
- Device factory reset triggers
- Mode-switching on single-button devices
- Wearable gadget controls

Experiment 4 | Measure Light Intensity

Sensor: Photo-Resistor (LDR) Module

Difficulty: ★ Beginner

Objective: Read the ambient light level and display it in the Serial Monitor.

How It Works

A Photo-Resistor (also called an LDR, or Light Dependent Resistor) changes its electrical resistance depending on how much light falls on it. In bright light its resistance drops; in darkness it rises. The sensor module converts this changing resistance into a changing voltage using a voltage divider circuit. The Arduino's analog pin reads this voltage and converts it to a number between 0 (0V) and 1023 (5V) - this is your light intensity reading.

Concepts Learned

- Analog Input - reading a range of values (0–1023)
- analogRead() - reads voltage as a number
- Light sensing
- Interpreting sensor values

Components Required

Component	Qty
Arduino Uno	1
Photo-Resistor Module	1
Jumper Wires	3

Wiring

Photo-Resistor Pin	Arduino Pin
S	A0
+	5V
-	GND

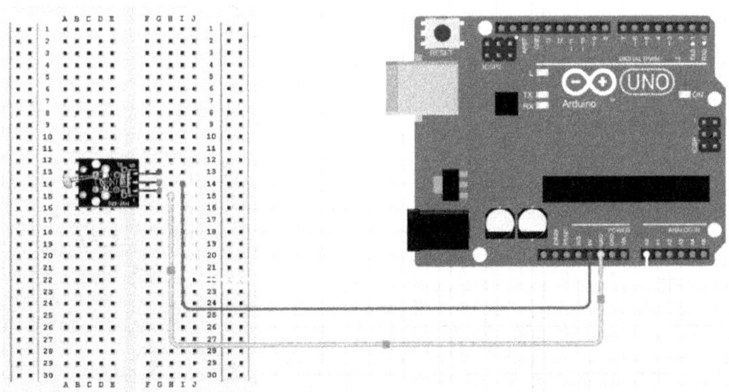

Arduino Code & Serial Monitor Output

```
const int ldrPin = A0;

void setup() {
  Serial.begin(9600);
}

void loop() {
  int lightValue = analogRead(ldrPin);
  Serial.print("Light Intensity: ");
  Serial.println(lightValue);
  delay(500);
}
```

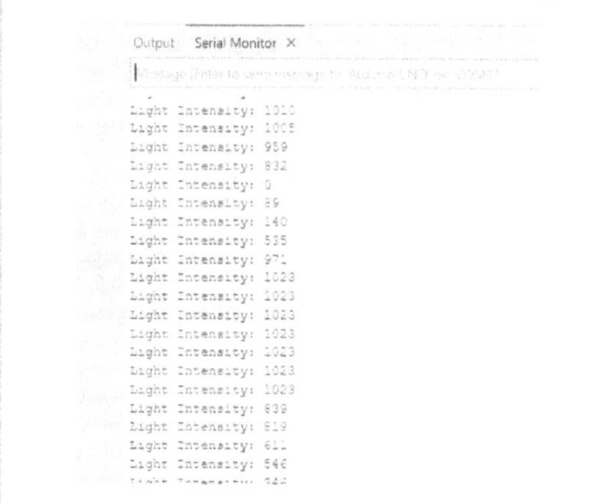

How the Code Works

const int ldrPin = A0 declares that the LDR is connected to the analog pin A0. Notice we use const - this means the value cannot accidentally be changed later in the code. There is no pinMode() call here because analog input pins do not need to be configured. In loop(), analogRead(ldrPin) reads the current voltage on the pin and converts it to a number from 0 to 1023. Serial.print() outputs the label and Serial.println() outputs the value followed by a new line. The delay(500) pauses for half a second between readings - enough to see changes without flooding the Serial Monitor.

Real-World Applications

- Automatic street lights
- Mobile phone brightness control
- Solar trackers
- Smart home lighting systems
- Greenhouse and plant growth monitoring

Experiment 5 | Day vs Night Detector

Sensor: Photo-Resistor (LDR) Module

Difficulty: ★ Beginner

Objective: Determine whether the environment is Day or Night based on a light threshold.

How It Works

The LDR (Light Dependent Resistor) changes its electrical resistance based on how much light hits it. In darkness the resistance is high; in bright light it drops. The Arduino reads this as a number between 0 and 1023 using analogRead(). By comparing that number to a threshold, we can decide whether it is day or night.

Concepts Learned

- Threshold comparisons
- if-else decision making
- Sensor-based classification
- Calibrating a threshold value

Components Required

Component	Qty
Arduino Uno	1
Photo-Resistor Module	1
Jumper Wires	3

Wiring

LDR Module Pin	Arduino Pin
S	A0
+	5V
-	GND

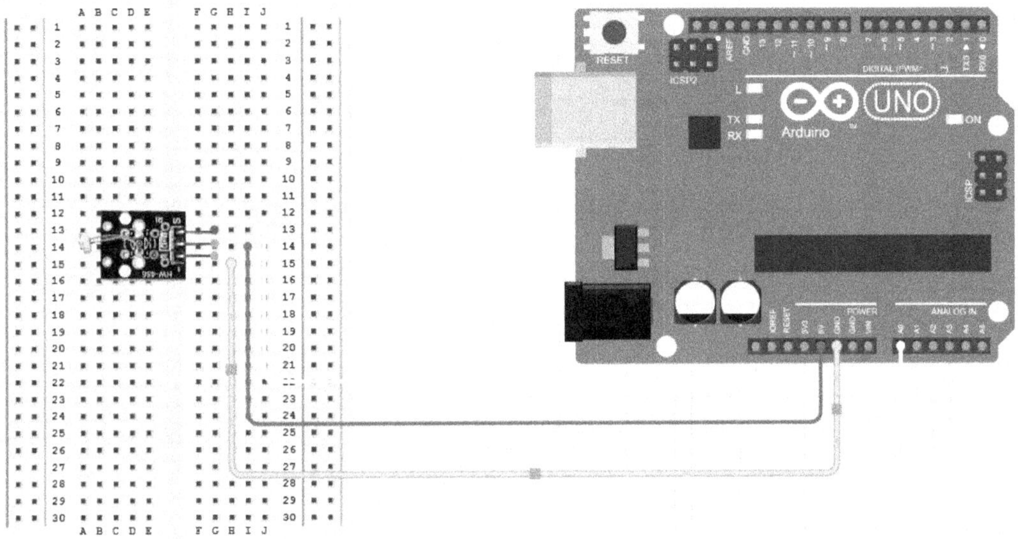

Arduino Code & Serial Monitor Output

```
const int ldrPin = A0;
const int threshold = 400;

void setup() {
  Serial.begin(9600);
}

void loop() {
  int lightValue = analogRead(ldrPin);
  Serial.print("Light: ");
  Serial.print(lightValue);
  if (lightValue > threshold) {
    Serial.println(" --> DAY");
  } else {
    Serial.println(" --> NIGHT");
  }
  delay(500);
}
```

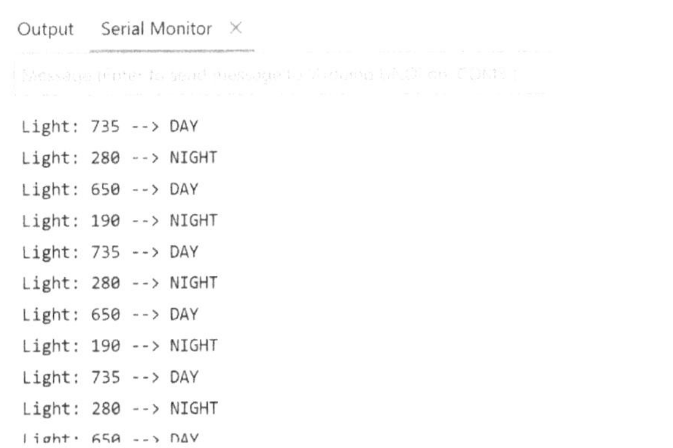

How the Code Works

The constant threshold = 400 is the dividing line between day and night - you can adjust this number to suit your environment. Inside loop(), analogRead(ldrPin) reads the current light level. The if-else block then compares it to the threshold and prints either DAY or NIGHT to the Serial Monitor. The delay(500) means it checks twice per second.

Real-World Applications

- Automatic street light switching
- Solar garden lights
- Smart home curtain control
- Energy-saving lighting systems
- Security lighting triggers

Experiment 6 | Light Threshold Monitor

Sensor: Photo-Resistor (LDR) Module
Difficulty: ★ Beginner
Objective: Monitor whether light intensity crosses a predefined threshold and display a warning.

How It Works

This experiment uses the same LDR sensor as before, but focuses on monitoring a specific threshold and generating a warning when it is crossed. This is the core idea behind most automated alert systems - watch a value, act when it passes a limit.

Concepts Learned

- Alert generation from sensor data
- Monitoring systems
- Real-world automation logic
- Setting threshold values

Components Required

Component	Qty
Arduino Uno	1
Photo-Resistor Module	1
Jumper Wires	3

Wiring

LDR Module Pin	Arduino Pin
S	A0
+	5V
-	GND

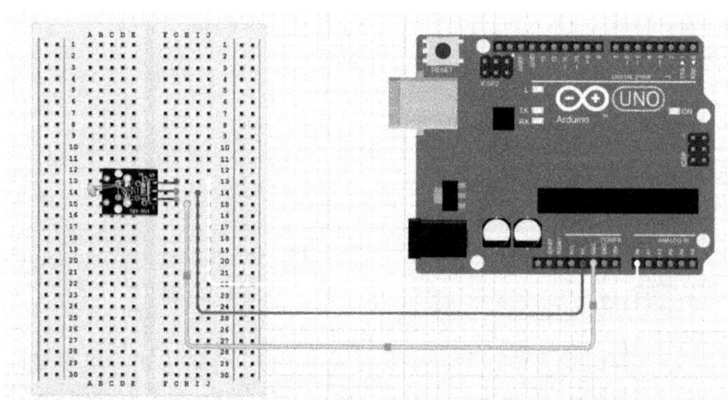

Arduino Code & Serial Monitor Output

```
const int ldrPin = A0;
const int threshold = 500;

void setup() {
  Serial.begin(9600);
}

void loop() {
  int lightValue = analogRead(ldrPin);
  Serial.print("Light: ");
  Serial.print(lightValue);
  if (lightValue > threshold) {
    Serial.println(" --> ABOVE
THRESHOLD");
  } else {
    Serial.println(" --> BELOW
THRESHOLD");
  }
  delay(500);
}
```

Output   Serial Monitor ×

Message (Enter to send message to 'Arduino UNO' on 'COM3')

```
Light: 735 --> ABOVE THRESHOLD
Light: 280 --> BELOW THRESHOLD
Light: 650 --> ABOVE THRESHOLD
Light: 190 --> BELOW THRESHOLD
Light: 723 --> ABOVE THRESHOLD
Light: 155 --> BELOW THRESHOLD
Light: 481 --> BELOW THRESHOLD
Light: 301 --> BELOW THRESHOLD
Light: 912 --> ABOVE THRESHOLD
Light: 87  --> BELOW THRESHOLD
Light: 654 --> ABOVE THRESHOLD
Light: 245 --> BELOW THRESHOLD
Light: 835 --> ABOVE THRESHOLD
Light: 123 --> BELOW THRESHOLD
Light: 760 --> ABOVE THRESHOLD
```

How the Code Works

threshold = 500 is the alert level. Every 500 milliseconds the code reads the light sensor and compares it. If the reading is above the threshold it prints ABOVE THRESHOLD, otherwise BELOW THRESHOLD. The structure is identical to Experiment 5 - the key learning here is that the same sensor and same code pattern can serve many different purposes just by changing the threshold value.

Real-World Applications

- Warehouse lighting monitors
- Smart agriculture systems
- Solar panel monitoring
- Security lighting systems
- Industrial light level monitoring

Experiment 7 | Sound Level Monitor

Sensor: KY-038 Sound Sensor

Difficulty: ★ Beginner

Objective: Measure ambient sound level and display the reading in the Serial Monitor.

How It Works

The KY-038 sound sensor has a small microphone that converts sound waves into a changing electrical voltage. The louder the sound, the higher the voltage spike. The Arduino reads this through its analog pin as a number from 0 to 1023. In a quiet room the reading will sit low and steady; a clap will cause a sudden spike to a much higher value.

Concepts Learned

- Analog sound sensing
- Reading microphone output
- Signal amplitude
- Mapping values to descriptive labels

Components Required

Component	Qty
Arduino Uno	1
KY-038 Sound Sensor	1
Jumper Wires	3

Wiring

Sound Sensor Pin	Arduino Pin
A0	A0
+	5V
G	GND

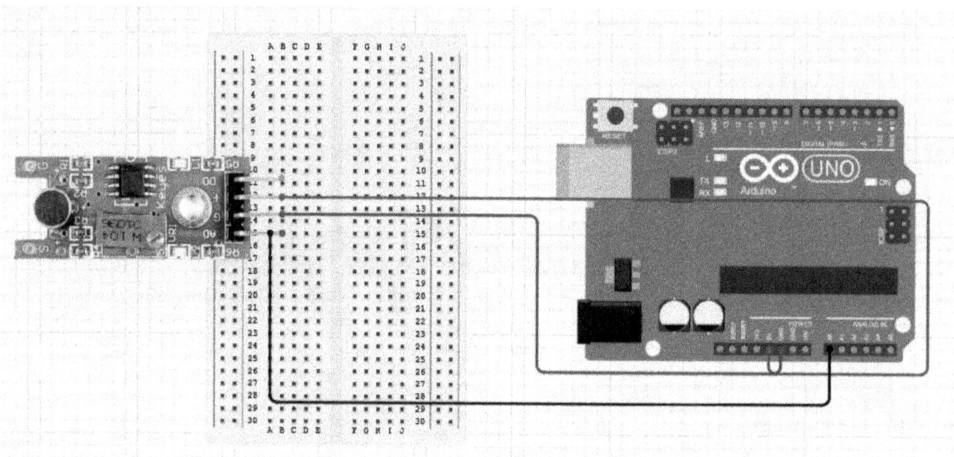

Arduino Code & Serial Monitor Output

```
const int soundPin = A0;

void setup() {
  Serial.begin(9600);
}

void loop() {
  int soundLevel = analogRead(soundPin);
  Serial.print("Sound Level: ");
  Serial.println(soundLevel);
  delay(100);
}
```

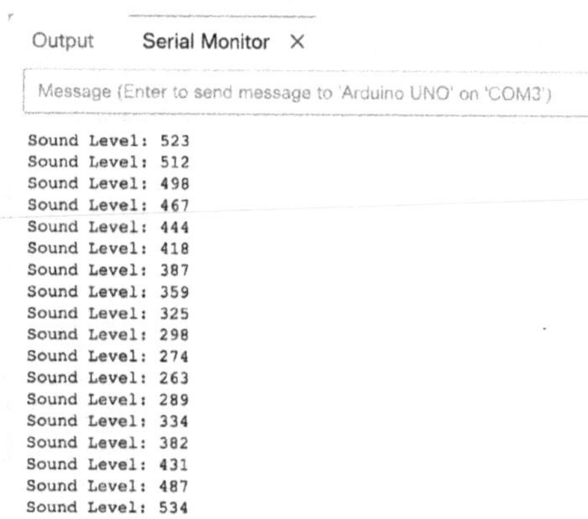

How the Code Works

analogRead(soundPin) continuously reads the microphone voltage. The result is printed directly to the Serial Monitor so you can observe how different sounds affect the reading. There are no thresholds here - this experiment is about observation. Try whispering, speaking normally, clapping, and tapping the desk while watching the numbers to understand the sensor's range.

Real-World Applications

- Noise level meters
- Library/office quiet monitors
- Industrial safety alerts
- Baby room monitors
- Sound-activated logging systems

Experiment 8 | Loud Sound Detection

Sensor: KY-038 Sound Sensor

Difficulty: ★ Beginner

Objective: Classify the sound level into named categories and print them to the Serial Monitor.

How It Works

Building on the previous experiment, we now classify the sound level into named categories. Instead of just showing raw numbers, the code maps ranges of values to descriptions like Quiet Room or Clap. This is how real noise-monitoring devices work - they convert numbers into meaningful labels.

Concepts Learned

- Multi-level threshold comparisons
- else-if chains
- Sound classification
- Real-time feedback

Components Required

Component	Qty
Arduino Uno	1
KY-038 Sound Sensor	1
Jumper Wires	3

Wiring

Sound Sensor Pin	Arduino Pin
A0	A0
+	5V
G	GND

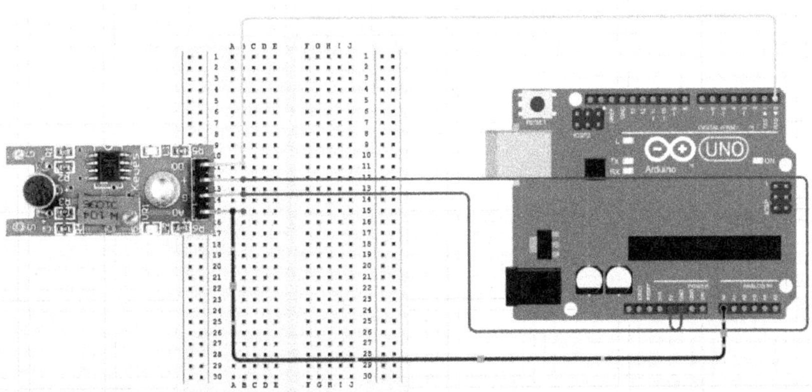

Arduino Code & Serial Monitor Output

```
const int soundPin = A0;

void setup() {
  Serial.begin(9600);
}

void loop() {
  int level = analogRead(soundPin);
  if (level <= 50)
Serial.println("Quiet Room");
  else if (level <= 150)
Serial.println("Conversation");
  else if (level <= 400)
Serial.println("Loud Speaking");
  else if (level <= 700)
Serial.println("Desk Tap");
  else
Serial.println("CLAP / LOUD NOISE");
  delay(100);
}
```

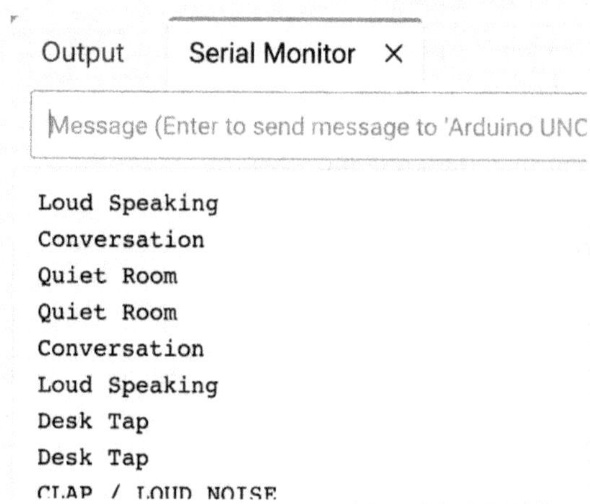

How the Code Works

The chain of else-if statements checks the sound level against five ranges in order from quietest to loudest. The first condition that is true will print its label and the rest are skipped. Notice the ranges - 0 to 50 is silence, while 800 or above is a clap. You may need to adjust these numbers after observing your own sensor readings from Experiment 7.

Real-World Applications

- Classroom noise monitors
- Sound-level warning systems
- Conference room monitors
- Construction site safety
- Hearing protection alerts

Experiment 9 | Clap Detector

Sensor: KY-038 Sound Sensor

Difficulty: ★ Beginner

Objective: Detect a clap event and print a message to the Serial Monitor.

How It Works

A clap produces a very short, very loud burst of sound - a spike in the sensor reading. By setting a threshold high enough to ignore normal conversation but low enough to catch a clap, we can detect this specific event. The delay(500) after detection prevents one clap from being counted multiple times.

Concepts Learned

- Impulse detection
- Single-threshold trigger
- Event-based output
- Debounce delay

Components Required

Component	Qty
Arduino Uno	1

Component	Qty
KY-038 Sound Sensor	1
Jumper Wires	3

Wiring

Sound Sensor Pin	Arduino Pin
A0	A0
+	5V
G	GND

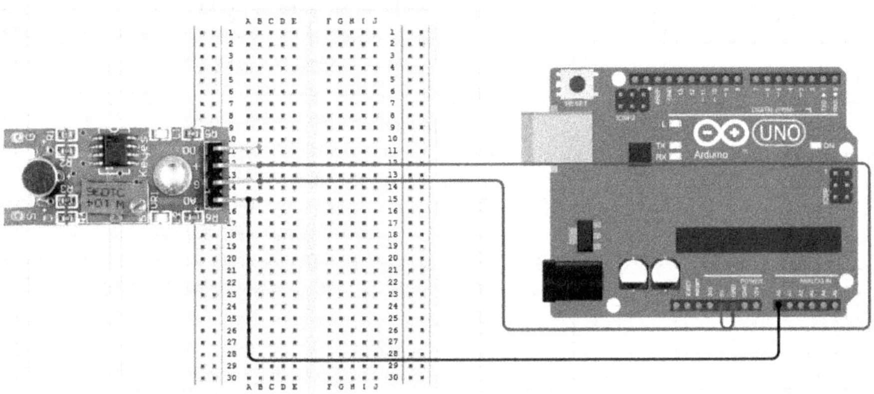

Arduino Code & Serial Monitor Output

```
const int soundPin = A0;
const int clapThreshold = 600;

void setup() {
  Serial.begin(9600);
}

void loop() {
  int soundLevel = analogRead(soundPin);
  if (soundLevel > clapThreshold) {
    Serial.println("CLAP DETECTED!");
    delay(500);
  }
}
```

How the Code Works

clapThreshold = 600 is set high enough to ignore background noise. When a sound spike exceeds this value, the code immediately prints CLAP DETECTED! and waits 500 milliseconds before checking again. That waiting period is the debounce - without it, one clap would trigger dozens of detections because the spike lasts several milliseconds.

Real-World Applications

- Clap-to-switch lights
- Hands-free device triggers
- Applause meters
- Interactive installations
- Sound-activated cameras

Experiment 10 | Voice Detection

Sensor: High-Sensitivity Voice Sensor
Difficulty: ★ Beginner
Objective: Detect the presence of human voice or sound and display a message.

How It Works

The high-sensitivity voice sensor uses a more sensitive microphone than the standard sound sensor. It has a built-in comparator that outputs a clean digital HIGH or LOW signal - HIGH when sound is detected above the sensitivity level set by its onboard potentiometer. This makes it much simpler to use than reading analog values.

Concepts Learned

- Digital sensor output
- Active LOW logic
- Sound-triggered events
- Using D0 pin of sound sensor

Components Required

Component	Qty
Arduino Uno	1
High-Sensitivity Voice Sensor	1
Jumper Wires	3

Wiring

Voice Sensor Pin	Arduino Pin
D0	D2
+	5V
G	GND

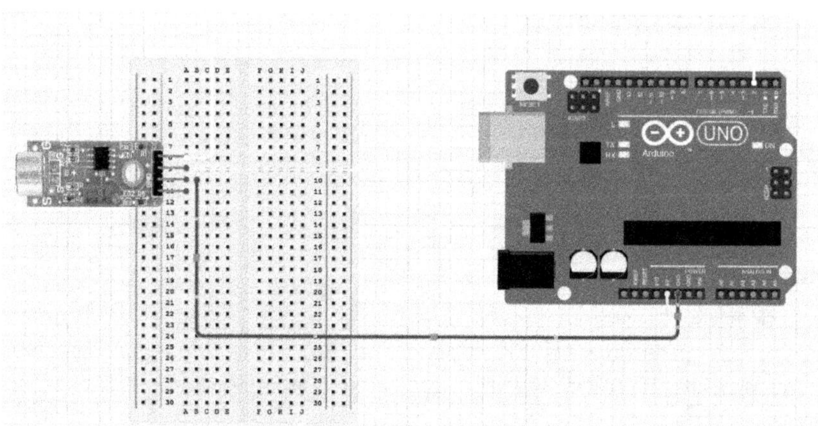

Arduino Code & Serial Monitor Output

```
const int voicePin = 2;

void setup() {
  pinMode(voicePin, INPUT);
  Serial.begin(9600);
}

void loop() {
  int voiceState = digitalRead(voicePin);
  if (voiceState == LOW) {
    Serial.println("VOICE DETECTED");
    delay(300);
  }
}
```

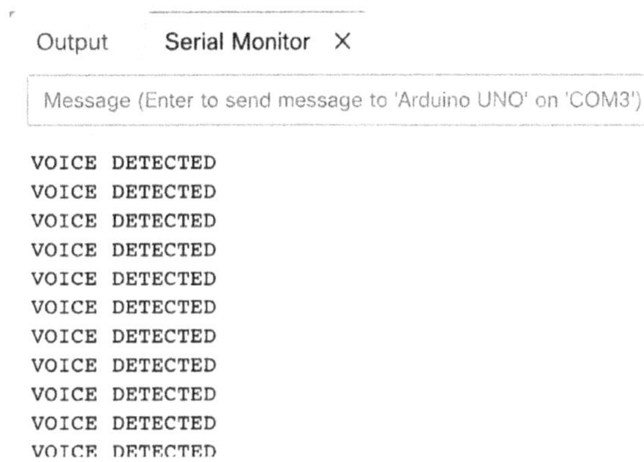

How the Code Works

pinMode(voicePin, INPUT) sets pin 2 to listen for signals. In the loop, digitalRead(voicePin) returns either HIGH or LOW. When it reads LOW - meaning sound was detected - the code prints VOICE DETECTED and waits 300 milliseconds to avoid multiple triggers from one sound. The sensitivity of the sensor itself can be adjusted by turning the small blue potentiometer on the module.

Real-World Applications

- Voice-activated lights
- Smart speaker wake detection
- Voice command triggers
- Hands-free device control
- Security alert systems

Experiment 11 | Sound Sensitivity Comparison

Sensor: High-Sensitivity Voice Sensor

Difficulty: ★ Beginner

Objective: Compare analog readings from the high-sensitivity sensor under different sound conditions.

How It Works

This experiment reads the raw analog output of the high-sensitivity sensor rather than its digital output. This lets you observe the actual signal strength rather than just a yes/no detection. It is useful for calibrating the sensor or comparing its sensitivity to the standard sound sensor.

Concepts Learned

- Analog vs digital sensor output
- Sensitivity calibration
- Comparative readings
- Data observation

Components Required

Component	Qty
Arduino Uno	1
High-Sensitivity Voice Sensor	1
Jumper Wires	3

Wiring

Voice Sensor Pin	Arduino Pin
A0	A0
+	5V
G	GND

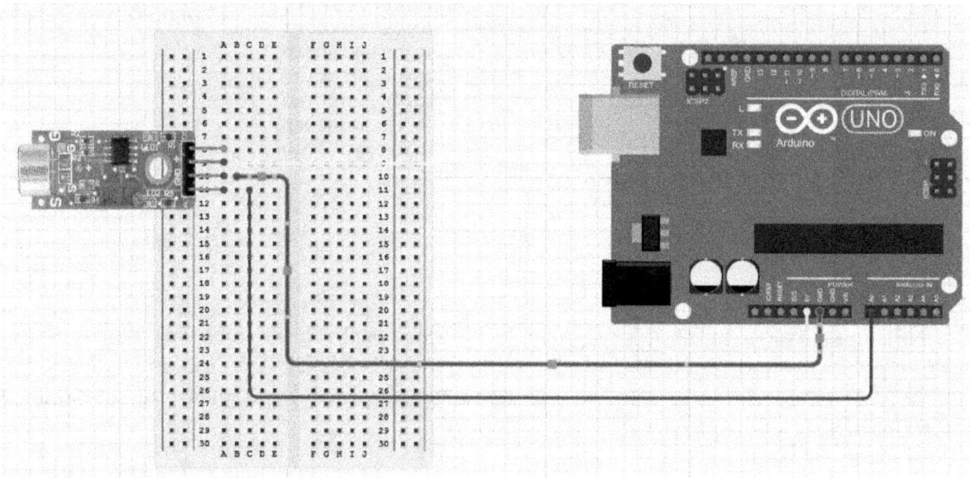

Arduino Code & Serial Monitor Output

```
const int sensorPin = A0;

void setup() {
  Serial.begin(9600);
}

void loop() {
  int value = analogRead(sensorPin);
  Serial.print("Sensitivity Reading: ");
  Serial.println(value);
  delay(100);
}
```

Output   Serial Monitor ×

Message (Enter to send message to 'Arduino UNO' on 'COM3')

```
Sensitivity Reading: 512
Sensitivity Reading: 487
Sensitivity Reading: 523
Sensitivity Reading: 498
Sensitivity Reading: 465
Sensitivity Reading: 445
Sensitivity Reading: 472
Sensitivity Reading: 501
Sensitivity Reading: 566
Sensitivity Reading: 603
Sensitivity Reading: 645
Sensitivity Reading: 678
Sensitivity Reading: 712
Sensitivity Reading: 689
```

How the Code Works

analogRead(sensorPin) returns a value between 0 and 1023. In a quiet room this will hover around a midpoint value. Louder sounds will push it further from that midpoint. Watch the Serial Monitor and notice how the high-sensitivity sensor reacts to softer sounds compared to the KY-038 from the previous experiments.

Real-World Applications

- Acoustic research tools
- Noise pollution mapping
- Microphone calibration
- Audio level loggers
- Lab sound experiments

Experiment 12 | Flame Detection

Sensor: Flame Sensor Module

Difficulty: ★ Beginner

Objective: Detect the presence of a flame using infrared light and display a warning.

How It Works

The flame sensor detects infrared light - the same invisible light that a flame or fire gives off. It has a photodiode that is most sensitive to wavelengths around 760–1100nm, which is the infrared range produced by fire. When infrared light hits the sensor, its digital output pin goes LOW, which we read with digitalRead().

Concepts Learned

- IR-based detection
- Digital flame output
- Fire safety logic
- Active LOW digital sensor

Components Required

Component	Qty
Arduino Uno	1
Flame Sensor Module	1
Jumper Wires	3

Wiring

Flame Sensor Pin	Arduino Pin
DO	D2
+	5V
G	GND

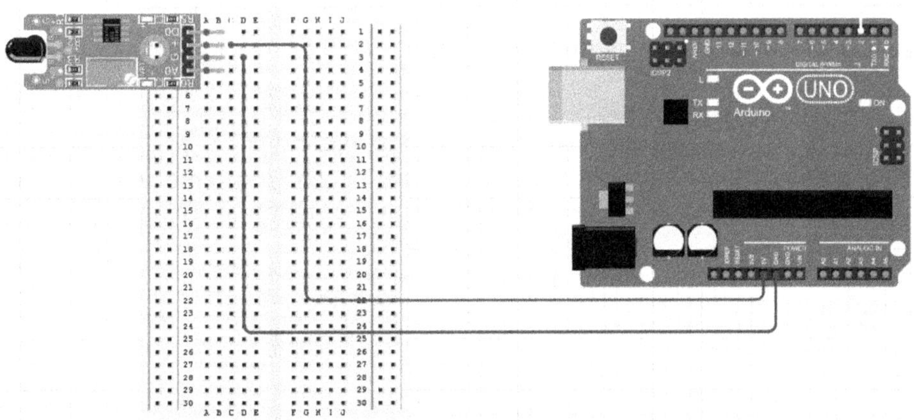

Arduino Code & Serial Monitor Output

```
const int flamePin = 2;

void setup() {
  pinMode(flamePin, INPUT);
  Serial.begin(9600);
}

void loop() {
  int flameState = digitalRead(flamePin);
  if (flameState == LOW) {
    Serial.println("FLAME DETECTED! DANGER!");
  } else {
    Serial.println("No Flame");
  }
  delay(200);
}
```

Output   Serial Monitor ×

Message (Enter to send message to 'Arduino UNO' on 'COM3')

```
No Flame
No Flame
FLAME DETECTED! DANGER!
No Flame
No Flame
No Flame
FLAME DETECTED! DANGER!
FLAME DETECTED! DANGER!
No Flame
No Flame
```

How the Code Works

flamePin is set as INPUT because we are reading from it. In the loop, when the sensor detects a flame it returns LOW - note the logic is inverted from what you might expect. If it reads LOW we print FLAME DETECTED!, otherwise No Flame. The delay(200) gives us five checks per second, which is fast enough for a reliable alarm.

Real-World Applications

- Home fire alarm systems
- Industrial burner monitoring
- Candle detection
- Gas stove safety
- Fireplace automatic dampers

Experiment 13 | Fire Distance Experiment

Sensor: Flame Sensor Module

Difficulty: ★ Beginner

Objective: Observe how the analog flame sensor value changes as a flame moves closer or further away.

How It Works

The analog output of the flame sensor gives more information than the digital output - instead of just yes or no, it tells you the intensity of the detected infrared light. The closer and brighter the flame, the lower the analog reading (more light = lower resistance = lower voltage reading on some sensor designs). This lets you estimate proximity.

Concepts Learned

- Analog flame sensing
- Distance-to-value relationship
- Sensor range
- Analog reading interpretation

Components Required

Component	Qty
Arduino Uno	1
Flame Sensor Module	1

Component	Qty
Jumper Wires	3

Wiring

Flame Sensor Pin	Arduino Pin
A0	A0
+	5V
G	GND

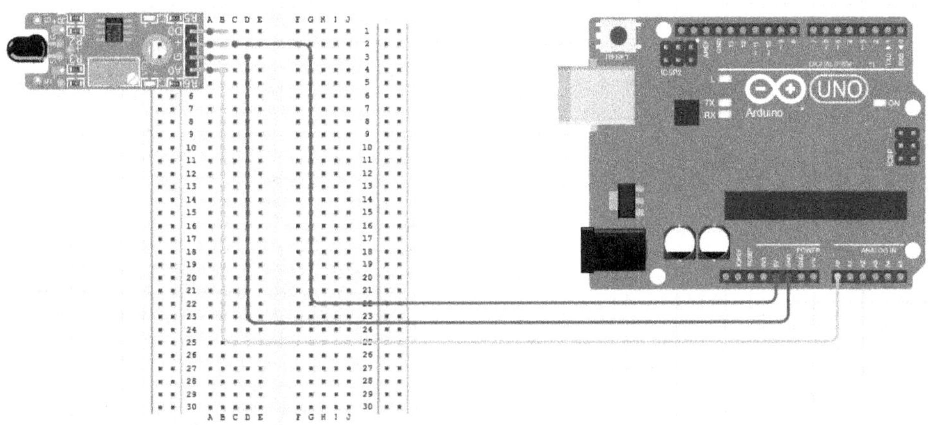

Arduino Code & Serial Monitor Output

```
const int flamePin = A0;

void setup() {
  Serial.begin(9600);
}

void loop() {
  int flameValue = analogRead(flamePin);
  Serial.print("Flame IR Value: ");
  Serial.println(flameValue);
  delay(300);
}
```

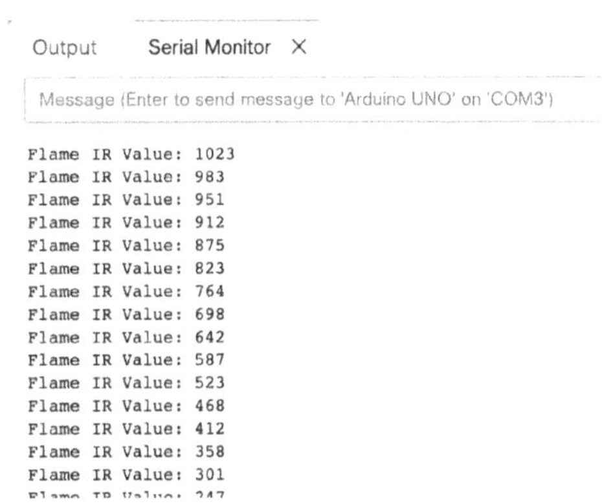

How the Code Works

analogRead(flamePin) returns a number that changes as you move a flame closer or further away. Watch the Serial Monitor carefully as you experiment - try a lighter at 10cm, 20cm, and 30cm away. Record the values. This is how you would calibrate a real fire detection system to trigger at a specific distance rather than just detecting any flame.

Real-World Applications

- Fire proximity alarms
- Furnace control systems
- Candle snuffer automation
- Firefighting robot navigation
- Infrared distance research

Experiment 14 | Read Temperature (DHT11)

Sensor: DHT11 Temperature & Humidity Sensor

Difficulty: ★ Beginner

Objective: Read and display temperature in Celsius from the DHT11 sensor.

How It Works

The DHT11 uses a capacitive humidity sensor and a thermistor to measure the surrounding air. It has a built-in chip that converts the raw readings into digital data and sends it over a single wire using a special timing protocol. The DHT library handles all this complex communication for you - you just call dht.readTemperature() and get the answer.

Concepts Learned

- DHT11 library usage
- Digital communication protocol
- Temperature reading
- Library installation

Components Required

Component	Qty
Arduino Uno	1
DHT11 Sensor	1
Jumper Wires	3

Wiring

DHT11 Pin	Arduino Pin
S	D2
+	5V
-	GND

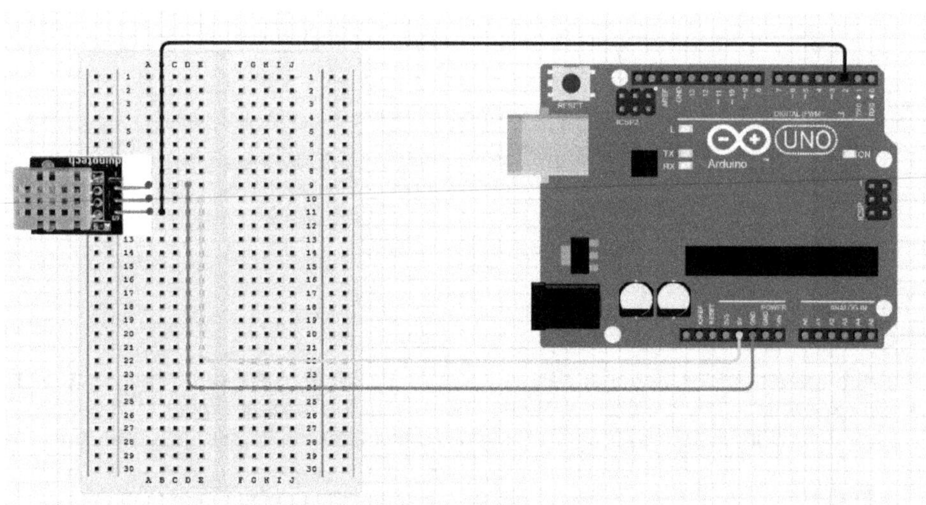

Arduino Code & Serial Monitor Output

```
#include <DHT.h>
#define DHTPIN 2
#define DHTTYPE DHT11
DHT dht(DHTPIN, DHTTYPE);

void setup() {
  Serial.begin(9600);
  dht.begin();
}

void loop() {
  float temp = dht.readTemperature();
  Serial.print("Temperature: ");
  Serial.print(temp);
  Serial.println(" C");
  delay(2000);
}
```

Output   Serial Monitor ×

Message (Enter to send message to 'Arduino UNO' on 'COM3')

```
Temperature: 29.00 C
Temperature: 29.10 C
Temperature: 28.90 C
Temperature: 29.20 C
Temperature: 29.30 C
Temperature: 29.40 C
Temperature: 29.10 C
Temperature: 29.00 C
Temperature: 28.80 C
Temperature: 28.70 C
Temperature: 28.60 C
Temperature: 28.50 C
Temperature: 28.70 C
Temperature: 28.90 C
Temperature: 29.00 C
```

How the Code Works

#include <DHT.h> loads the library. DHT dht(2, DHT11) creates a sensor object connected to pin 2. In setup(), dht.begin() initialises communication. In loop(), dht.readTemperature() talks to the sensor and returns the temperature as a decimal number. The delay(2000) is important - the DHT11 can only take a new reading every two seconds, so asking faster than that returns incorrect values.

Real-World Applications

- Indoor climate control
- Weather stations
- Greenhouse monitoring
- HVAC systems
- Data logging systems

Experiment 15 | Read Humidity (DHT11)

Sensor: DHT11 Temperature & Humidity Sensor
Difficulty: ★ Beginner
Objective: Read and display relative humidity from the DHT11 sensor.

How It Works

Humidity is the amount of water vapour in the air, measured as a percentage of how much the air could theoretically hold at that temperature. The DHT11 measures this using a capacitive element - two electrodes with a moisture-absorbing material between them. More moisture changes the capacitance, which the sensor converts to a humidity percentage.

Concepts Learned

- Humidity measurement
- DHT library functions
- Relative humidity concept
- Sensor warm-up delay

Components Required

Component	Qty
Arduino Uno	1

Component	Qty
DHT11 Sensor	1
Jumper Wires	3

Wiring

DHT11 Pin	Arduino Pin
S	D2
+	5V
-	GND

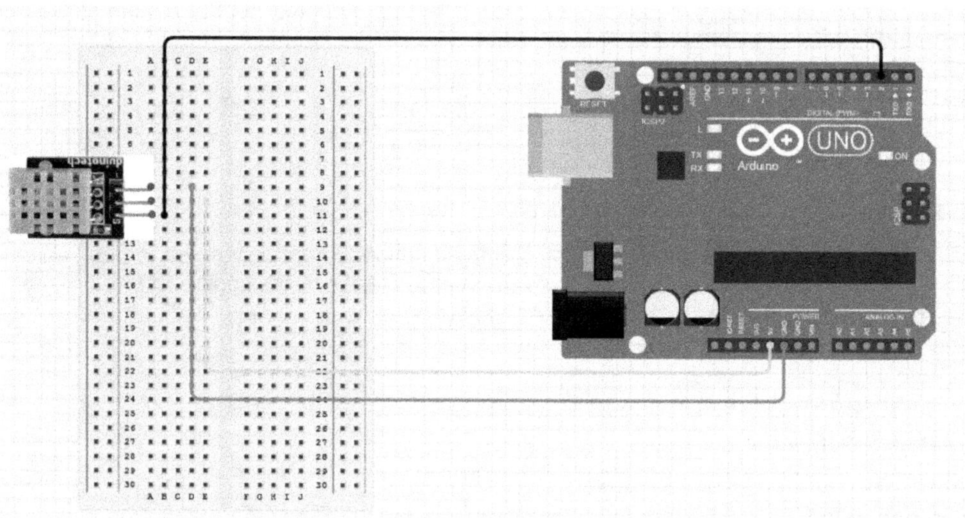

Arduino Code & Serial Monitor Output

```
#include <DHT.h>
#define DHTPIN 2
#define DHTTYPE DHT11
DHT dht(DHTPIN, DHTTYPE);

void setup() {
  Serial.begin(9600);
  dht.begin();
}

void loop() {
  float humidity = dht.readHumidity();
  Serial.print("Humidity: ");
  Serial.print(humidity);
  Serial.println(" %");
  delay(2000);
}
```

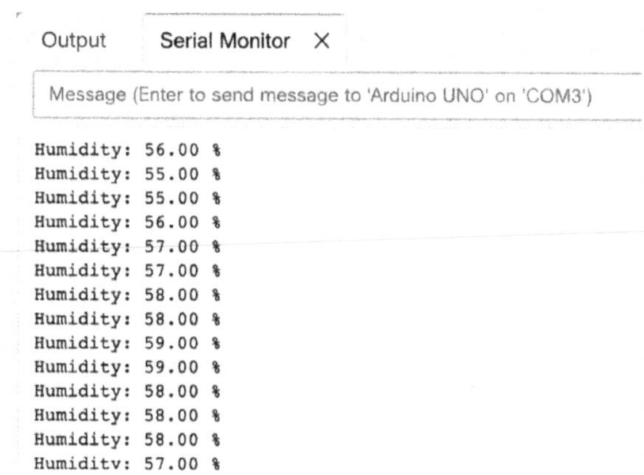

How the Code Works

The code is almost identical to Experiment 14 but calls dht.readHumidity() instead of dht.readTemperature(). The result is a floating-point number representing relative humidity from 0 to 100 percent. The DHT11 is accurate to about ±5% humidity, which is good enough for most projects. Again, the 2-second delay is required by the sensor's hardware.

Real-World Applications

- Humidity-controlled storage rooms
- Cigar/wine humidors
- Museum artifact preservation
- Server room monitoring
- Plant growth chambers

Experiment 16 | Comfort Zone Monitor

Sensor: DHT11 Temperature & Humidity Sensor

Difficulty: ★ Beginner

Objective: Read both temperature and humidity, then classify comfort level as Comfortable, Hot, Cold, or Humid.

How It Works

Human comfort depends on a combination of temperature and humidity - not just one alone. A temperature of 25°C feels pleasant when humidity is low, but sticky and uncomfortable when humidity is high. This experiment reads both values simultaneously and applies a set of rules to classify the overall comfort level.

Concepts Learned

- Multi-variable monitoring
- Combined sensor reading
- Comfort index logic
- Nested conditions

Components Required

Component	Qty
Arduino Uno	1
DHT11 Sensor	1
Jumper Wires	3

Wiring

DHT11 Pin	Arduino Pin
S	D2
+	5V
-	GND

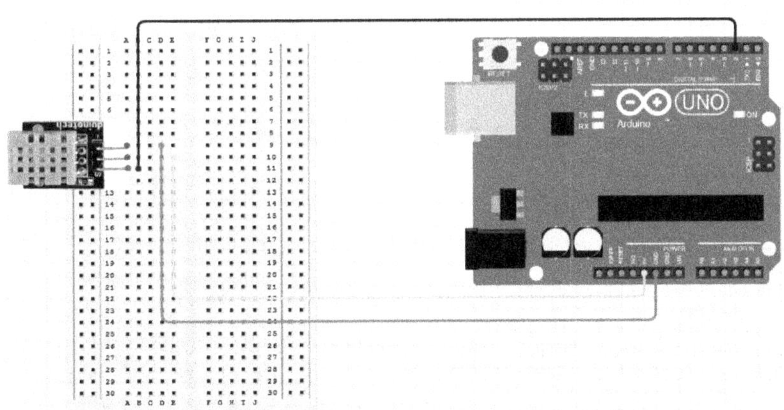

Arduino Code & Serial Monitor Output

```
#include <DHT.h>
#define DHTPIN 2
#define DHTTYPE DHT11
DHT dht(DHTPIN, DHTTYPE);

void setup() {
  Serial.begin(9600);
  dht.begin();
}

void loop() {
  float t = dht.readTemperature();
  float h = dht.readHumidity();
  Serial.print("Temp: "); Serial.print(t);
Serial.print("C  ");
  Serial.print("Humidity: ");
Serial.print(h); Serial.print("%  ");
  if (t >= 18 && t <= 26 && h >= 30 && h
<= 60) {
    Serial.println("Status: COMFORTABLE");
  } else if (t > 26) {
    Serial.println("Status: TOO HOT");
  } else if (t < 18) {
    Serial.println("Status: TOO COLD");
  } else {
    Serial.println("Status: TOO HUMID");
  }
  delay(2000);
}
```

Output   Serial Monitor ×

Message (Enter to send message to 'Arduino UNO' on 'COM3')

```
Temp: 21.30C  Humidity: 45.00%  Status: COMFORTABLE
Temp: 22.00C  Humidity: 44.00%  Status: COMFORTABLE
Temp: 23.10C  Humidity: 50.00%  Status: COMFORTABLE
Temp: 24.20C  Humidity: 48.00%  Status: COMFORTABLE
Temp: 25.60C  Humidity: 47.00%  Status: COMFORTABLE
Temp: 27.10C  Humidity: 45.00%  Status: TOO HOT
Temp: 28.30C  Humidity: 42.00%  Status: TOO HOT
Temp: 29.00C  Humidity: 40.00%  Status: TOO HOT
Temp: 26.80C  Humidity: 65.00%  Status: TOO HUMID
Temp: 25.40C  Humidity: 62.00%  Status: TOO HUMID
Temp: 24.10C  Humidity: 61.00%  Status: TOO HUMID
```

How the Code Works

Both temperature and humidity are read in the same loop iteration. The if-else chain checks the most important condition first - if both are in the ideal range (18–26°C and 30–60% humidity) it prints COMFORTABLE. The remaining else-if blocks catch specific problem conditions. Notice how the logic builds up in layers: first check for ideal, then check what is wrong if not ideal.

Real-World Applications

- Smart thermostats
- Office comfort monitors
- Baby room environment control
- Gym climate systems
- Hotel room automation

Experiment 17 | Digital Temperature Reading (DS18B20)

Sensor: DS18B20 Temperature Sensor

Difficulty: ★ Beginner

Objective: Read accurate temperature using the DS18B20 one-wire digital sensor.

How It Works

The DS18B20 communicates using the OneWire protocol - a clever system that sends digital data over a single wire. Unlike the DHT11, it is waterproof in its standard form and accurate to ±0.5°C. Multiple DS18B20 sensors can even share the same wire, each with a unique address. The 4.7kΩ resistor between the signal wire and 5V is essential - it is called a pull-up resistor and keeps the signal stable.

Concepts Learned

- OneWire communication protocol
- DallasTemperature library
- High-accuracy temperature sensing
- Library-based sensor reading

Components Required

Component	Qty
Arduino Uno	1
DS18B20 Sensor	1
4.7kΩ Resistor	1
Jumper Wires	3

Wiring

DS18B20 Pin	Arduino Pin
Signal	D2
VCC	5V
GND	GND

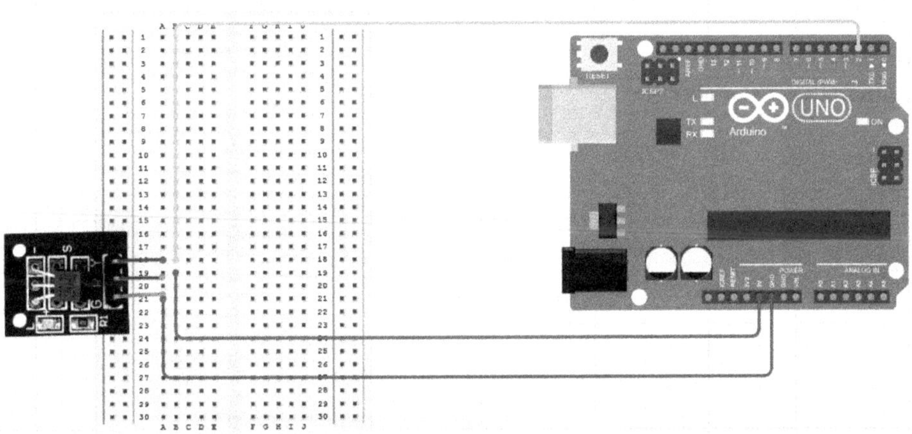

Arduino Code & Serial Monitor Output

```
#include <OneWire.h>
#include <DallasTemperature.h>
#define ONE_WIRE_BUS 2
OneWire oneWire(ONE_WIRE_BUS);
DallasTemperature sensors(&oneWire);

void setup() {
  Serial.begin(9600);
  sensors.begin();
}

void loop() {
  sensors.requestTemperatures();
  float tempC =
sensors.getTempCByIndex(0);
  Serial.print("Temperature: ");
  Serial.print(tempC);
  Serial.println(" C");
  delay(1000);
}
```

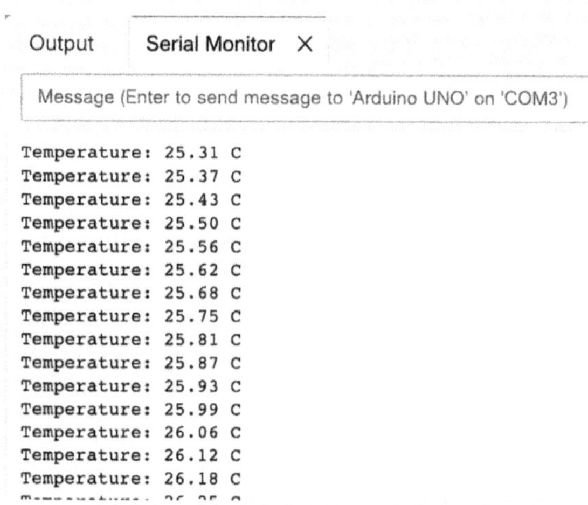

How the Code Works

The OneWire and DallasTemperature libraries work together. sensors.requestTemperatures() tells the sensor to start a measurement, and getTempCByIndex(0) retrieves the result from the first sensor on the wire. The index 0 means the first sensor - if you had multiple sensors on the same wire you would use 0, 1, 2, and so on to read each one separately.

Real-World Applications

- Aquarium temperature monitoring
- Food storage systems
- Medical equipment
- Outdoor weather stations
- Industrial process control

Experiment 18 | Temperature Logger

Sensor: DS18B20 Temperature Sensor

Difficulty: ★ Beginner

Objective: Log temperature readings over time with a timestamp using millis().

How It Works

A temperature logger records readings over time rather than just showing the current value. By printing the elapsed time alongside each reading, you create a time series of data that can be copied from the Serial Monitor into a spreadsheet for analysis. This is the foundation of all data logging systems.

Concepts Learned

- Time-stamped logging
- millis() for elapsed time
- Data logging concept
- Formatted Serial output

Components Required

Component	Qty
Arduino Uno	1
DS18B20 Sensor	1
4.7kΩ Resistor	1
Jumper Wires	3

Wiring

DS18B20 Pin	Arduino Pin
Signal	D2
VCC	5V
GND	GND

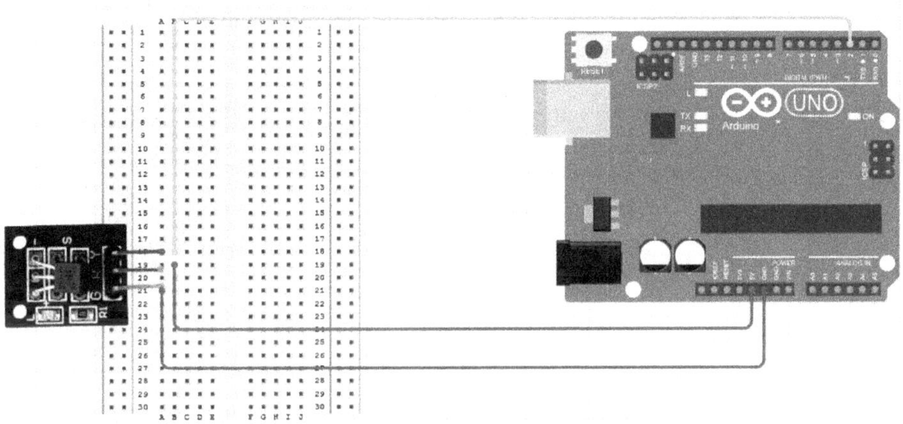

Arduino Code & Serial Monitor Output

```
#include <OneWire.h>
#include <DallasTemperature.h>
#define ONE_WIRE_BUS 2
OneWire oneWire(ONE_WIRE_BUS);
DallasTemperature sensors(&oneWire);

void setup() {
  Serial.begin(9600);
  sensors.begin();
  Serial.println("Time(ms) | Temp(C)");
}

void loop() {
  sensors.requestTemperatures();
  float tempC =
sensors.getTempCByIndex(0);
  Serial.print(millis());
  Serial.print(" ms  | ");
  Serial.print(tempC);
  Serial.println(" C");
```

Output   Serial Monitor ×

Message (Enter to send message to 'Arduino UNO' on 'COM3')

```
Time(ms) | Temp(C)
  0 ms    | 25.31 C
 2000 ms  | 25.37 C
 4000 ms  | 25.43 C
 6000 ms  | 25.50 C
 8000 ms  | 25.56 C
10000 ms  | 25.62 C
12000 ms  | 25.68 C
14000 ms  | 25.75 C
16000 ms  | 25.81 C
18000 ms  | 25.87 C
20000 ms  | 25.93 C
22000 ms  | 25.99 C
24000 ms  | 26.06 C
26000 ms  | 26.12 C
```

```
  delay(2000);
}
```

How the Code Works

millis() returns the number of milliseconds since the Arduino was powered on. By printing this alongside each temperature reading we get a timestamp for every entry. The header line in setup() (Time(ms) | Temp(C)) creates column labels so the data is easy to read. Notice we only read the sensor every 2000 milliseconds - faster than this and the DHT11 gives unreliable readings.

Real-World Applications

- Cold chain logistics monitoring
- Science lab experiments
- Server room temperature logs
- Food safety compliance
- Environmental research

Experiment 19 | Analog Temperature Reading

Sensor: Analog Temperature Sensor

Difficulty: ★ Beginner

Objective: Read temperature from an analog sensor and convert the raw value to Celsius.

How It Works

The analog temperature sensor outputs a voltage that changes linearly with temperature. At 0°C it outputs 0.5V, and every 10°C increase adds 0.1V to the output. To convert the raw Arduino reading (0–1023) back into a temperature, we must reverse this process using simple maths.

Concepts Learned

- Analog-to-temperature conversion
- Voltage divider output
- Math in Arduino (map/formula)
- Sensor calibration

Components Required

Component	Qty
Arduino Uno	1
Analog Temperature Sensor	1
Jumper Wires	3

Wiring

Sensor Pin	Arduino Pin
S	A0
+	5V
-	GND

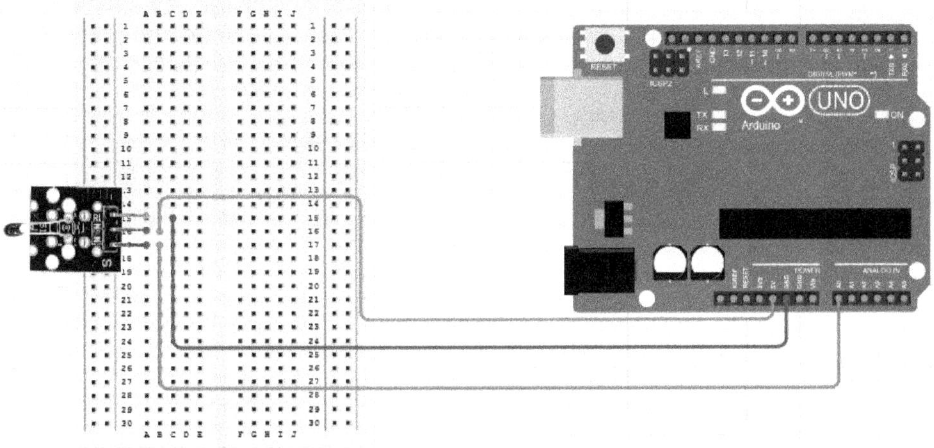

Arduino Code & Serial Monitor Output

```
const int tempPin = A0;

void setup() {
  Serial.begin(9600);
}

void loop() {
  int rawValue = analogRead(tempPin);
  float voltage = rawValue * (5.0 /
1023.0);
  float tempC = (voltage - 0.5) * 100.0;
  Serial.print("Temperature: ");
  Serial.print(tempC);
  Serial.println(" C");
  delay(1000);
}
```

Output   Serial Monitor ×

Message (Enter to send message to 'Arduino UNO' on 'COM3')

```
Temperature: 23.15 C
Temperature: 23.21 C
Temperature: 23.28 C
Temperature: 23.33 C
Temperature: 23.39 C
Temperature: 23.46 C
Temperature: 23.52 C
Temperature: 23.57 C
Temperature: 23.64 C
Temperature: 23.70 C
Temperature: 23.77 C
Temperature: 23.83 C
```

How the Code Works

analogRead returns a number from 0 to 1023 representing a voltage of 0 to 5V. The line voltage = rawValue * (5.0 / 1023.0) converts it back to volts. Then tempC = (voltage - 0.5) * 100.0 applies the sensor's formula to get the temperature in Celsius. This kind of unit conversion is extremely common in electronics - always check your sensor's datasheet for the formula.

Real-World Applications

- Simple thermometers
- Analog control loops
- Low-cost temperature monitoring
- Motor temperature guards
- Battery temperature sensing

Experiment 20 | Compare Analog vs Digital Temperature

Sensor: Analog Temperature Sensor & DS18B20

Difficulty: ★ Beginner

Objective: Read temperature from both an analog and a digital sensor simultaneously and compare their outputs.

How It Works

No two sensors are perfectly identical. Comparing readings from an analog sensor and a digital sensor on the same Arduino at the same time reveals their differences in accuracy, response time, and precision. This experiment teaches an important real-world lesson: always understand your sensor's limitations before relying on it.

Concepts Learned

- Multi-sensor reading
- Analog vs digital accuracy
- Sensor comparison
- Formatted output

Components Required

Component	Qty
Arduino Uno	1
Analog Temperature Sensor	1
DS18B20 Sensor	1
4.7kΩ Resistor	1
Jumper Wires	5

Wiring

Sensor	Pin
Analog Sensor S	A0
Analog Sensor +	5V
DS18B20 Signal	D2
DS18B20 VCC	5V
All GND	GND

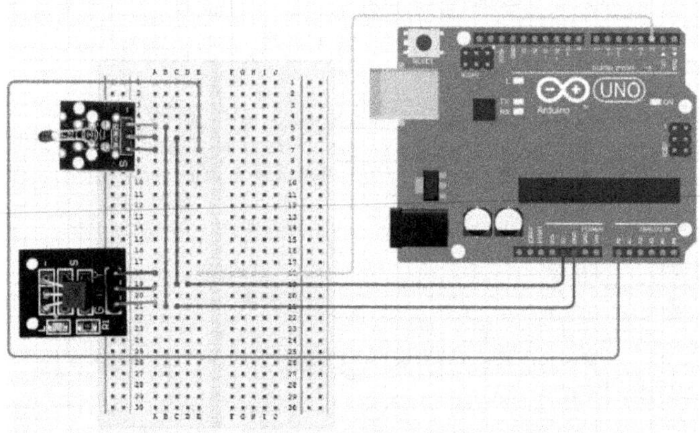

Arduino Code & Serial Monitor Output

```
#include <OneWire.h>
#include <DallasTemperature.h>
OneWire oneWire(2);
DallasTemperature digital(&oneWire);
const int analogPin = A0;

void setup() {
  Serial.begin(9600);
  digital.begin();
}

void loop() {
  int raw = analogRead(analogPin);
  float analogTemp = ((raw * 5.0 / 1023.0)
- 0.5) * 100.0;
  digital.requestTemperatures();
  float digitalTemp =
digital.getTempCByIndex(0);
  Serial.print("Analog: ");
Serial.print(analogTemp); Serial.print(" C
|  ");
  Serial.print("Digital: ");
Serial.print(digitalTemp);
Serial.println(" C");
  delay(2000);
}
```

Output   Serial Monitor ×

Message (Enter to send message to 'Arduino UNO' on 'COM3')

```
Analog: 23.17 C  |  Digital: 25.31 C
Analog: 23.21 C  |  Digital: 25.37 C
Analog: 23.26 C  |  Digital: 25.43 C
Analog: 23.31 C  |  Digital: 25.50 C
Analog: 23.36 C  |  Digital: 25.56 C
Analog: 23.41 C  |  Digital: 25.62 C
Analog: 23.46 C  |  Digital: 25.68 C
Analog: 23.51 C  |  Digital: 25.75 C
Analog: 23.56 C  |  Digital: 25.81 C
Analog: 23.61 C  |  Digital: 25.87 C
Analog: 23.66 C  |  Digital: 25.93 C
Analog: 23.71 C  |  Digital: 25.99 C
Analog: 23.76 C  |  Digital: 26.06 C
```

How the Code Works

Both sensors are read in the same loop() so the readings happen almost simultaneously. The analog sensor uses the voltage formula from Experiment 19, while the digital sensor uses the DallasTemperature library. The formatted output lines up both values side by side in the Serial Monitor. Look for differences between the two readings - these reveal calibration offsets and measurement noise.

Real-World Applications

- Sensor accuracy testing
- Quality control
- Redundant temperature systems
- Educational demonstrations
- Calibration references

Experiment 21 | Orientation Detection

Sensor: Tilt Sensor

Difficulty: ★ Beginner

Objective: Detect whether the tilt sensor is upright or tilted and display the orientation.

How It Works

Inside the tilt switch is a small metal ball and two electrical contacts. When upright, the ball rests between the contacts completing the circuit. When tilted, the ball rolls away from the contacts and breaks the circuit. The Arduino detects this open/closed state as HIGH or LOW on its input pin.

Concepts Learned

- Digital tilt sensing
- Orientation states

- Mechanical switch logic
- Physical computing

Components Required

Component	Qty
Arduino Uno	1
Tilt Switch Module	1
Jumper Wires	3

Wiring

Tilt Sensor Pin	Arduino Pin
S	D2
+	5V
-	GND

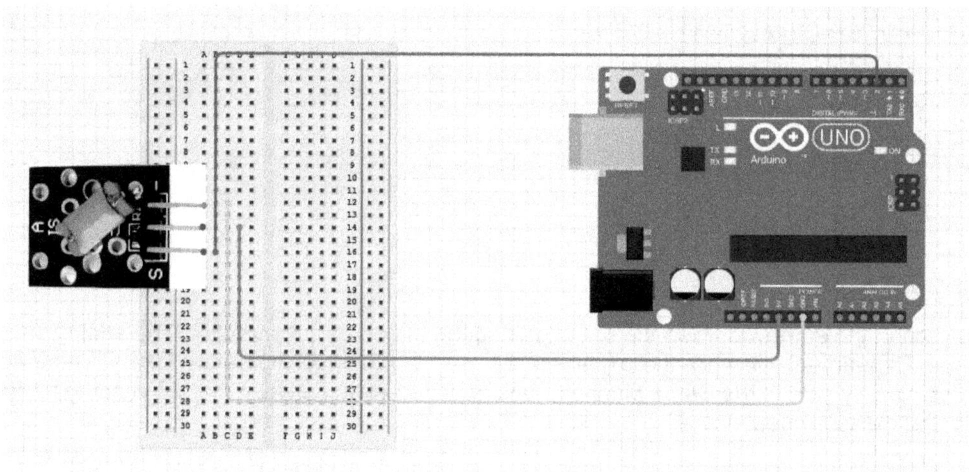

Arduino Code & Serial Monitor Output

```
const int tiltPin = 2;

void setup() {
  pinMode(tiltPin, INPUT_PULLUP);
  Serial.begin(9600);
}

void loop() {
  int state = digitalRead(tiltPin);
  if (state == LOW) {
    Serial.println("TILTED");
  } else {
    Serial.println("Upright");
  }
  delay(200);
}
```

Output　Serial Monitor ×

Message (Enter to send message to 'Arduino UNO' on 'COM3')

```
Upright
Upright
Upright
Upright
Upright
Upright
Upright
Upright
Upright
TILTED
TILTED
TILTED
TILTED
TILTED
```

How the Code Works

INPUT_PULLUP is used here instead of plain INPUT. This activates an internal resistor inside the Arduino that keeps the pin at HIGH when nothing is connected to it - it prevents random floating values. When the switch tilts and opens the circuit, the pin reads HIGH. When it closes the circuit (by returning upright), the pin reads LOW. This inverted logic is normal for switches.

Real-World Applications

- Anti-tip furniture alerts
- Pinball machine tilt detection
- Drone orientation monitoring
- Medical bed angle alarms
- Vehicle rollover detection

Experiment 22 | Tilt Counter

Sensor: Tilt Sensor

Difficulty: ★ Beginner

Objective: Count how many times the tilt sensor has been tilted.

How It Works

Counting tilts requires detecting the moment the sensor changes state - not just reading its current state. If we just checked the state continuously, a single tilt would count hundreds of times while the sensor is in the tilted position. Edge detection solves this by only counting when the state transitions from upright to tilted.

Concepts Learned

- Edge detection on tilt sensor
- State change counting
- Event accumulation
- Debounce

Components Required

Component	Qty
Arduino Uno	1
Tilt Switch Module	1
Jumper Wires	3

Wiring

Tilt Sensor Pin	Arduino Pin
S	D2
+	5V
-	GND

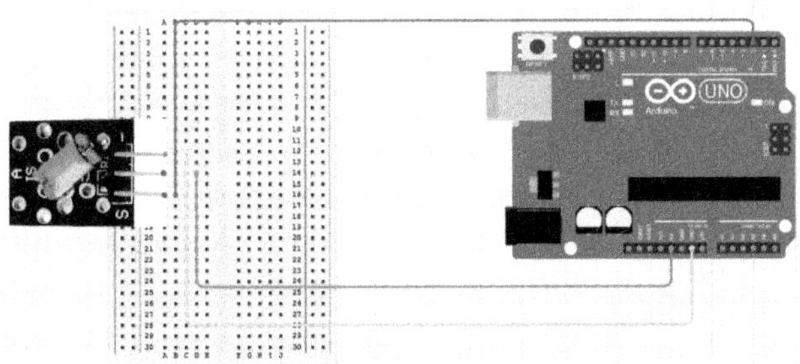

Arduino Code & Serial Monitor Output

```
const int tiltPin = 2;
int lastState = HIGH;
int count = 0;

void setup() {
  pinMode(tiltPin, INPUT_PULLUP);
  Serial.begin(9600);
}

void loop() {
  int state = digitalRead(tiltPin);
  if (state == LOW && lastState == HIGH) {
    count++;
    Serial.print("Tilt Count: ");
    Serial.println(count);
    delay(200);
  }
  lastState = state;
}
```

Output | Serial Monitor ×

Message (Enter to send message to 'Arduino UNO' on 'COM3')

```
Tilt Count: 1
Tilt Count: 2
Tilt Count: 3
Tilt Count: 4
Tilt Count: 5
Tilt Count: 6
Tilt Count: 7
Tilt Count: 8
Tilt Count: 9
Tilt Count: 10
Tilt Count: 11
Tilt Count: 12
Tilt Count: 13
Tilt Count: 14
Tilt Count: 15
```

How the Code Works

lastState stores the previous reading. In each loop iteration we compare the current state to the last state. Only when the state is LOW (tilted) AND lastState was HIGH (was upright) do we increment the counter - this is the falling edge of the signal. Storing the reading in lastState at the end of the loop prepares for the next comparison. The delay(200) is debounce - tilt switches can bounce electrically when they change state.

Real-World Applications

- Shake counters for exercise
- Bottle shake counters
- Packaging quality checks
- Vending machine tilt detection
- Earthquake event counters

Experiment 23 | Mercury Tilt Detection

Sensor: Mercury Switch

Difficulty: ★ Beginner

Objective: Detect tilt using the mercury switch and display orientation status.

How It Works

A mercury switch works on the same principle as a tilt switch but uses a small bead of liquid mercury instead of a metal ball. Mercury conducts electricity, so when it slides to one end of the glass tube it bridges the contacts and completes the circuit. Note: mercury switches are being phased out in modern electronics due to environmental concerns.

Concepts Learned

- Mercury switch operation
- Digital input reading
- Electrical contact detection
- Safety note: mercury handling

Components Required

Component	Qty
Arduino Uno	1
Mercury Switch Module	1
Jumper Wires	3

Wiring

Mercury Switch Pin	Arduino Pin
S	D2
+	5V
-	GND

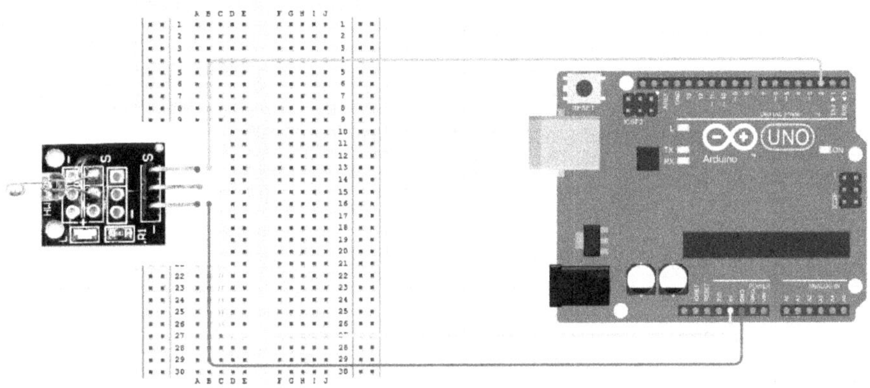

Arduino Code & Serial Monitor Output

```
const int mercuryPin = 2;

void setup() {
  pinMode(mercuryPin, INPUT_PULLUP);
  Serial.begin(9600);
}

void loop() {
  int state = digitalRead(mercuryPin);
  if (state == LOW) {
    Serial.println("TILTED - Circuit
Closed");
  } else {
    Serial.println("Upright - Circuit
Open");
  }
  delay(200);
}
```

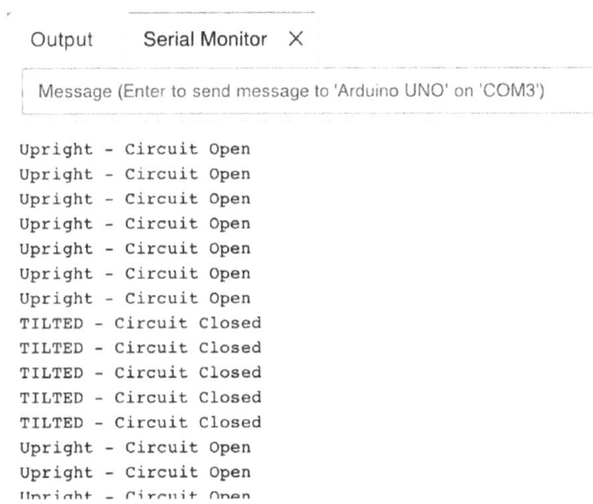

How the Code Works

The code is identical in structure to the tilt switch experiments. INPUT_PULLUP keeps the pin stable when the circuit is open. LOW means the mercury is bridging the contacts (circuit closed, module tilted), HIGH means the mercury has moved away (circuit open, module upright). Watch the Serial Monitor as you slowly tilt the sensor to find the exact angle at which it switches.

Real-World Applications

- Old-style thermostat tilt switches
- Appliance angle detection
- Retro arcade tilt detection
- Mechanical alarm systems
- Level indicators

Experiment 24 | Position Alarm

Sensor: Mercury Switch
Difficulty: ★ Beginner
Objective: Trigger an alarm message when an object is moved from its original position.

How It Works

A position alarm works by recording the original state of the sensor at startup, then continuously comparing the current state to that original. If they ever differ, the object has been moved. This is a classic approach in security - the system does not need to know what position is 'safe', it just knows if anything changed.

Concepts Learned

- Initial state storage
- Position change detection
- State machine basics
- Alarm triggering

Components Required

Component	Qty
Arduino Uno	1
Mercury Switch Module	1
Jumper Wires	3

Wiring

Mercury Switch Pin	Arduino Pin
S	D2
+	5V
-	GND

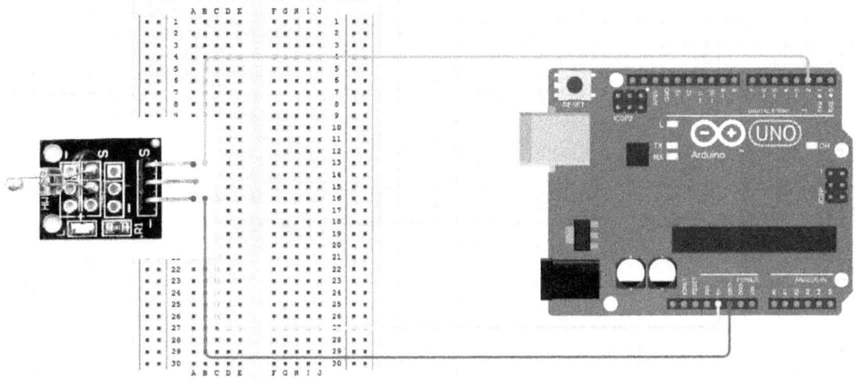

Arduino Code & Serial Monitor Output

```
const int mercuryPin = 2;
int initialState;

void setup() {
  pinMode(mercuryPin, INPUT_PULLUP);
  Serial.begin(9600);
  initialState = digitalRead(mercuryPin);
  Serial.println("Position set. Monitoring...");
}

void loop() {
  int currentState = digitalRead(mercuryPin);
  if (currentState != initialState) {
    Serial.println("ALARM! Object moved!");
  } else {
    Serial.println("OK - Position unchanged");
  }
  delay(500);
}
```

Output   Serial Monitor ×

Message (Enter to send message to 'Arduino UNO' on 'COM3')

```
Position set. Monitoring...
OK - Position unchanged
OK - Position unchanged
OK - Position unchanged
OK - Position unchanged
OK - Position unchanged
OK - Position unchanged
OK - Position unchanged
ALARM! Object moved!
ALARM! Object moved!
ALARM! Object moved!
ALARM! Object moved!
ALARM! Object moved!
```

How the Code Works

initialState = digitalRead(mercuryPin) captures the starting position in setup() and saves it. In loop(), we read the current state and compare it to initialState using the != (not equal) operator. Any difference triggers the alarm message. This approach works for any binary sensor - reed switches, tilt sensors, or buttons - not just mercury switches.

Real-World Applications

- Anti-theft object alarms
- Picture frame tampering alerts
- Museum exhibit protection
- Safe door monitoring
- Equipment position tracking

Experiment 25 | Vibration Detection

Sensor: Shock Switch Module
Difficulty: ★ Beginner
Objective: Detects vibration or impact using the shock sensor.

How It Works

The shock sensor contains a thin conductive spring mounted inside a tube. When the sensor experiences a sudden impact or vibration, the spring wobbles and momentarily makes contact with the outer electrode, creating a very brief electrical pulse. This pulse is what the Arduino detects. The faster or harder the impact, the more pulses it generates.

Concepts Learned

- Shock/vibration sensing
- Momentary contact detection
- Short pulse reading
- Sensitivity awareness

Components Required

Component	Qty
Arduino Uno	1
Shock Switch Module	1
Jumper Wires	3

Wiring

Shock Sensor Pin	Arduino Pin
S	D2
+	5V
-	GND

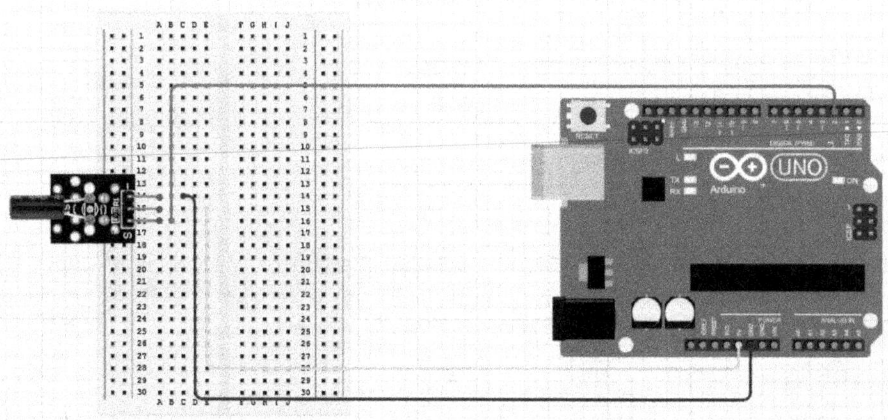

Arduino Code & Serial Monitor Output

```
const int shockPin = 2;

void setup() {
  pinMode(shockPin, INPUT_PULLUP);
  Serial.begin(9600);
}

void loop() {
  int state = digitalRead(shockPin);
  if (state == LOW) {
    Serial.println("VIBRATION DETECTED!");
    delay(200);
  }
}
```

Output   Serial Monitor ×

Message (Enter to send message to 'Arduino UNO' on 'COM3')

```
VIBRATION DETECTED!
VIBRATION DETECTED!
VIBRATION DETECTED!
VIBRATION DETECTED!
VIBRATION DETECTED!
VIBRATION DETECTED!
VIBRATION DETECTED!
VIBRATION DETECTED!
VIBRATION DETECTED!
VIBRATION DETECTED!
VIBRATION DETECTED!
VIBRATION DETECTED!
VIBRATION DETECTED!
```

How the Code Works

Because the shock pulse is very brief, we use INPUT_PULLUP to keep the pin stable between events. The code checks for a LOW reading - the moment of contact - and immediately prints VIBRATION DETECTED. The delay(200) after detection prevents the same impact from triggering multiple readings. Try tapping the sensor lightly versus harder to see how it responds.

Real-World Applications

- Earthquake early warning
- Vehicle impact detection
- Machinery vibration monitoring
- Package drop detection
- Anti-theft car alarms

Experiment 26 | Impact Counter

Sensor: Shock Switch Module

Difficulty: ★ Beginner

Objective: Count the number of impacts or taps detected by the shock sensor.

How It Works

Counting impacts uses the same edge-detection pattern as the tilt counter and button counter. Each time the shock sensor makes a new contact (state goes from HIGH to LOW), we add one to the count. The cumulative total is always available in the count variable and printed after every new impact.

Concepts Learned

- Impact event counting
- Edge detection on shock signal
- Debounce for vibration
- Cumulative event tracking

Components Required

Component	Qty
Arduino Uno	1
Shock Switch Module	1
Jumper Wires	3

Wiring

Shock Sensor Pin	Arduino Pin
S	D2
+	5V
-	GND

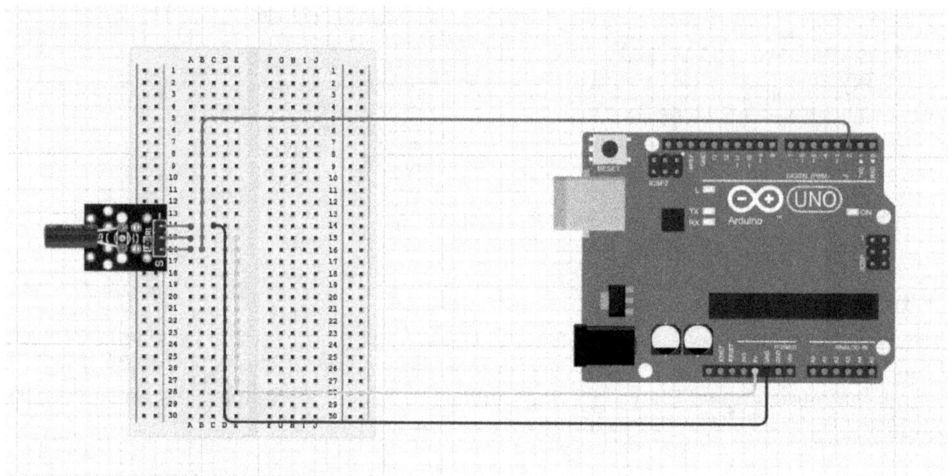

Arduino Code & Serial Monitor Output

```
const int shockPin = 2;
int count = 0;
int lastState = HIGH;

void setup() {
  pinMode(shockPin, INPUT_PULLUP);
  Serial.begin(9600);
}

void loop() {
  int state = digitalRead(shockPin);
  if (state == LOW && lastState == HIGH) {
    count++;
    Serial.print("Impact Count: ");
    Serial.println(count);
    delay(150);
  }
  lastState = state;
}
```

Output | Serial Monitor ×

Message (Enter to send message to 'Arduino UNO' on 'COM3')

```
Impact Count: 1
Impact Count: 2
Impact Count: 3
Impact Count: 4
Impact Count: 5
Impact Count: 6
Impact Count: 7
Impact Count: 8
Impact Count: 9
Impact Count: 10
Impact Count: 11
Impact Count: 12
Impact Count: 13
Impact Count: 14
Impact Count: 15
```

How the Code Works

lastState tracks whether the previous reading was a contact or not. The condition state == LOW && lastState == HIGH detects only the start of a new impact, not its duration. count++ increments the total, which is then printed. This pattern - detect rising or falling edge, increment counter, print - is one of the most reusable patterns in Arduino programming.

Real-World Applications

- Drum hit counters
- Sports impact trackers
- Package handling quality

- Knock pattern detection
- Industrial wear monitoring

Experiment 27 | Magnetic Field Detection

Sensor: Hall Sensor
Difficulty: ★ Beginner
Objective: Detect the presence of a magnetic field using the Hall effect sensor.

How It Works

The Hall effect is a phenomenon where a magnetic field causes electrons in a conductor to deflect sideways, creating a small voltage difference. A Hall sensor measures this effect. The digital Hall sensor outputs LOW when a magnetic field is present and HIGH when there is none, making it act like a contactless switch.

Concepts Learned

- Hall effect principle
- Digital magnetic sensing
- Magnet polarity detection
- Binary field detection

Components Required

Component	Qty
Arduino Uno	1
Hall Sensor Module	1
Jumper Wires	3

Wiring

Hall Sensor Pin	Arduino Pin
S	D2
+	5V
-	GND

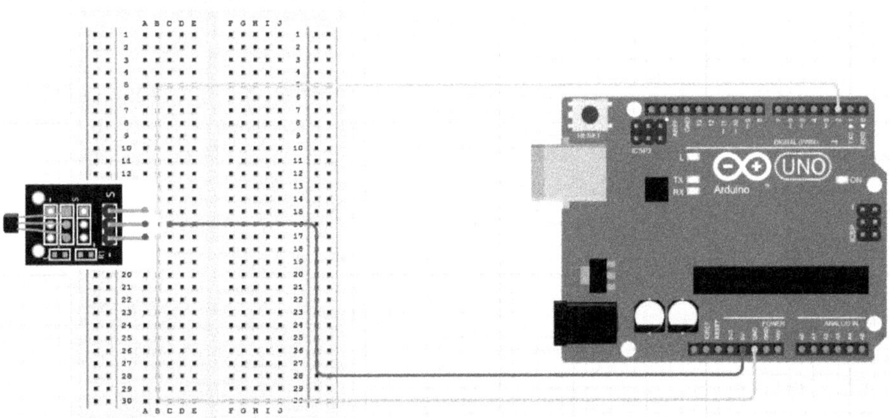

Arduino Code & Serial Monitor Output

```
const int hallPin = 2;

void setup() {
  pinMode(hallPin, INPUT);
  Serial.begin(9600);
}

void loop() {
  int state = digitalRead(hallPin);
  if (state == LOW) {
    Serial.println("Magnetic Field
DETECTED");
  } else {
    Serial.println("No Magnetic Field");
  }
  delay(200);
}
```

```
Output    Serial Monitor ×

Message (Enter to send message to 'Arduino UNO' on 'COM3')

No Magnetic Field
No Magnetic Field
No Magnetic Field
No Magnetic Field
No Magnetic Field
No Magnetic Field
No Magnetic Field
Magnetic Field DETECTED
Magnetic Field DETECTED
Magnetic Field DETECTED
Magnetic Field DETECTED
Magnetic Field DETECTED
Magnetic Field DETECTED
No Magnetic Field
No Magnetic Field
```

How the Code Works

The code structure is identical to the reed switch and tilt sensor experiments. When a magnet is brought near, digitalRead returns LOW and we print Magnetic Field DETECTED. The key advantage over a reed switch is that the Hall sensor has no moving parts - it uses electronics to detect magnetism, so it is faster, more precise, and lasts much longer.

Real-World Applications

- Proximity switches
- Door/lid position sensors
- Electric motor speed sensors
- Anti-theft systems
- Brushless motor control

Experiment 28 | Magnet Distance Experiment

Sensor: Hall Sensor

Difficulty: ★ Beginner

Objective: Observe how the hall sensor reading changes as a magnet moves closer and further away.

How It Works

The digital Hall sensor has a detection range - it switches state only when the magnetic field is strong enough to exceed its threshold. As you move a magnet closer, the field strength increases. There is a point where the sensor suddenly switches from FAR to NEAR. This switching distance depends on the strength of the magnet and the sensor's sensitivity.

Concepts Learned

- Magnetic field strength vs distance
- Sensor saturation
- Proximity experiment
- Observation and inference

Components Required

Component	Qty
Arduino Uno	1

Component	Qty
Hall Sensor Module	1
Small Magnet	1
Jumper Wires	3

Wiring

Hall Sensor Pin	Arduino Pin
S	D2
+	5V
-	GND

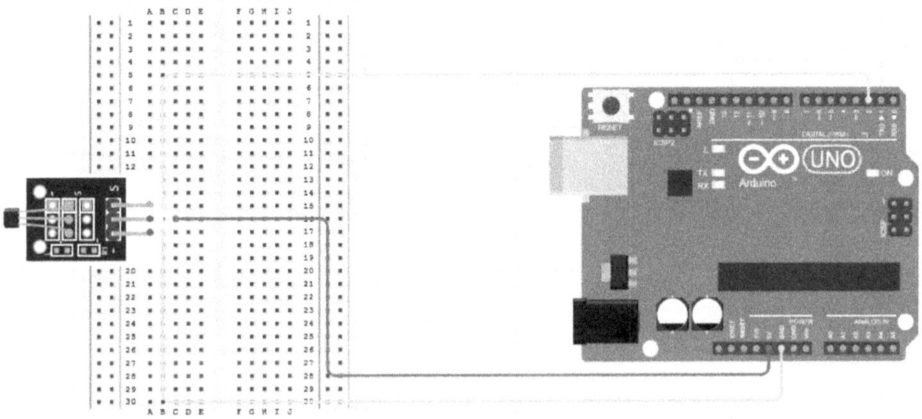

Arduino Code & Serial Monitor Output

```
const int hallPin = 2;

void setup() {
  pinMode(hallPin, INPUT);
  Serial.begin(9600);
}

void loop() {
  int state = digitalRead(hallPin);
  Serial.print("Hall State: ");
  Serial.println(state == LOW ? "NEAR
(magnet close)" : "FAR (no magnet)");
  delay(200);
}
```

Output   Serial Monitor ×

Message (Enter to send message to 'Arduino UNO' on 'COM3')

```
Hall State: FAR (no magnet)
Hall State: FAR (no magnet)
Hall State: FAR (no magnet)
Hall State: FAR (no magnet)
Hall State: FAR (no magnet)
Hall State: FAR (no magnet)
Hall State: FAR (no magnet)
Hall State: FAR (no magnet)
Hall State: FAR (no magnet)
Hall State: NEAR (magnet close)
Hall State: NEAR (magnet close)
Hall State: NEAR (magnet close)
Hall State: NEAR (magnet close)
```

How the Code Works

The ternary operator in the print statement (state == LOW ? 'NEAR' : 'FAR') is a compact way of writing an if-else. It reads: if state is LOW, print NEAR, otherwise print FAR. Try different magnets and note how the switching distance changes. A strong neodymium magnet will trigger the sensor from much further away than a weak ferrite magnet.

Real-World Applications

- Magnetic proximity sensors
- Gear tooth counters
- Contactless position sensing
- Linear actuator limit switches
- Reed-switch replacement systems

Experiment 29 | Magnetic Strength Measurement

Sensor: Linear Hall Sensor

Difficulty: ★ Beginner

Objective: Read the analog output of the linear Hall sensor to measure magnetic field strength.

How It Works

Unlike the digital Hall sensor, the linear Hall sensor outputs an analog voltage that varies smoothly with magnetic field strength. With no magnet present it outputs approximately 2.5V - the midpoint of its range. A North pole pushes the reading higher; a South pole pushes it lower. This lets you measure both the strength and polarity of a magnetic field.

Concepts Learned

- Linear Hall effect
- Analog magnetic measurement
- Voltage proportional to field
- Midpoint = no field (512)

Components Required

Component	Qty
Arduino Uno	1
Linear Hall Sensor Module	1
Jumper Wires	3

Wiring

Linear Hall Pin	Arduino Pin
S	A0
+	5V
-	GND

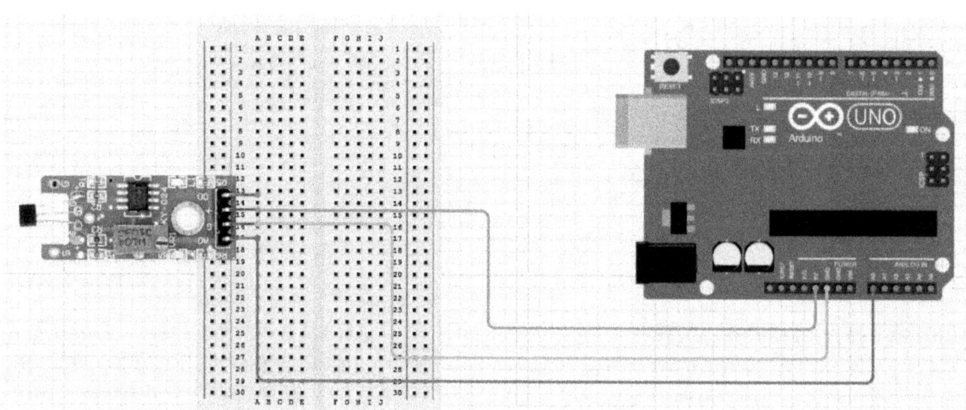

Arduino Code & Serial Monitor Output

```
const int hallPin = A0;

void setup() {
  Serial.begin(9600);
}

void loop() {
  int value = analogRead(hallPin);
  Serial.print("Magnetic Strength: ");
  Serial.println(value);
  // ~512 = no field, >512 = N pole, <512
= S pole
  delay(200);
}
```

Output | Serial Monitor ×

Message (Enter to send message to 'Arduino UNO' on 'COM3')

```
Magnetic Strength: 512
Magnetic Strength: 511
Magnetic Strength: 513
Magnetic Strength: 510
Magnetic Strength: 511
Magnetic Strength: 512
Magnetic Strength: 512
Magnetic Strength: 513
Magnetic Strength: 511
Magnetic Strength: 512
Magnetic Strength: 560
Magnetic Strength: 573
Magnetic Strength: 589
Magnetic Strength: 610
Magnetic Strength: 632
Magnetic Strength: 648
Magnetic Strength: 663
Magnetic Strength: 678
Magnetic Strength: 689
Magnetic Strength: 695
```

How the Code Works

analogRead returns a number around 512 with no magnet present (512 represents roughly 2.5V on a 5V Arduino). Values above 512 indicate a North pole field; values below 512 indicate a South pole field. The further from 512, the stronger the field. The comment in the code reminds you of this interpretation. Try rotating a magnet around the sensor and watch the value change continuously.

Real-World Applications

- Current sensing circuits
- Magnetic field mapping
- Electric motor feedback
- Contactless potentiometers
- Joystick position sensing

Experiment 30 | Magnetic Position Detector

Sensor: Linear Hall Sensor

Difficulty: ★ Beginner

Objective: Determine the position (left, centre, right) of a magnet relative to the sensor.

How It Works

By setting two threshold values - one above and one below the neutral midpoint - we can divide the sensor's output into three zones: South pole detected, neutral, and North pole detected. This turns the continuous analog reading into a position or polarity detector.

Concepts Learned

- Threshold-based position detection
- Multiple value zones
- Bipolar Hall sensing
- Spatial classification

Components Required

Component	Qty
Arduino Uno	1
Linear Hall Sensor Module	1
Small Magnet	1

Component	Qty
Jumper Wires	3

Wiring

Linear Hall Pin	Arduino Pin
S	A0
+	5V
-	GND

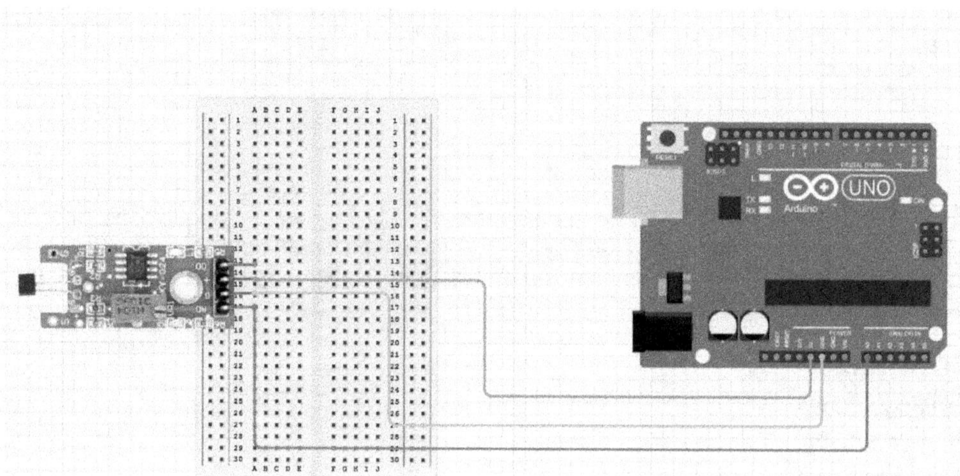

Arduino Code & Serial Monitor Output

```
const int hallPin = A0;

void setup() {
  Serial.begin(9600);
}

void loop() {
  int value = analogRead(hallPin);
  Serial.print("Value: ");
Serial.print(value); Serial.print(" -->
");
  if (value < 450) {
    Serial.println("South Pole (below
centre)");
  } else if (value > 570) {
    Serial.println("North Pole (above
centre)");
  } else {
    Serial.println("Neutral / No Magnet");
  }
  delay(200);
}
```

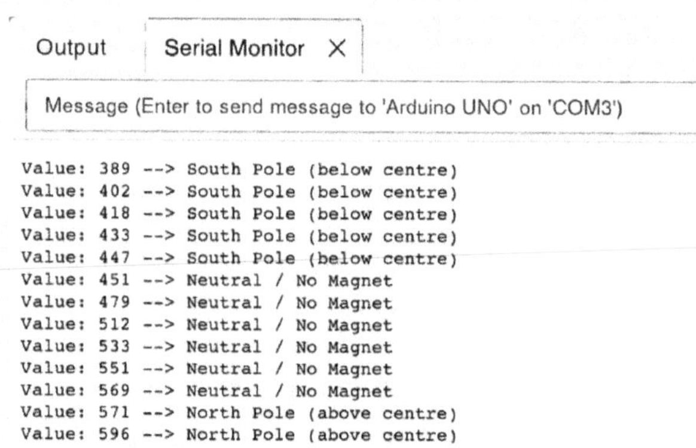

How the Code Works

The code checks if the value is below 450 (South pole), above 570 (North pole), or between the two (neutral). The band between 450 and 570 acts as a dead zone that prevents the output from flickering when the sensor is near the boundary. You can widen or narrow this band by adjusting the two threshold values.

Real-World Applications

- Joystick position reading
- Linear encoder systems
- Valve position detection
- Dial position sensors
- Magnetic card readers

Experiment 31 | Magnetic Switch Operation

Sensor: Reed Switch Module
Difficulty: ★ Beginner
Objective: Understand how a reed switch opens and closes in the presence of a magnet.

How It Works

A reed switch contains two thin magnetic metal contacts sealed inside a glass tube. When a magnet is brought close, the magnetic field causes both contacts to bend toward each other and touch, completing the circuit. Remove the magnet and the contacts spring apart again. Reed switches are used everywhere from door sensors to bicycle speedometers.

Concepts Learned

- Reed switch operation
- Normally open contact
- Magnetic circuit switching
- Contact bounce

Components Required

Component	Qty
Arduino Uno	1
Reed Switch Module	1
Jumper Wires	3

Wiring

Reed Switch Pin	Arduino Pin
S	D2
+	5V
-	GND

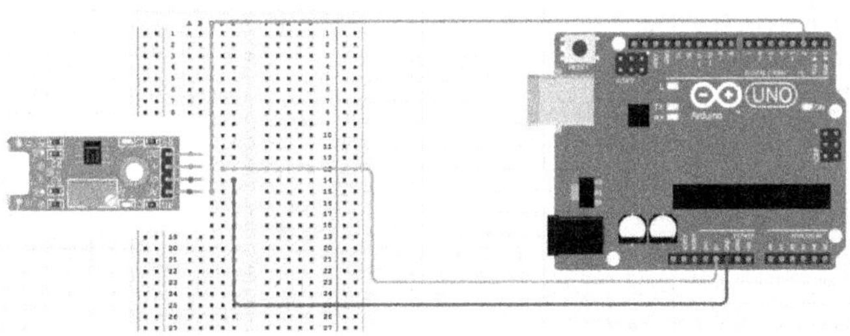

Arduino Code & Serial Monitor Output

```
const int reedPin = 2;

void setup() {
  pinMode(reedPin, INPUT_PULLUP);
  Serial.begin(9600);
}

void loop() {
  int state = digitalRead(reedPin);
  if (state == LOW) {
    Serial.println("Reed Switch: CLOSED (Magnet near)");
  } else {
    Serial.println("Reed Switch: OPEN (No magnet)");
  }
  delay(200);
}
```

Output | Serial Monitor ×

Message (Enter to send message to 'Arduino UNO' on 'COM3')

```
Reed Switch: OPEN (No magnet)
Reed Switch: OPEN (No magnet)
Reed Switch: OPEN (No magnet)
Reed Switch: OPEN (No magnet)
Reed Switch: OPEN (No magnet)
Reed Switch: OPEN (No magnet)
Reed Switch: OPEN (No magnet)
Reed Switch: OPEN (No magnet)
Reed Switch: CLOSED (Magnet near)
Reed Switch: CLOSED (Magnet near)
Reed Switch: CLOSED (Magnet near)
Reed Switch: CLOSED (Magnet near)
Reed Switch: CLOSED (Magnet near)
Reed Switch: CLOSED (Magnet near)
```

How the Code Works

INPUT_PULLUP keeps the pin HIGH when the circuit is open (no magnet). When the magnet closes the reed switch, the circuit is completed, pulling the pin to GND - which reads as LOW. So LOW means closed (magnet near) and HIGH means open (no magnet). This inverted logic is standard for switches and you will see it throughout this book.

Real-World Applications

- Door and window sensors
- Flow meters
- Level gauges
- Tamper detection
- Speed sensors in bicycles

Experiment 32 | Door Open Detector

Sensor: Reed Switch Module

Difficulty: ★ Beginner

Objective: Simulate a door sensor that prints an alert when the door is opened.

How It Works

A door sensor uses a reed switch mounted on the door frame and a magnet mounted on the door itself. When the door closes, the magnet lines up with the reed switch and closes the circuit. When the door opens, the magnet moves away and the circuit opens. This experiment simulates exactly that by detecting changes in the reed switch state rather than just reporting its current state.

Concepts Learned

- Reed switch as door sensor
- Alert on state change
- One-time trigger vs continuous
- Magnet placement logic

Components Required

Component	Qty
Arduino Uno	1

Component	Qty
Reed Switch Module	1
Magnet	1
Jumper Wires	3

Wiring

Reed Switch Pin	Arduino Pin
S	D2
+	5V
-	GND

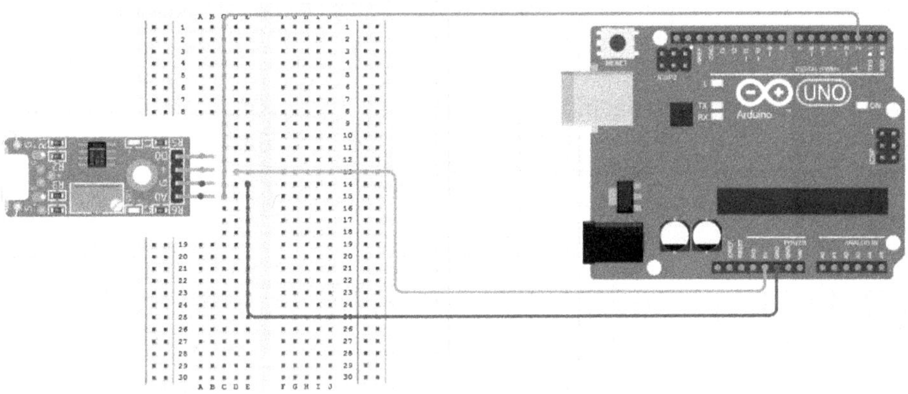

Arduino Code & Serial Monitor Output

```
const int reedPin = 2;
int lastState = LOW;

void setup() {
  pinMode(reedPin, INPUT_PULLUP);
  Serial.begin(9600);
  Serial.println("Door monitor active.");
}

void loop() {
  int state = digitalRead(reedPin);
  if (state == HIGH && lastState == LOW) {
    Serial.println("DOOR OPENED!");
  }
  if (state == LOW && lastState == HIGH) {
    Serial.println("Door closed.");
  }
  lastState = state;
  delay(100);
}
```

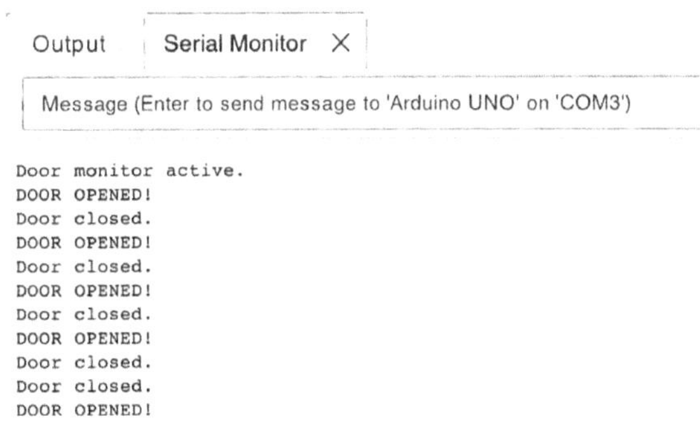

How the Code Works

lastState starts as LOW (door assumed closed, magnet present). When state changes to HIGH it means the circuit just opened - the door was opened. When it goes back to LOW the door was closed again. Only printing on state changes (not continuously) keeps the output clean and readable. This edge-triggered approach is used in virtually every door alarm on the market.

Real-World Applications

- Home security door sensors
- Smart lock entry logging
- Refrigerator door alerts
- Mailbox notification
- Cabinet tamper detection

Experiment 33 | Compact Magnetic Detection

Sensor: Mini Reed Switch

Difficulty: ★ Beginner

Objective: Use the mini reed switch to detect a magnetic field in a compact form factor.

How It Works

The mini reed switch works on exactly the same principle as the full-size reed switch - a magnetic field closes its contacts. The only difference is physical size. Smaller switches are used in compact devices like hearing aids, medication dispensers, and wearables where space is limited.

Concepts Learned

- Miniature reed switch
- Compact sensor form factor
- Digital binary detection
- Wiring small components

Components Required

Component	Qty
Arduino Uno	1
Mini Reed Switch Module	1
Jumper Wires	3

Wiring

Mini Reed Switch	Arduino Pin
S	D2
+	5V
-	GND

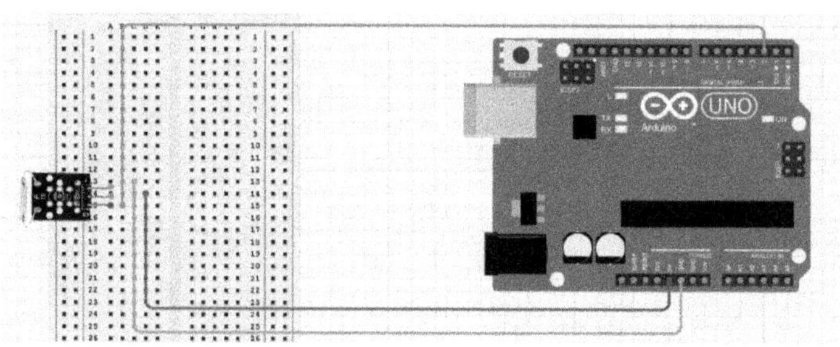

Arduino Code & Serial Monitor Output

```
const int reedPin = 2;

void setup() {
  pinMode(reedPin, INPUT_PULLUP);
  Serial.begin(9600);
}

void loop() {
  if (digitalRead(reedPin) == LOW) {
    Serial.println("Magnet Detected");
  } else {
    Serial.println("No Magnet");
  }
  delay(200);
}
```

Output Serial Monitor ×

Message (Enter to send message to 'Arduino UNO' on 'COM3')

```
No Magnet
No Magnet
No Magnet
No Magnet
No Magnet
No Magnet
No Magnet
No Magnet
Magnet Detected
Magnet Detected
Magnet Detected
Magnet Detected
Magnet Detected
Magnet Detected
Magnet Detected
```

How the Code Works

The code is the simplest reed switch example in this book - just read the pin and print the result. INPUT_PULLUP keeps the signal stable. LOW means the magnet is close and the switch is closed. Try different magnets and different approach angles to understand the switch's sensitivity and activation zone.

Real-World Applications

- Wearable device magnet clasps
- Compact security sensors
- Toy magnetic switches
- Hearing aid controls
- Compact flow meters

Experiment 34 | Read Remote Button

Sensor: IR Receiver Module
Difficulty: ★ Beginner
Objective: Receive IR signals from a TV remote and display the button codes.

How It Works

TV remote controls use infrared light to send commands. Each button press transmits a unique pattern of infrared pulses at 38kHz - too fast to see but detectable by the IR receiver. The receiver decodes the pulse pattern into a hexadecimal code number. The IRremote library handles all the complex timing and decoding, giving you a simple number you can work with.

Concepts Learned

- IR communication protocol
- IRremote library
- Hex code decoding
- Remote control operation

Components Required

Component	Qty
Arduino Uno	1
IR Receiver Module	1
TV Remote Control	1

Component	Qty
Jumper Wires	3

Wiring

IR Receiver Pin	Arduino Pin
S	D2
+	5V
-	GND

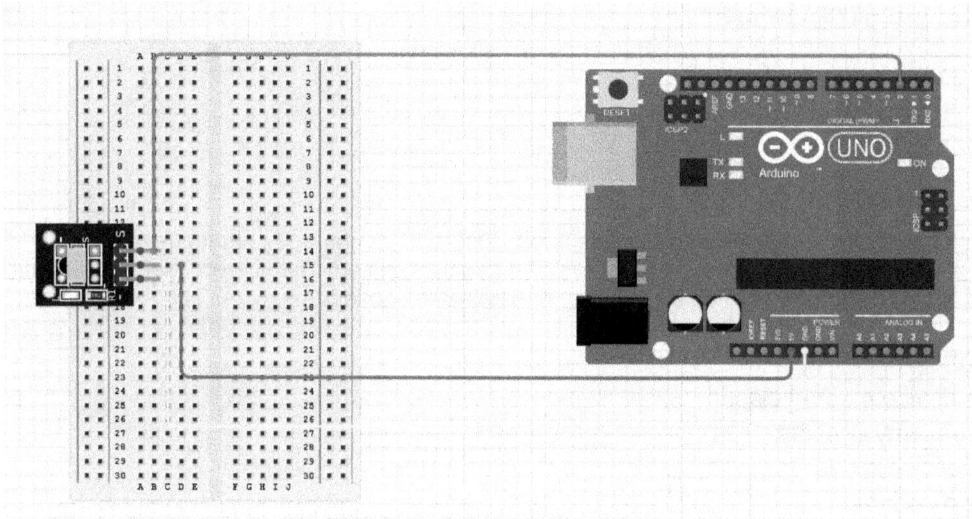

Arduino Code & Serial Monitor Output

```
#include <IRremote.h>
const int irPin = 2;
IRrecv irrecv(irPin);
decode_results results;

void setup() {
  Serial.begin(9600);
  irrecv.enableIRIn();
}

void loop() {
  if (irrecv.decode(&results)) {
    Serial.print("Button Code: 0x");
    Serial.println(results.value, HEX);
    irrecv.resume();
  }
}
```

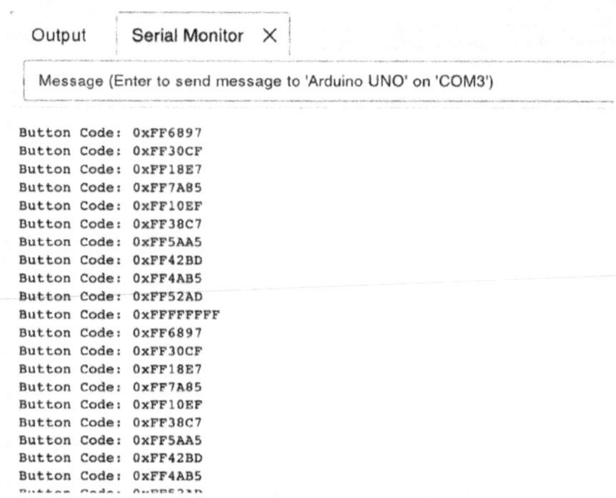

How the Code Works

irrecv.enableIRIn() starts the receiver listening for signals. In loop(), irrecv.decode(&results) checks if a complete signal has been received. If so, results.value contains the button code as a hexadecimal number, which is printed with the HEX formatting option. irrecv.resume() resets the receiver to listen for the next signal - without this line, it would only ever decode one button press.

Real-World Applications

- Custom remote controls
- Robotics IR control
- Presentation clickers
- Home automation remotes
- IR-controlled toys

Experiment 35 | Decode Remote Signals

Sensor: IR Receiver Module
Difficulty: ★ Beginner
Objective: Map specific IR button codes to named actions and display them.

How It Works

Once you know the hex codes for your remote's buttons (from Experiment 34), you can map each one to a named action. Every remote brand uses different codes - the codes in this example are from a common NEC-protocol remote and may not match yours. Use the output from Experiment 34 to find your own remote's codes and update the case values.

Concepts Learned

- Switch-case on hex codes
- Named button mapping
- Protocol decoding
- Remote control customisation

Components Required

Component	Qty
Arduino Uno	1
IR Receiver Module	1
TV Remote Control	1
Jumper Wires	3

Wiring

IR Receiver Pin	Arduino Pin
S	D2
+	5V
-	GND

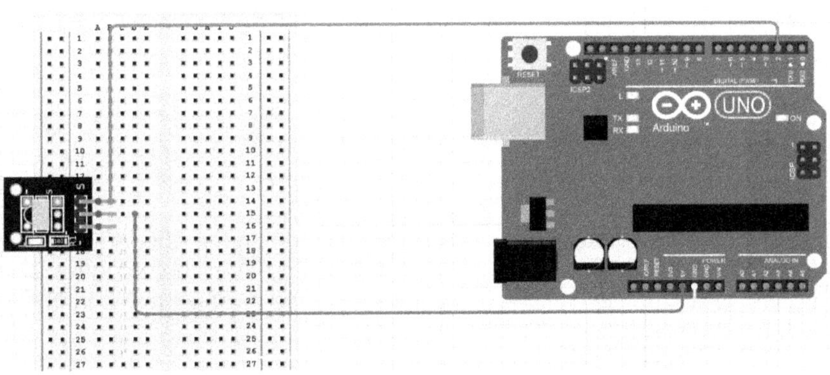

Arduino Code & Serial Monitor Output

```
#include <IRremote.h>
const int irPin = 2;
IRrecv irrecv(irPin);
decode_results results;

void setup() {
  Serial.begin(9600);
  irrecv.enableIRIn();
}

void loop() {
  if (irrecv.decode(&results)) {
    switch (results.value) {
      case 0xFF629D: Serial.println("UP");
break;
      case 0xFFA857:
Serial.println("DOWN");  break;
      case 0xFF22DD:
Serial.println("LEFT");  break;
      case 0xFFC23D:
Serial.println("RIGHT"); break;
      case 0xFF02FD: Serial.println("OK");
break;
      default: Serial.println("UNKNOWN");
    }
    irrecv.resume();
  }
}
```

Output | Serial Monitor ×

Message (Enter to send message to 'Arduino UNO' on 'COM3')

```
UP
DOWN
LEFT
RIGHT
OK
UP
UP
LEFT
OK
RIGHT
DOWN
DOWN
```

How the Code Works

The switch statement is more efficient than a chain of if-else when comparing one variable against many values. Each case checks if results.value matches a specific code. break stops execution and exits the switch after a match is found. The default case at the end catches any unrecognised codes. Replace the hex values with the ones you captured from Experiment 34.

Real-World Applications

- Universal remote decoders
- Smart TV assistants
- IR-controlled robots
- Custom home automation
- Escape room puzzles

Experiment 36 | Send IR Signal

Sensor: IR Emitter Module

Difficulty: ★ Beginner

Objective: Transmit a custom IR signal and observe it being sent.

How It Works

The IR emitter module contains an infrared LED - it emits invisible light in the 850–950nm wavelength range. By pulsing this light at exactly 38kHz in specific patterns, it can mimic any TV remote control. The IRremote library takes care of generating the correct pulse timing - you just provide the protocol (NEC in this case) and the code number.

Concepts Learned

- IR signal transmission
- IRremote send library
- 38kHz carrier frequency
- Simulating a remote control

Components Required

Component	Qty
Arduino Uno	1
IR Emitter Module	1
Jumper Wires	3

Wiring

IR Emitter Pin	Arduino Pin
S	D3
+	5V
-	GND

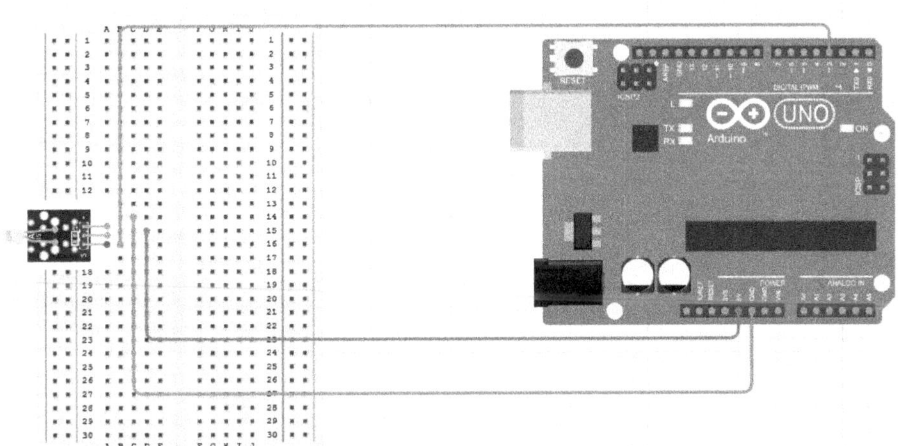

Arduino Code & Serial Monitor Output

```
#include <IRremote.h>
IRsend irsend;

void setup() {
  Serial.begin(9600);
}

void loop() {
  irsend.sendNEC(0xFF629D, 32);  // Send
NEC code
  Serial.println("IR Signal Sent:
0xFF629D");
  delay(1000);
}
```

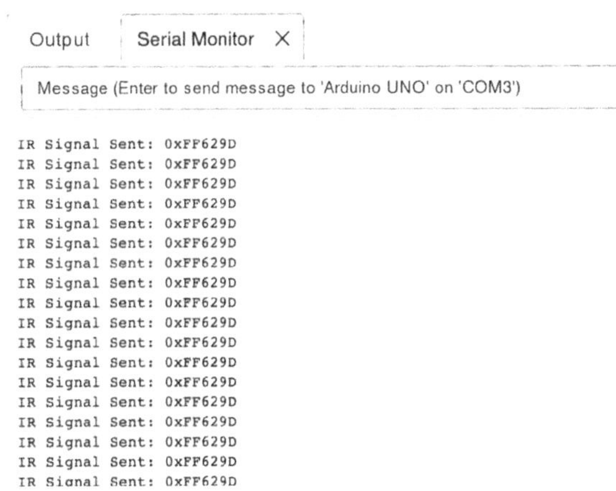

How the Code Works

irsend.sendNEC(0xFF629D, 32) transmits the code 0xFF629D using the NEC protocol, with 32 as the number of bits. The 38kHz carrier frequency is generated automatically by the library. After sending, we print a confirmation to the Serial Monitor. To control a real device, replace 0xFF629D with the code your device expects - use Experiment 35 to find the right codes.

Real-World Applications

- TV/AC control from Arduino
- Custom remote emulation
- IR repeater systems
- Smart home control hubs
- Automated appliance testers

Experiment 37 | Object Detection

Sensor: Obstacle Avoidance Sensor

Difficulty: ★ Beginner

Objective: Detect nearby objects using the infrared obstacle avoidance sensor.

How It Works

The obstacle avoidance sensor has both an infrared emitter and a receiver. It constantly emits infrared light forward. When an object is close enough, the light bounces back and hits the receiver. The sensor's onboard comparator circuit compares the reflected signal strength to a threshold set by the small blue potentiometer, and flips its output LOW when an obstacle is detected.

Concepts Learned

- IR reflection detection
- Object proximity sensing
- Digital obstacle output
- Adjustable sensitivity

Components Required

Component	Qty
Arduino Uno	1
Obstacle Avoidance Sensor	1
Jumper Wires	3

Wiring

Obstacle Sensor Pin	Arduino Pin
OUT	D2
VCC	5V
GND	GND

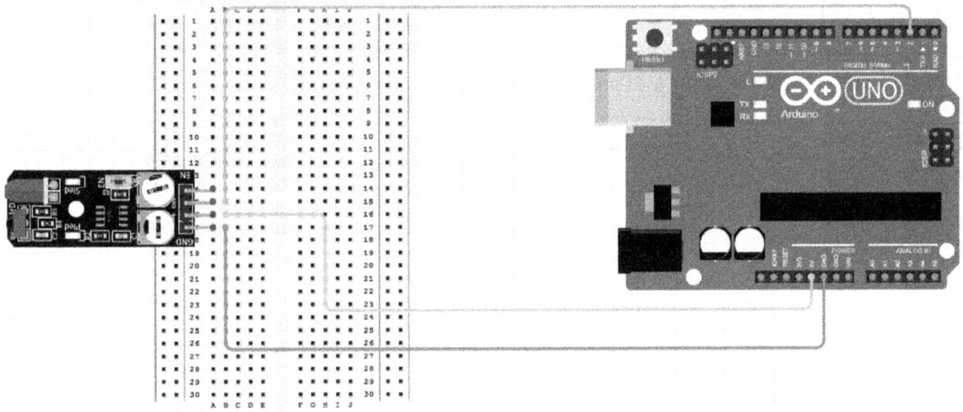

Arduino Code & Serial Monitor Output

```
const int obstaclePin = 2;

void setup() {
  pinMode(obstaclePin, INPUT);
  Serial.begin(9600);
}

void loop() {
  int state = digitalRead(obstaclePin);
  if (state == LOW) {
    Serial.println("OBSTACLE DETECTED!");
  } else {
    Serial.println("Path Clear");
  }
  delay(200);
}
```

Output | Serial Monitor ×

Message (Enter to send message to 'Arduino UNO' on 'COM3')

```
Path Clear
Path Clear
Path Clear
Path Clear
Path Clear
Path Clear
Path Clear
Path Clear
OBSTACLE DETECTED!
OBSTACLE DETECTED!
OBSTACLE DETECTED!
OBSTACLE DETECTED!
Path Clear
Path Clear
```

How the Code Works

The sensor output is LOW when an obstacle is detected and HIGH when the path is clear. Inside loop(), we read the pin and print the appropriate message. The key practical skill here is potentiometer adjustment - turn it clockwise to increase range, counter-clockwise to decrease it. Set it too sensitive and it triggers on distant walls; too low and it misses nearby objects.

Real-World Applications

- Robot obstacle avoidance
- Automatic braking systems
- Conveyor object detection
- Automatic door openers
- Anti-collision systems

Experiment 38 | Distance Threshold Detection

Sensor: Obstacle Avoidance Sensor
Difficulty: ★ Beginner
Objective: Use the onboard potentiometer to adjust detection range and observe changes.

How It Works

The same obstacle sensor hardware from Experiment 37 is used here, but the focus shifts to calibration. By adjusting the onboard potentiometer while watching the Serial Monitor, you can set the exact detection range for your specific application. This hands-on calibration experience is fundamental to working with real sensors.

Concepts Learned

- Potentiometer sensitivity adjustment
- Detection range tuning
- Physical calibration
- Threshold concepts

Components Required

Component	Qty
Arduino Uno	1
Obstacle Avoidance Sensor	1
Jumper Wires	3

Wiring

Obstacle Sensor Pin	Arduino Pin
OUT	D2
VCC	5V
GND	GND

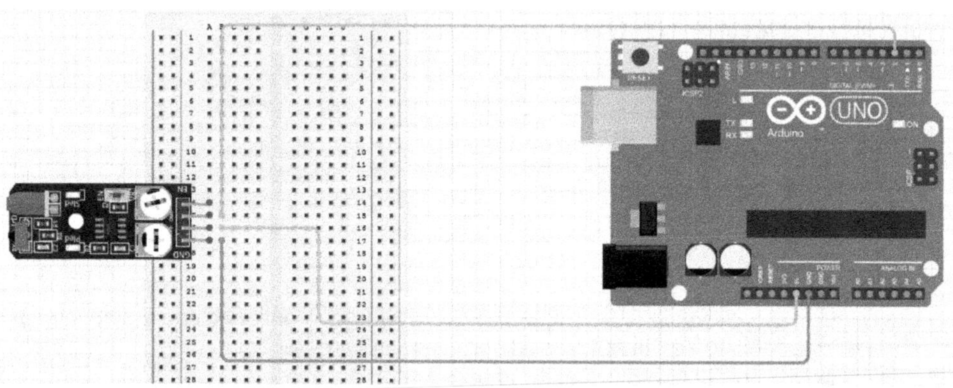

Arduino Code & Serial Monitor Output

```
const int sensorPin = 2;

void setup() {
  pinMode(sensorPin, INPUT);
  Serial.begin(9600);
  Serial.println("Adjust potentiometer to
set detection range.");
}

void loop() {
  int val = digitalRead(sensorPin);
```

Output | Serial Monitor ×

Message (Enter to send message to 'Arduino UNO' on 'COM3')

```
Adjust potentiometer to set detection range.
OUT OF RANGE
OUT OF RANGE
OUT OF RANGE
OUT OF RANGE
OUT OF RANGE
IN RANGE
IN RANGE
IN RANGE
IN RANGE
IN RANGE
IN RANGE
```

```
  Serial.println(val == LOW ? "IN RANGE" :
"OUT OF RANGE");
  delay(200);
}
```

How the Code Works

The code itself is simple - just read and print IN RANGE or OUT OF RANGE. The real experiment is physical: hold an object at your desired detection distance, then turn the potentiometer until the output just switches to IN RANGE. Back it off slightly to create a reliable trigger point. This process - adjusting a physical component while monitoring software output - is called hardware calibration.

Real-World Applications

- Adjustable proximity switches
- Robot sensor tuning
- Auto door range setting
- Part detection on lines
- Parking sensor calibration

Experiment 39 | Black Line Detection

Sensor: Tracking Sensor
Difficulty: ★ Beginner
Objective: Detect a black line on a white surface using the tracking (line-following) sensor.

How It Works

The tracking sensor works by shining infrared light downward and measuring how much reflects back. White or light surfaces reflect a lot of infrared light, giving a HIGH reading. Black or dark surfaces absorb most of the infrared light, reflecting very little, giving a LOW reading. This simple difference in reflectivity is how line-following robots navigate.

Concepts Learned

- IR reflection on surfaces
- White vs black surface response
- Line-following principle
- Low/high logic on surface colour

Components Required

Component	Qty
Arduino Uno	1
Tracking Sensor	1
Jumper Wires	3

Wiring

Tracking Sensor Pin	Arduino Pin
OUT	D2
VCC	5V
GND	GND

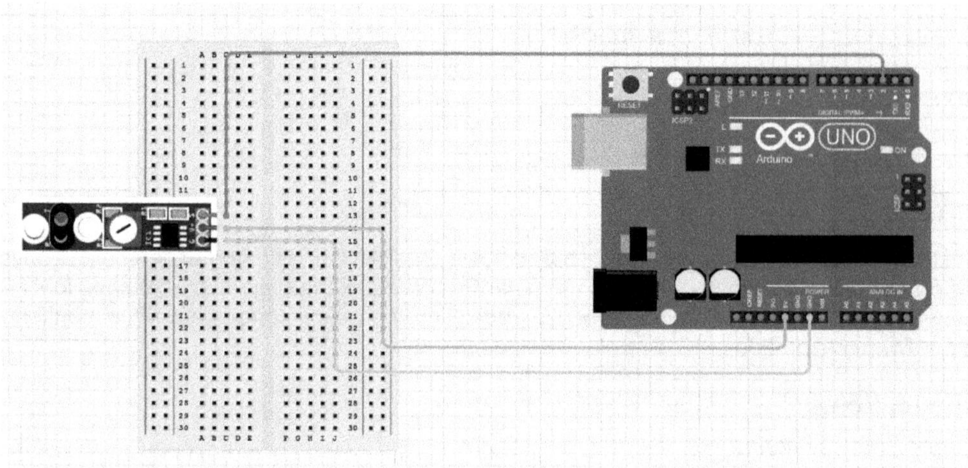

Arduino Code & Serial Monitor Output

```
const int trackPin = 2;

void setup() {
  pinMode(trackPin, INPUT);
  Serial.begin(9600);
}

void loop() {
  int state = digitalRead(trackPin);
  if (state == LOW) {
    Serial.println("BLACK LINE detected");
  } else {
    Serial.println("White surface");
  }
  delay(100);
}
```

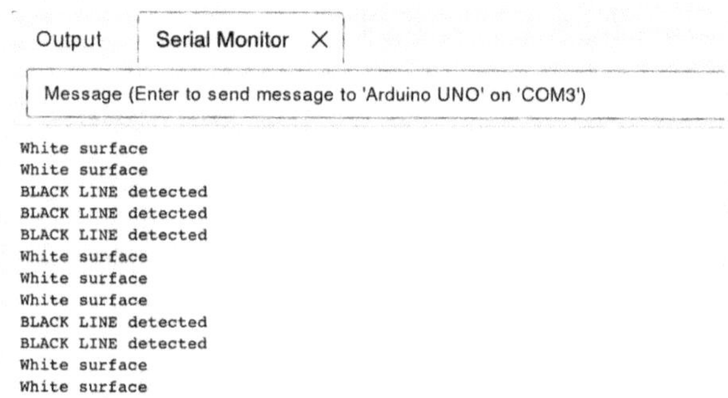

How the Code Works

When the sensor is over a black line, it reads LOW and we print BLACK LINE detected. Over a white surface it reads HIGH. The 100-millisecond delay is short enough to track a moving line in a robot. In a real line-following robot you would have two or more of these sensors side by side - when the left sensor sees black, turn left; when the right sensor sees black, turn right.

Real-World Applications

- Line-following robots
- Automated guided vehicles
- Barcode edge detection
- Conveyor tracking systems
- Maze-solving robots

Experiment 40 | White Surface Detection

Sensor: Tracking Sensor

Difficulty: ★ Beginner

Objective: Confirm detection of a white surface (high reflectivity) vs a dark surface.

How It Works

This is the inverse perspective of Experiment 39 - instead of detecting the black line, we confirm detection of the white surface. Understanding both states is important because in some applications (like detecting the end of a track) you want to know when white is seen, not when black is seen.

Concepts Learned

- Surface reflectivity
- Sensor output inversion
- IR absorption vs reflection
- Calibration with surfaces

Components Required

Component	Qty
Arduino Uno	1
Tracking Sensor	1
Jumper Wires	3

Wiring

Tracking Sensor Pin	Arduino Pin
OUT	D2
VCC	5V
GND	GND

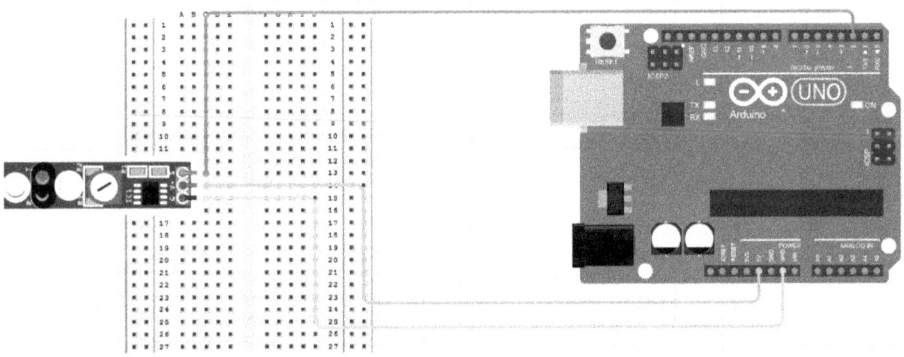

Arduino Code & Serial Monitor Output

```
const int trackPin = 2;

void setup() {
  pinMode(trackPin, INPUT);
  Serial.begin(9600);
}

void loop() {
  int state = digitalRead(trackPin);
  Serial.println(state == HIGH ? "WHITE
surface (high reflectivity)" : "DARK
surface (low reflectivity)");
  delay(100);
```

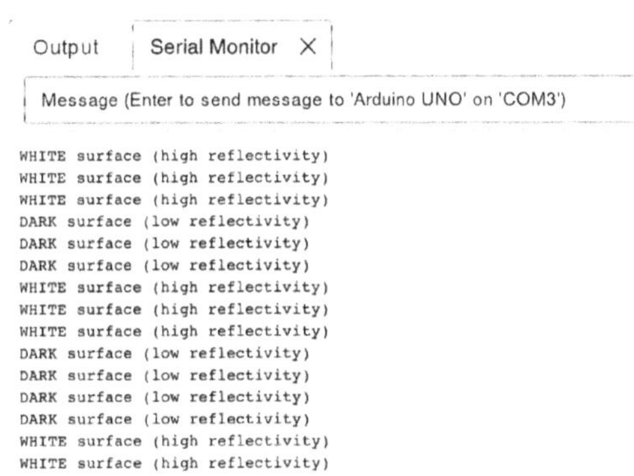

```
}
```

How the Code Works

The condition state == HIGH now means white surface detected. We use the ternary operator to print the appropriate message in a single line. Notice the phrasing - we describe white as high reflectivity and dark as low reflectivity. This is the physical reason for the sensor's output, and understanding the physics helps you predict how it will behave on unusual surfaces like grey, shiny, or transparent materials.

Real-World Applications

- Surface quality inspection
- Optical sorting machines
- Label detection
- Printed mark reading
- Package surface scanning

Experiment 41 | Position Tracking

Sensor: Rotary Encoder
Difficulty: ★★ Intermediate
Objective: Track the absolute position of a rotary encoder by counting pulses.

How It Works

A rotary encoder has a disc with evenly spaced teeth or slots and two sensors - CLK and DT - offset from each other slightly. As you turn the shaft, the teeth alternately block and unblock each sensor, generating a series of pulses. The order in which CLK and DT pulse tells you the direction of rotation. Counting total pulses gives you the position.

Concepts Learned

- Rotary encoder operation
- Pulse counting
- Interrupt-based counting
- Position accumulation

Components Required

Component	Qty
Arduino Uno	1
Rotary Encoder Module	1
Jumper Wires	4

Wiring

Encoder Pin	Arduino Pin
CLK	D2
DT	D3
VCC	5V
GND	GND

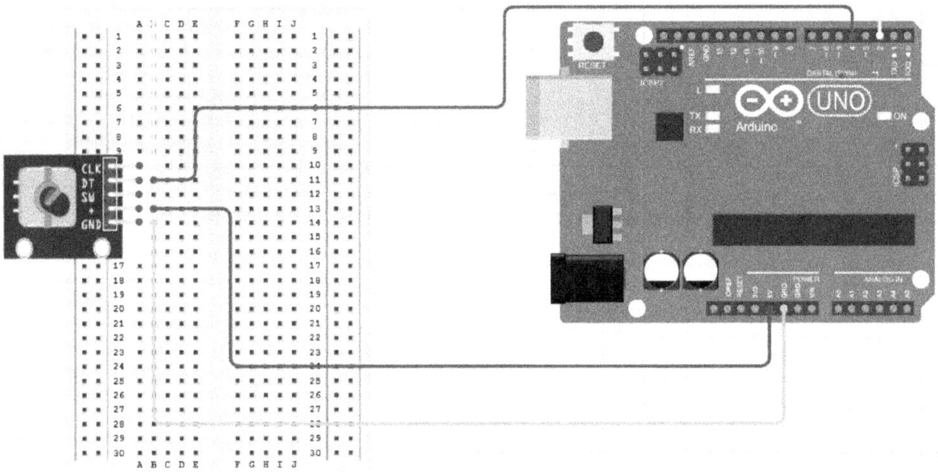

Arduino Code & Serial Monitor Output

```
const int clkPin = 2;
const int dtPin  = 3;
int position = 0;
int lastClk;

void setup() {
  pinMode(clkPin, INPUT);
  pinMode(dtPin,  INPUT);
  Serial.begin(9600);
  lastClk = digitalRead(clkPin);
}

void loop() {
  int currentClk = digitalRead(clkPin);
  if (currentClk != lastClk && currentClk
== HIGH) {
    if (digitalRead(dtPin) != currentClk)
position++;
    else
position--;
    Serial.print("Position: ");
    Serial.println(position);
  }
  lastClk = currentClk;
}
```

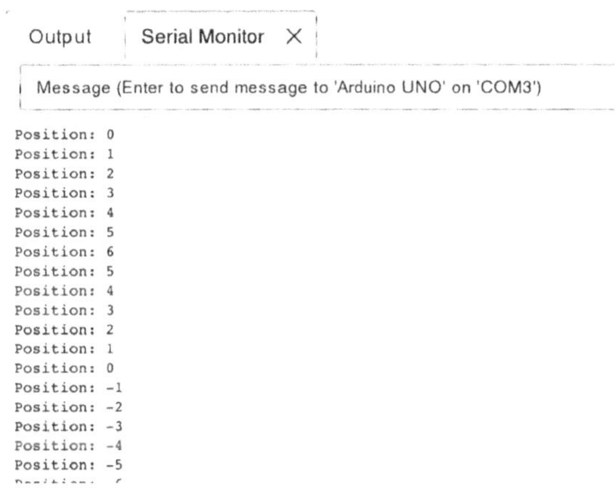

How the Code Works

lastClk stores the previous CLK state. When CLK changes and its new value is HIGH, a full pulse has completed. We then check if DT differs from CLK - if it does, rotation is clockwise and we increment position; if DT matches CLK, rotation is counter-clockwise and we decrement. Printing after every pulse gives you a live position readout in the Serial Monitor.

Real-World Applications

- CNC machine position
- Camera focus knobs

- Volume control dials
- Printer head tracking
- Robot joint position

Experiment 42 | Direction Detection

Sensor: Rotary Encoder
Difficulty: ★★ Intermediate
Objective: Detect whether the rotary encoder is being turned clockwise or counter-clockwise.

How It Works

Direction detection uses the same quadrature encoding principle as position tracking. The key insight is that CLK and DT pulse in a specific sequence depending on rotation direction. Clockwise rotation means DT is already LOW when CLK goes HIGH. Counter-clockwise means DT is HIGH when CLK goes HIGH. By checking DT at the exact moment CLK rises, we determine direction.

Concepts Learned

- Quadrature encoding
- Phase relationship
- CW vs CCW detection
- Interrupt-driven logic

Components Required

Component	Qty
Arduino Uno	1
Rotary Encoder Module	1
Jumper Wires	4

Wiring

Encoder Pin	Arduino Pin
`CLK`	`D2`
`DT`	`D3`
`VCC`	`5V`
`GND`	`GND`

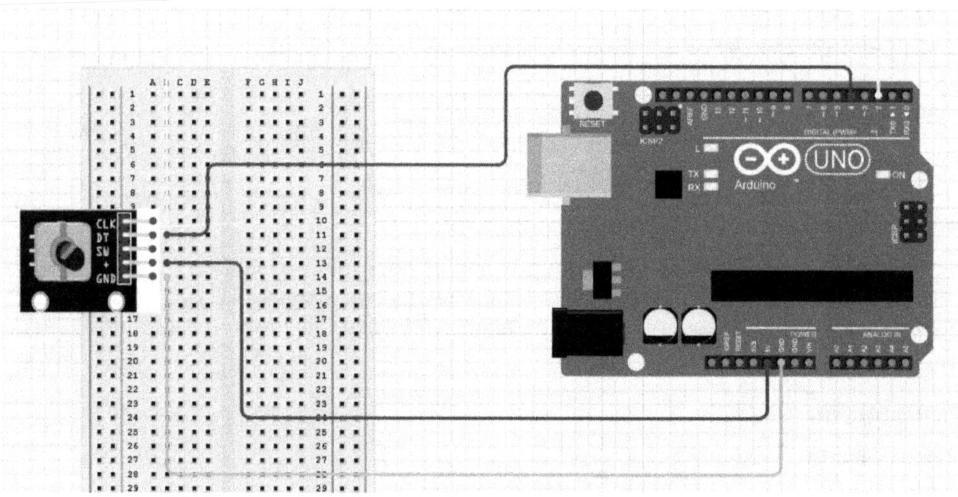

Arduino Code & Serial Monitor Output

```
const int clkPin = 2;
const int dtPin  = 3;
int lastClk;

void setup() {
  pinMode(clkPin, INPUT);
  pinMode(dtPin,  INPUT);
  Serial.begin(9600);
  lastClk = digitalRead(clkPin);
}

void loop() {
  int currentClk = digitalRead(clkPin);
  if (currentClk != lastClk && currentClk
== HIGH) {
    if (digitalRead(dtPin) != currentClk)
{
      Serial.println("Clockwise");
    } else {
      Serial.println("Counter-Clockwise");
    }
  }
  lastClk = currentClk;
}
```

Output | Serial Monitor ×

Message (Enter to send message to 'Arduino UNO' on 'COM3')

```
Clockwise
Clockwise
Clockwise
Counter-Clockwise
Counter-Clockwise
Clockwise
Clockwise
Counter-Clockwise
Counter-Clockwise
Counter-Clockwise
Clockwise
Clockwise
```

How the Code Works

The condition digitalRead(dtPin) != currentClk checks whether DT and CLK are in opposite states at the moment of the CLK rising edge. If they differ, direction is clockwise. If they match, it is counter-clockwise. This is exactly the same logic as Experiment 41 - the only difference is that we print a direction name instead of updating a position counter.

Real-World Applications

- Scroll knobs on devices
- Zoom in/out controls
- Pan/tilt camera heads
- Electric motor direction control
- Navigation wheel input

Experiment 43 | Speed Measurement

Sensor: Rotary Encoder
Difficulty: ★★ Intermediate
Objective: Calculate the rotational speed (RPM) of an encoder shaft.

How It Works

Speed is calculated by counting how many pulses arrive in a known time window. If the encoder has 20 slots per revolution, then 20 pulses equals one full rotation. Count pulses for one second, divide by 20 to get revolutions per second, multiply by 60 to get RPM. Using Arduino's interrupt system means no pulses are missed even at high speeds.

Concepts Learned

- RPM calculation
- Time-based measurement
- Pulses per revolution

- millis() timing

Components Required

Component	Qty
Arduino Uno	1
Rotary Encoder Module	1
Jumper Wires	4

Wiring

Encoder Pin	Arduino Pin
CLK	D2
DT	D3
VCC	5V
GND	GND

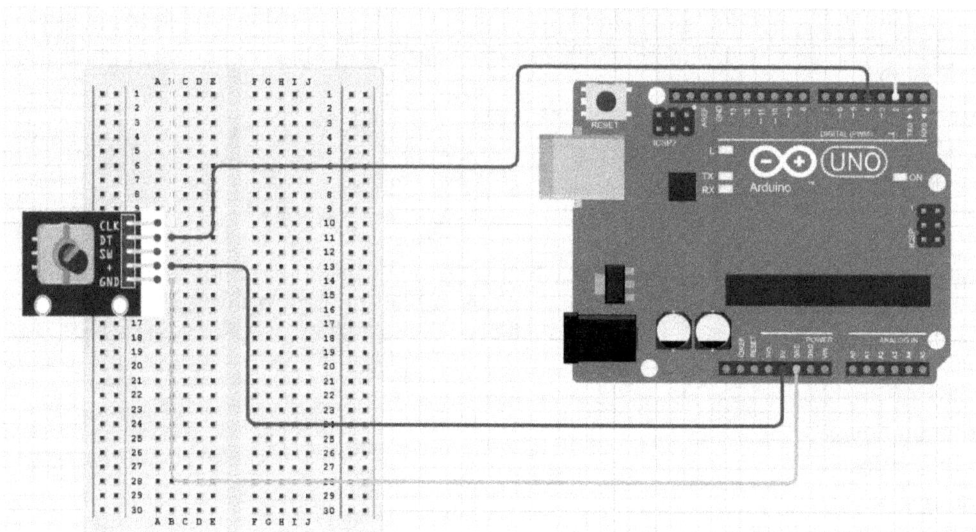

Arduino Code & Serial Monitor Output

```
const int clkPin = 2;
volatile int pulseCount = 0;
unsigned long lastTime = 0;
const int pulsesPerRev = 20;

void countPulse() { pulseCount++; }

void setup() {
  Serial.begin(9600);

attachInterrupt(digitalPinToInterrupt(clkP
in), countPulse, RISING);
}
```

Output | Serial Monitor ×

Message (Enter to send message to 'Arduino UNO' on 'COM3')

```
RPM: 0.00
RPM: 12.00
RPM: 24.00
RPM: 36.00
RPM: 48.00
RPM: 60.00
RPM: 72.00
RPM: 84.00
RPM: 96.00
RPM: 108.00
RPM: 120.00
RPM: 132.00
RPM: 144.00
RPM: 156.00
```

```
void loop() {
  if (millis() - lastTime >= 1000) {
    float rpm = (pulseCount /
(float)pulsesPerRev) * 60.0;
    Serial.print("RPM: ");
Serial.println(rpm);
    pulseCount = 0;
    lastTime = millis();
  }
}
```

How the Code Works

attachInterrupt sets up the Arduino to call countPulse() automatically every time the CLK pin rises - this is an interrupt, meaning it runs instantly regardless of what else the code is doing. In loop(), every second we calculate RPM from the accumulated pulse count, print it, and reset the counter to zero. The volatile keyword on pulseCount is required for variables shared between main code and interrupt functions.

Real-World Applications

- Electric motor RPM meters
- Turbine speed monitoring
- Conveyor belt speed
- Anemometers (wind speed)
- Bicycle speedometers

Experiment 44 | X Axis Reading

Sensor: Joystick Module
Difficulty: ★ Beginner
Objective: Read the X-axis analog value from the joystick module.

How It Works

The joystick contains two potentiometers - one for each axis - connected to a mechanical gimbal. Moving the stick left or right turns the X-axis potentiometer; moving it forward or back turns the Y-axis potentiometer. Each potentiometer acts as a voltage divider, producing a voltage between 0V and 5V that the Arduino reads as 0 to 1023. At rest, both axes sit near the midpoint value of 512.

Concepts Learned

- Potentiometer-based joystick
- Analog centre point (512)
- Axis reading
- Dead zone concept

Components Required

Component	Qty
Arduino Uno	1
Joystick Module	1
Jumper Wires	4

Wiring

Joystick Pin	Arduino Pin
VRX	A0

Joystick Pin	Arduino Pin
VCC	5V
GND	GND

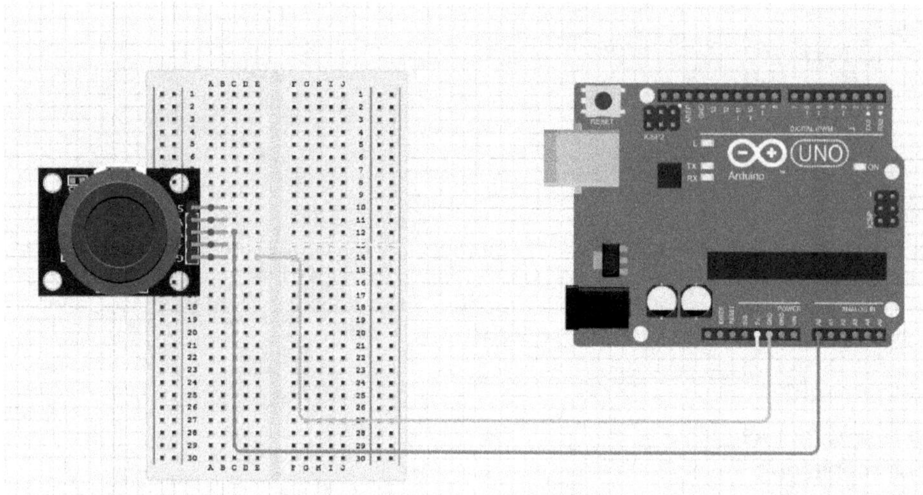

Arduino Code & Serial Monitor Output

```
const int xPin = A0;

void setup() {
  Serial.begin(9600);
}

void loop() {
  int xValue = analogRead(xPin);
  Serial.print("X Axis: ");
  Serial.println(xValue);
  // ~512=centre, 0=left, 1023=right
  delay(200);
}
```

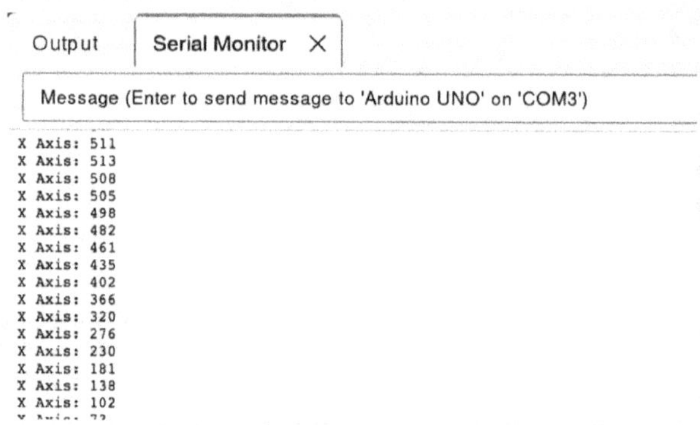

How the Code Works

analogRead(xPin) returns a number between 0 and 1023. The comment explains the mapping: 0 means fully left, 1023 means fully right, and 512 is centre. Try pushing the joystick to each extreme while watching the Serial Monitor. In a real application you would use these numbers to control speed, position, or direction - for example, values below 512 drive a motor in reverse, above 512 drive it forward.

Real-World Applications

- Game controllers
- Robot directional control
- RC car steering
- Drone throttle input
- Pan-tilt camera control

Experiment 45 | Y Axis Reading

Sensor: Joystick Module
Difficulty: ★ Beginner
Objective: Read the Y-axis analog value from the joystick module.

How It Works

The Y axis works identically to the X axis but responds to forward and backward movement of the joystick. In a typical setup, pushing the stick forward gives a low Y value (0) and pulling back gives a high value (1023), though this can vary between joystick modules. Always test your specific module to confirm the orientation.

Concepts Learned

- Dual-axis joystick
- Y-axis orientation
- Analog range mapping
- Directional input

Components Required

Component	Qty
Arduino Uno	1
Joystick Module	1
Jumper Wires	4

Wiring

Joystick Pin	Arduino Pin
VRY	A1
VCC	5V
GND	GND

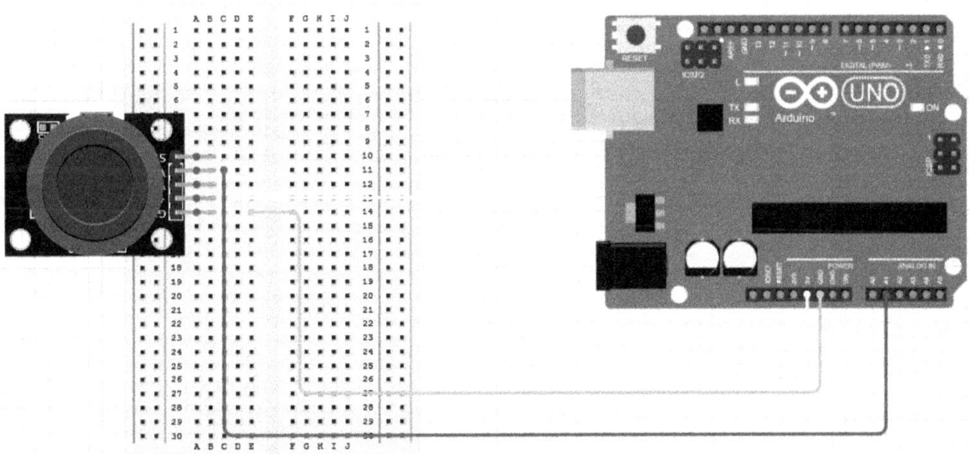

Arduino Code & Serial Monitor Output

```
const int yPin = A1;

void setup() {
  Serial.begin(9600);
}

void loop() {
  int yValue = analogRead(yPin);
  Serial.print("Y Axis: ");
  Serial.println(yValue);
  // ~512=centre, 0=up, 1023=down
  delay(200);
}
```

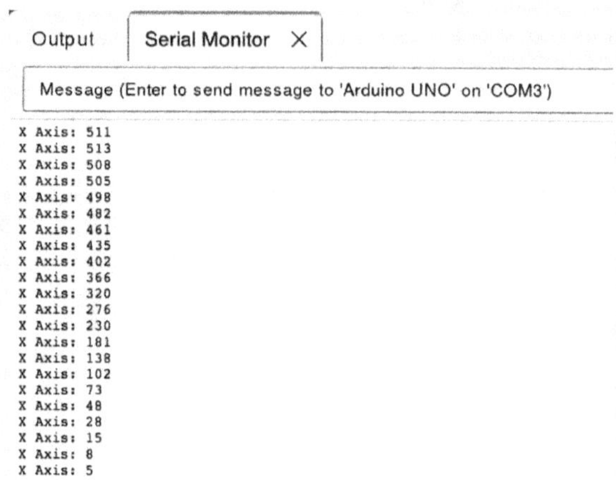

How the Code Works

This experiment reads A1 instead of A0, which is the Y-axis potentiometer. Everything else is identical to Experiment 44. Try combining both axes at once - this is what the next experiments will do. Notice that moving the stick diagonally affects both X and Y simultaneously, and the centre position for Y may not be exactly 512 on your specific module.

Real-World Applications

- Vertical camera tilt
- Elevator control input
- Submarine depth control
- Scroll input device
- Vertical flight control

Experiment 46 | Push Button Reading (Joystick)

Sensor: Joystick Module
Difficulty: ★ Beginner
Objective: Read the built-in push button of the joystick module (press down on the stick).

How It Works

The joystick's push button is a normal momentary switch built into the stick shaft - pressing down on the stick activates it. It works exactly like the button module from Experiments 1–3. This gives the joystick three inputs: X position, Y position, and a click. Most game controllers use this pattern for the thumbstick click.

Concepts Learned

- Joystick click button
- Active LOW switch
- Button within joystick module
- Multi-function input device

Components Required

Component	Qty
Arduino Uno	1
Joystick Module	1
Jumper Wires	4

Wiring

Joystick Pin	Arduino Pin
SW	D2
VCC	5V
GND	GND

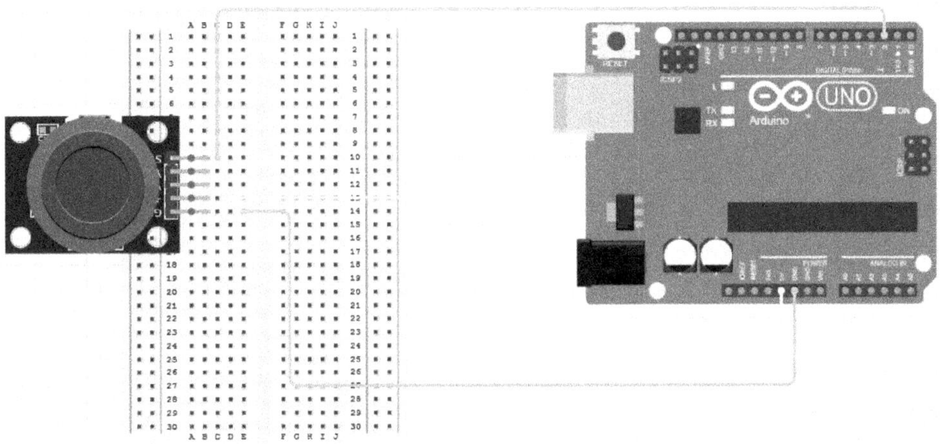

Arduino Code & Serial Monitor Output

```
const int swPin = 2;

void setup() {
  pinMode(swPin, INPUT_PULLUP);
  Serial.begin(9600);
}

void loop() {
  if (digitalRead(swPin) == LOW) {
    Serial.println("Joystick PRESSED");
    Serial.println(" ");
    delay(200);
  }
}
```

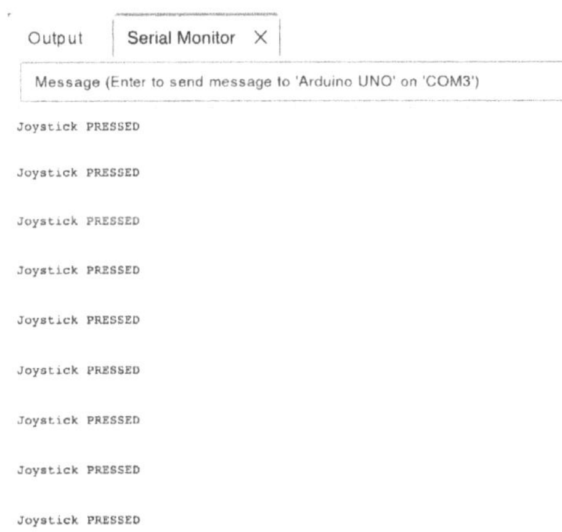

How the Code Works

INPUT_PULLUP is used because the switch connects the pin to ground when pressed. This gives us a LOW reading when pressed and HIGH when released. The if statement checks for LOW and prints JOYSTICK PRESSED with a 200ms debounce delay. You can combine this with the X and Y readings from the previous experiments to build a complete three-axis input controller.

Real-World Applications

- Game controller select button
- Confirm action in menus
- Robot gripper trigger
- Camera shutter button
- Mode selection click

Experiment 47 | Touch Detection

Sensor: Metal Touch Sensor
Difficulty: ★ Beginner
Objective: Detect when the metal touch pad is touched by a finger.

How It Works

The metal touch sensor detects the electrical capacitance of a human finger. Your body naturally holds a small electrical charge. When you touch the metal pad, this charge affects the sensor's input circuit, causing it to output HIGH. It does not need physical pressure - just contact with skin is enough. This is the same technology used in smartphone touchscreens.

Concepts Learned

- Capacitive touch sensing
- Human body capacitance
- Touch trigger output
- Simple touch interface

Components Required

Component	Qty
Arduino Uno	1
Metal Touch Sensor	1
Jumper Wires	3

Wiring

Touch Sensor Pin	Arduino Pin
S	D2
+	5V
-	GND

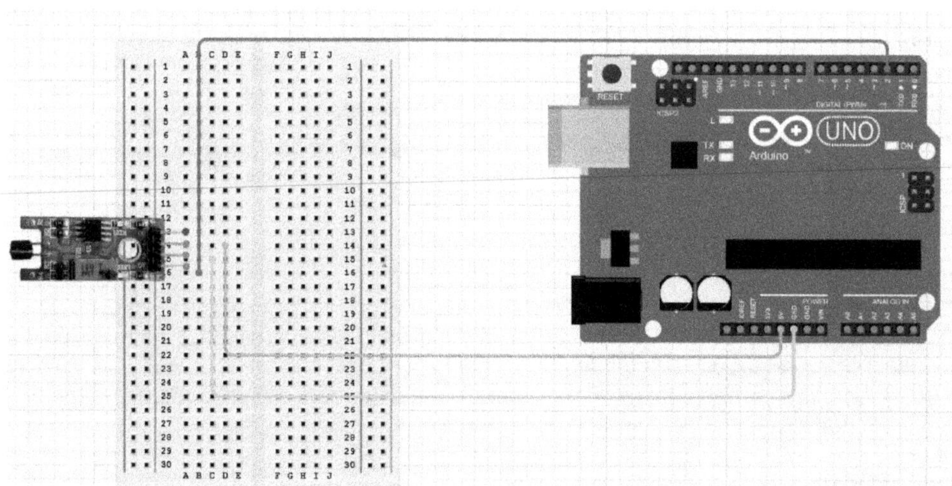

Arduino Code & Serial Monitor Output

```
const int touchPin = 2;

void setup() {
  pinMode(touchPin, INPUT);
  Serial.begin(9600);
}

void loop() {
  if (digitalRead(touchPin) == HIGH) {
    Serial.println("TOUCHED!");
    Serial.println(" ");
    delay(200);
  }
}
```

```
Output    Serial Monitor ×
Message (Enter to send message to 'Arduino UNO' on 'COM3')
TOUCHED!

TOUCHED!

TOUCHED!

TOUCHED!

TOUCHED!

TOUCHED!

TOUCHED!
```

How the Code Works

Unlike buttons, the touch sensor output is HIGH when touched (not LOW). This is because it detects added capacitance rather than a circuit closure. The if statement checks for HIGH and prints TOUCHED! with a 200ms delay to prevent multiple triggers from one touch. The sensor is sensitive - even hovering your finger very close may trigger it depending on the sensitivity setting.

Real-World Applications

- Touchscreen buttons
- Touch-activated lights
- Elevator touch panels
- Smart furniture control
- Capacitive keypads

Experiment 48 | Touch Counter

Sensor: Metal Touch Sensor
Difficulty: ★ Beginner
Objective: Count and display the number of times the touch sensor has been activated.

How It Works

Touch counting uses the same edge-detection pattern as button counting and tilt counting. We track the state change from not-touched (LOW) to touched (HIGH) to count individual touch events. This single-direction edge detection means lifting your finger and touching again counts as two separate events.

Concepts Learned

- Touch event counting
- State change detection
- Rising edge on touch
- Debounce for touch sensors

Components Required

Component	Qty
Arduino Uno	1
Metal Touch Sensor	1
Jumper Wires	3

Wiring

Touch Sensor Pin	Arduino Pin
S	D2
+	5V
-	GND

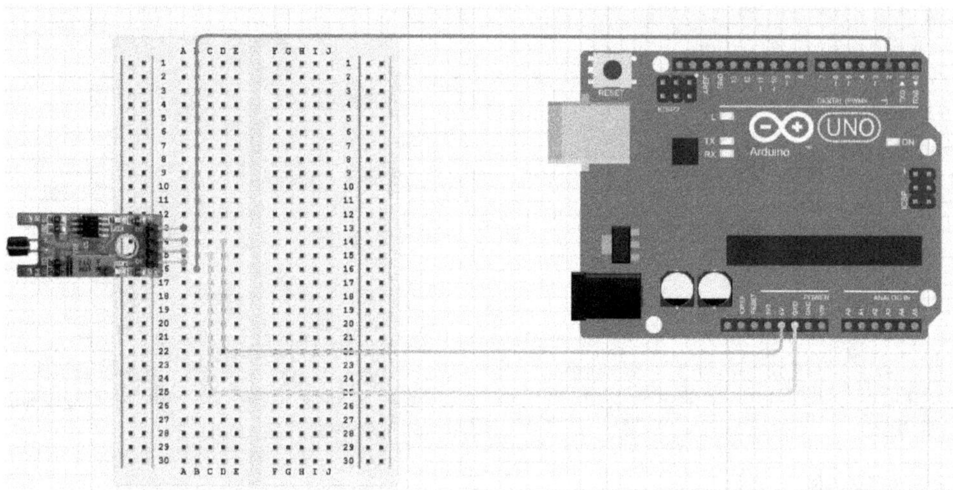

Arduino Code & Serial Monitor Output

```
const int touchPin = 2;
int count = 0;
int lastState = LOW;

void setup() {
  pinMode(touchPin, INPUT);
  Serial.begin(9600);
}

void loop() {
  int state = digitalRead(touchPin);
  if (state == HIGH && lastState == LOW) {
    count++;
    Serial.print("Touch Count: ");
    Serial.println(count);
    delay(150);
  }
  lastState = state;
}
```

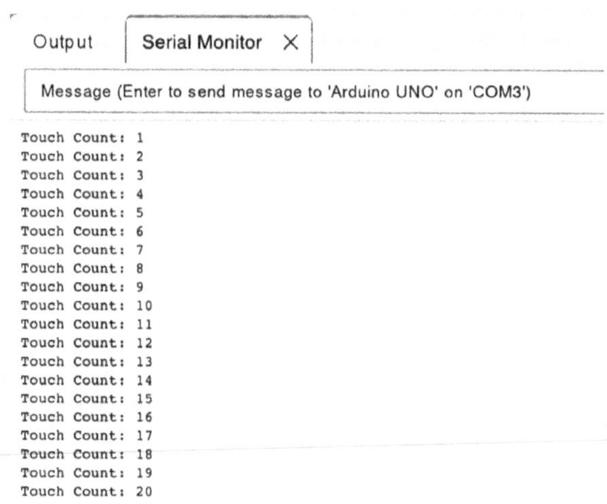

How the Code Works

lastState starts at LOW. When the state goes HIGH and lastState was LOW - meaning a new touch just started - we increment count and print it. The delay(150) is shorter than for buttons because touch sensors are less prone to mechanical bounce. The counter accumulates indefinitely, so if you reset the Arduino it starts from zero again.

Real-World Applications

- Touch-based voting systems
- Product sample touch counters

- Interactive museum exhibits
- Tap payment counters
- Kids touch learning games

Experiment 49 | Pulse Detection

Sensor: Heartbeat Sensor
Difficulty: ★★ Intermediate
Objective: Detect individual heartbeat pulses using the heartbeat sensor.

How It Works

The heartbeat sensor shines a small LED light through your fingertip. Blood absorbs light differently depending on whether it is oxygenated or not. Each heartbeat pushes a fresh pulse of oxygenated blood through your finger, creating a tiny change in how much light passes through. The sensor detects this as a repeating wave pattern in its analog output.

Concepts Learned

- Optical pulse detection
- Finger placement technique
- Signal noise in bio-sensors
- Pulse event detection

Components Required

Component	Qty
Arduino Uno	1
Heartbeat Sensor	1
Jumper Wires	3

Wiring

Heartbeat Sensor Pin	Arduino Pin
S	A0
+	5V
-	GND

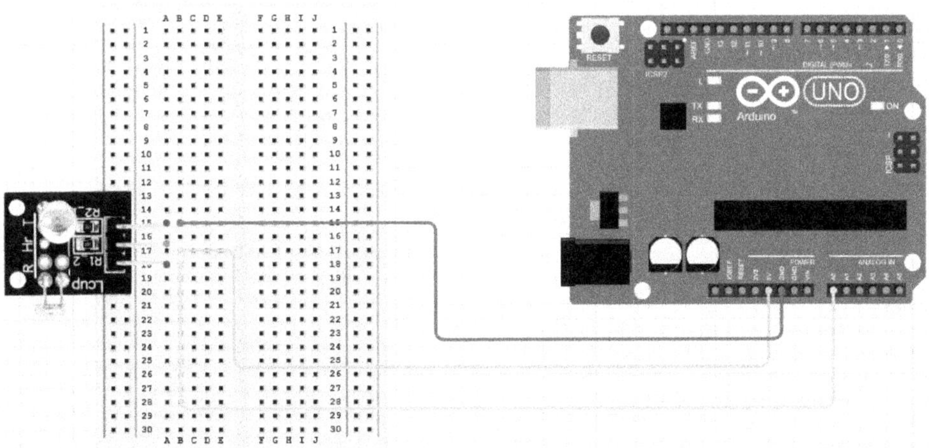

Arduino Code & Serial Monitor Output

```
const int pulsePin = A0;
int threshold = 550;
bool pulseDetected = false;

void setup() {
  Serial.begin(9600);
}

void loop() {
  int value = analogRead(pulsePin);
  Serial.println(value);
  if (value > threshold && !pulseDetected)
{
    Serial.println("-- PULSE --");
    pulseDetected = true;
  }
  if (value < threshold) pulseDetected =
false;
  delay(10);
}
```

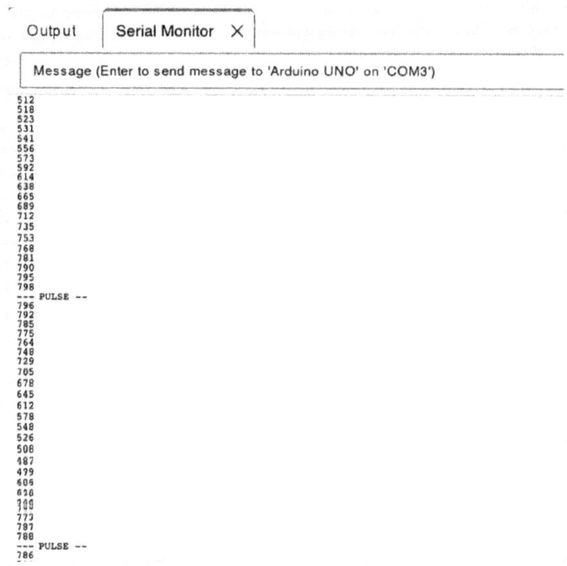

How the Code Works

Place your finger gently on the sensor and keep it still. The raw analog readings will appear in the Serial Monitor - you will see a wave pattern that rises and falls with each heartbeat. The threshold = 550 is the level at which we call a peak a pulse. When the signal crosses above this threshold, PULSE is printed. You may need to adjust the threshold up or down for your specific sensor and finger placement.

Real-World Applications

- Heart rate monitors
- Fitness trackers
- Medical pulse oximeters
- Stress monitoring devices
- Sleep quality tracking

Experiment 50 | BPM Measurement

Sensor: Heartbeat Sensor

Difficulty: ★★ Intermediate

Objective: Calculate beats per minute (BPM) from the heartbeat sensor.

How It Works

BPM (beats per minute) is calculated from the time between consecutive heartbeat pulses. If the time between two beats is 800 milliseconds, then one minute (60,000 milliseconds) divided by 800 gives 75 BPM. This experiment measures that interval using millis() and performs the division to give a live BPM reading.

Concepts Learned

- BPM calculation
- Time between pulses
- Inter-beat interval
- Smoothing readings

Components Required

Component	Qty
Arduino Uno	1
Heartbeat Sensor	1
Jumper Wires	3

Wiring

Heartbeat Sensor Pin	Arduino Pin
S	A0
+	5V
-	GND

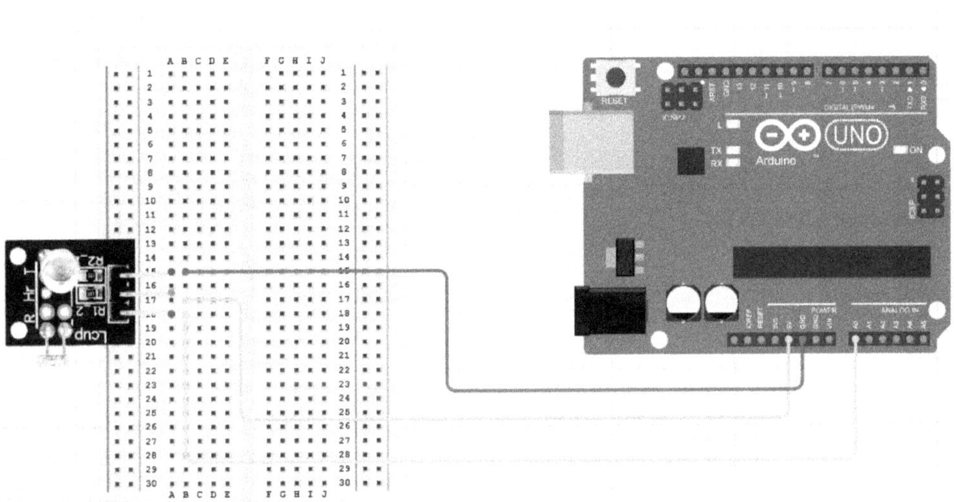

Arduino Code & Serial Monitor Output

```
const int pulsePin = A0;
const int threshold = 550;
unsigned long lastBeat = 0;
bool above = false;

void setup() {
  Serial.begin(9600);
}

void loop() {
  int value = analogRead(pulsePin);
  if (value > threshold && !above) {
    unsigned long now = millis();
    if (lastBeat != 0) {
      long interval = now - lastBeat;
      float bpm = 60000.0 / interval;
      Serial.print("BPM: ");
Serial.println(bpm);
    }
```

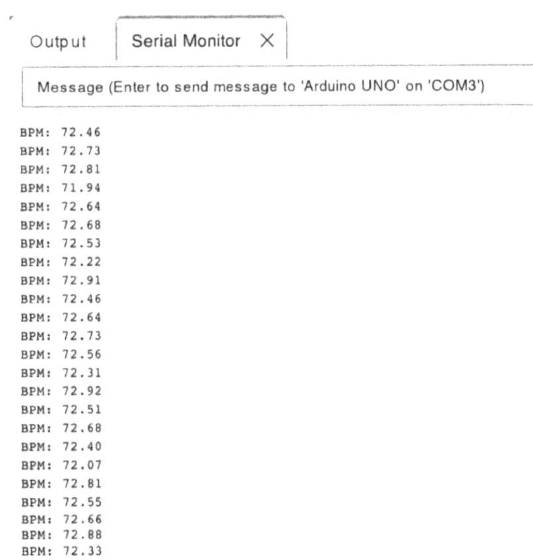

```
      lastBeat = now;
      above = true;
    }
    if (value < threshold) above = false;
    delay(10);
  }
```

How the Code Works

lastBeat stores the timestamp of the previous heartbeat. When a new beat is detected, we subtract lastBeat from the current time to get the interval in milliseconds. Dividing 60000 by this interval gives BPM. The above flag prevents counting the same beat peak multiple times as the signal stays high for a few milliseconds. For accurate readings keep your finger perfectly still and average several readings.

Real-World Applications

- Fitness wristbands
- Sports performance monitors
- Hospital patient monitors
- Telemedicine devices
- Wearable health trackers

Experiment 51 | Object Counting

Sensor: Photo Interrupter Module

Difficulty: ★ Beginner

Objective: Count objects passing through the photo interrupter beam.

How It Works

The photo interrupter has an infrared LED on one side and a phototransistor on the other. When nothing is between them the light shines directly onto the transistor, keeping the output HIGH. When an object passes through the gap and blocks the beam, the output drops to LOW. This creates a clean, reliable detection signal with no contact required.

Concepts Learned

- Beam break detection
- Object counting logic
- Opto-interrupter operation
- Rising/falling edge counting

Components Required

Component	Qty
Arduino Uno	1
Photo Interrupter Module	1
Jumper Wires	3

Wiring

Photo Interrupter Pin	Arduino Pin
OUT	D2
VCC	5V
GND	GND

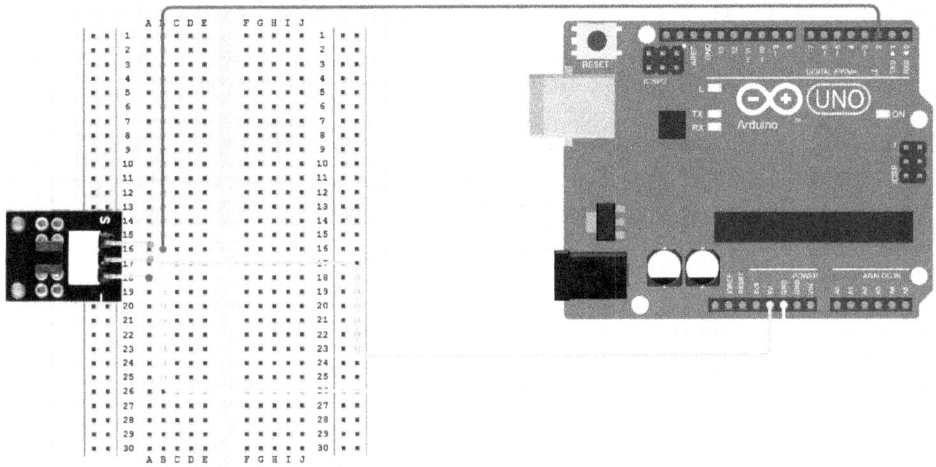

Arduino Code & Serial Monitor Output

```
const int irPin = 2;
int count = 0;
int lastState = HIGH;

void setup() {
  pinMode(irPin, INPUT);
  Serial.begin(9600);
}

void loop() {
  int state = digitalRead(irPin);
  if (state == LOW && lastState == HIGH) {
    count++;
    Serial.print("Objects counted: ");
    Serial.println(count);
  }
  lastState = state;
  delay(50);
}
```

Output | Serial Monitor ×

Message (Enter to send message to 'Arduino UNO' on 'COM3')

```
Objects counted: 1
Objects counted: 2
Objects counted: 3
Objects counted: 4
Objects counted: 5
Objects counted: 6
Objects counted: 7
Objects counted: 8
Objects counted: 9
Objects counted: 10
Objects counted: 11
Objects counted: 12
Objects counted: 13
Objects counted: 14
Objects counted: 15
```

How the Code Works

lastState starts HIGH (beam unbroken). When state drops to LOW - meaning the beam was just broken - we increment count and print it. When the state returns to HIGH we are ready to count the next object. The 50ms delay reduces the chance of counting one object multiple times if it vibrates in the beam. Try passing a piece of card through repeatedly to see the count increment.

Real-World Applications

- Conveyor production counters
- Pill counting machines
- Cash counting machines
- People counters
- Package sorting systems

Experiment 52 | Rotation Counting

Sensor: Photo Interrupter Module

Difficulty: ★★ Intermediate

Objective: Count rotations of a slotted disc passing through the photo interrupter.

How It Works

When a disc with evenly spaced slots is placed in the photo interrupter beam and spun, each slot that passes creates one beam-break event. By counting how many times the beam is broken per second and dividing by the number of slots on the disc, we calculate rotations per second. Using an interrupt ensures no slots are missed even at high speeds.

Concepts Learned

- Slotted encoder disc
- Rotations from pulses
- Interrupt-based counting
- Slots per revolution

Components Required

Component	Qty
Arduino Uno	1
Photo Interrupter Module	1
Slotted Disc	1
Jumper Wires	3

Wiring

Photo Interrupter Pin	Arduino Pin
OUT	D2
VCC	5V
GND	GND

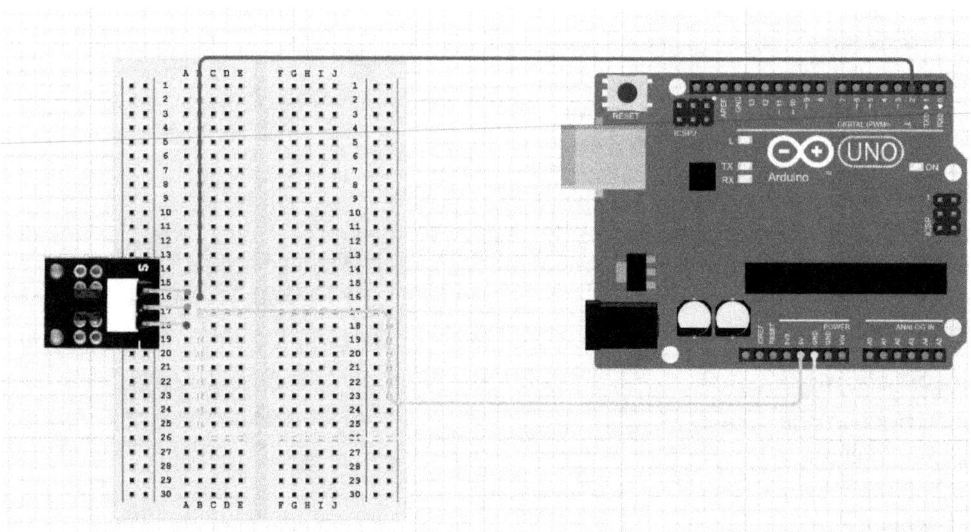

Arduino Code & Serial Monitor Output

```
const int irPin = 2;
volatile int slotCount = 0;
const int slotsPerRev = 20;
unsigned long lastCalc = 0;

void countSlot() { slotCount++; }

void setup() {
  Serial.begin(9600);

attachInterrupt(digitalPinToInterrupt(irPi
n), countSlot, FALLING);
}

void loop() {
  if (millis() - lastCalc >= 1000) {
    int revs = slotCount / slotsPerRev;
    Serial.print("Rotations/sec: ");
Serial.println(revs);
    slotCount = 0;
    lastCalc = millis();
  }
}
```

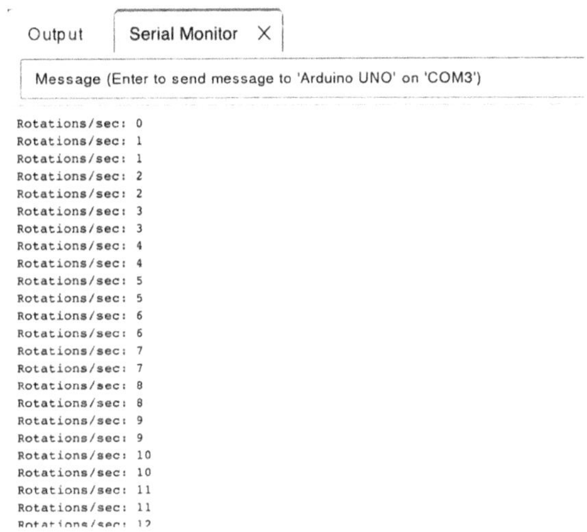

How the Code Works

attachInterrupt triggers countSlot() every time the beam is broken (FALLING edge). In loop(), every second we calculate how many complete revolutions occurred by dividing slotCount by slotsPerRev. The slotsPerRev constant must match your actual disc - count the slots physically and update this number. After calculating, slotCount resets to zero for the next second's measurement.

Real-World Applications

- Motor RPM monitoring
- Wheel speed sensors
- Flow meter turbines
- CNC axis encoders
- Fan speed measurement

Experiment 53 | Laser Transmission

Sensor: Laser Module
Difficulty: ★ Beginner
Objective: Activate the laser module and confirm it is transmitting.

How It Works

The laser module contains a laser diode - a tiny semiconductor that emits a highly focused, coherent beam of red light at around 650nm wavelength. Unlike an ordinary LED which scatters light in all directions, a laser beam stays narrow over a long distance. The module simply needs power and a HIGH signal on its control pin to activate.

Concepts Learned

- Laser diode operation
- Digital output control
- Laser safety basics
- On/off laser control

Components Required

Component	Qty
Arduino Uno	1
Laser Module	1
Jumper Wires	3

Wiring

Laser Module Pin	Arduino Pin
S	D3
+	5V
-	GND

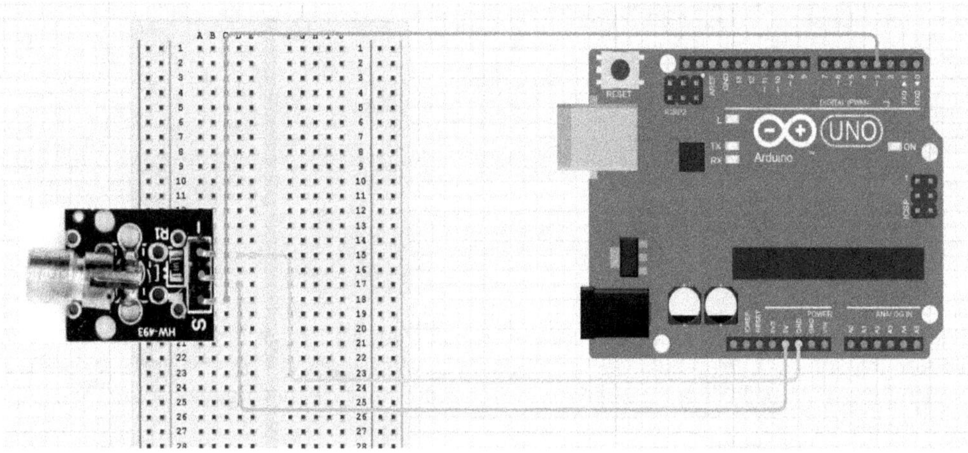

Arduino Code & Serial Monitor Output

```
const int laserPin = 3;

void setup() {
  pinMode(laserPin, OUTPUT);
  Serial.begin(9600);
}

void loop() {
  digitalWrite(laserPin, HIGH);
  Serial.println("Laser ON");
  delay(1000);
  digitalWrite(laserPin, LOW);
  Serial.println("Laser OFF");
  delay(1000);
}
```

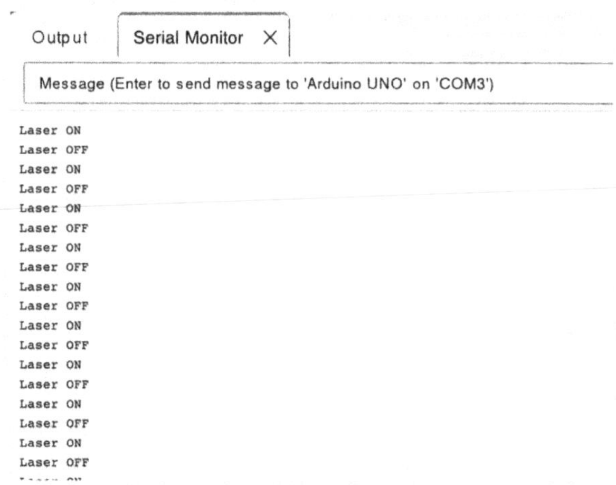

How the Code Works

pinMode(laserPin, OUTPUT) sets pin 3 to output mode. digitalWrite(laserPin, HIGH) turns the laser on. The code alternates between HIGH and LOW with 1-second delays, printing status each time. Always point the laser away from your eyes. In a real application you would keep the laser on continuously (just set it HIGH in setup) and only turn it off when needed.

Real-World Applications

- Laser tripwire systems
- Optical communication
- Laser alignment tools
- Laser pointer control
- Barcode scanners

Experiment 54 | Beam Alignment

Sensor: Laser Module & LDR
Difficulty: ★★ Intermediate
Objective: Detect when a laser beam hits an LDR receiver, indicating correct alignment.

How It Works

When the laser beam hits the LDR, it creates a very bright spot of light that drives the LDR reading high. If the beam is blocked or misaligned, the LDR reading drops below the threshold. This combination creates a tripwire - any interruption of the beam is instantly detectable. The beam can cross a room, making this useful for perimeter detection.

Concepts Learned

- Laser-LDR pairing
- Beam alignment feedback
- Light intensity threshold
- Transmitter-receiver system

Components Required

Component	Qty
Arduino Uno	1
Laser Module	1
Photo-Resistor Module	1
Jumper Wires	5

Wiring

Component	Arduino Pin
`Laser S`	D3
`LDR S`	A0
`Both +`	5V
`Both -`	GND

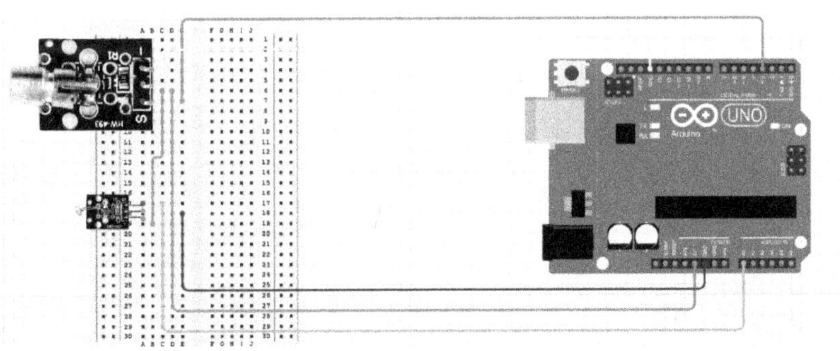

Arduino Code & Serial Monitor Output

```
const int laserPin = 3;
const int ldrPin   = A0;
const int threshold = 700;

void setup() {
  pinMode(laserPin, OUTPUT);
  Serial.begin(9600);
  digitalWrite(laserPin, HIGH);
}

void loop() {
  int ldrVal = analogRead(ldrPin);
  Serial.print("LDR: ");
Serial.print(ldrVal);
  if (ldrVal > threshold) {
    Serial.println(" --> BEAM ALIGNED!");
  } else {
    Serial.println(" --> Beam broken or
misaligned");
  }
  delay(300);
}
```

```
Output    Serial Monitor X
Message (Enter to send message to 'Arduino UNO' on 'COM3')

LDR:  324  --> Beam broken or misaligned
LDR:  298  --> Beam broken or misaligned
LDR:  311  --> Beam broken or misaligned
LDR:  342  --> Beam broken or misaligned
LDR:  287  --> Beam broken or misaligned
LDR:  315  --> Beam broken or misaligned
LDR:  299  --> Beam broken or misaligned
LDR:  327  --> Beam broken or misaligned
LDR:  301  --> Beam broken or misaligned
LDR:  338  --> Beam broken or misaligned
LDR:  712  --> BEAM ALIGNED!
LDR:  753  --> BEAM ALIGNED!
LDR:  801  --> BEAM ALIGNED!
LDR:  872  --> BEAM ALIGNED!
LDR:  915  --> BEAM ALIGNED!
LDR:  964  --> BEAM ALIGNED!
LDR: 1012  --> BEAM ALIGNED!
LDR:  978  --> BEAM ALIGNED!
LDR:  882  --> BEAM ALIGNED!
LDR:  756  --> BEAM ALIGNED!
LDR:  701  --> BEAM ALIGNED!
LDR:  543  --> Beam broken or misaligned
LDR:  412  --> Beam broken or misaligned
LDR:  387  --> Beam broken or misaligned
LDR:  328  --> Beam broken or misaligned
```

How the Code Works

The laser is turned on in setup() and left on permanently. In loop(), we read the LDR and compare it to beamThreshold. If the reading is high, the beam is hitting the LDR and all is fine. If it drops below threshold, the beam is broken or misaligned and the alarm triggers. Place the laser and LDR facing each other across a gap, align carefully, then note the aligned reading to set a good threshold value.

Real-World Applications

- Laser tripwire alarms
- Optical level measurement
- Automatic gate beams
- Quality control scanners
- Precision alignment tools

Experiment 55 | Tilt Controlled LED Effect

Sensor: Magic Light Cup Module

Difficulty: ★ Beginner

Objective: Observe the Magic Light Cup module's built-in tilt-triggered LED colour-change effect.

How It Works

The Magic Light Cup module contains an RGB LED and a tilt sensor wired together internally. When the module is tilted, the built-in circuit switches the LED colour. Two of these modules wired together create the appearance of liquid light pouring from one cup to another. In this experiment we just read its tilt state to understand the underlying mechanism.

Concepts Learned

- Pre-built sensor modules
- Tilt activation
- LED control inside module
- Demonstration experiment

Components Required

Component	Qty
Arduino Uno	1
Magic Light Cup Module	1
Jumper Wires	3

Wiring

Magic Cup Pin	Arduino Pin
S	D2
+	5V
-	GND

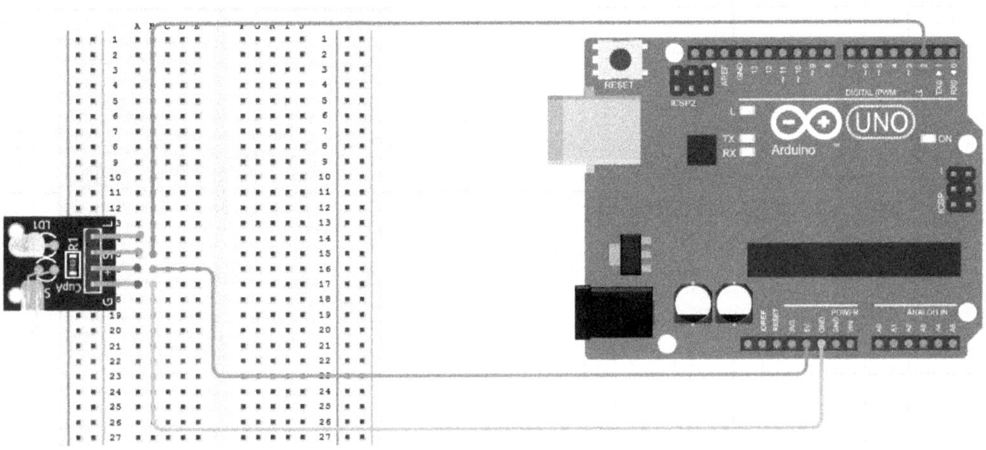

Arduino Code & Serial Monitor Output

```
const int cupPin = 2;

void setup() {
  pinMode(cupPin, INPUT);
  Serial.begin(9600);
}

void loop() {
  int state = digitalRead(cupPin);
  if (state == HIGH) {
    Serial.println("Cup TILTED - LED
effect active");
  } else {
    Serial.println("Cup upright");
  }
  delay(200);
}
```

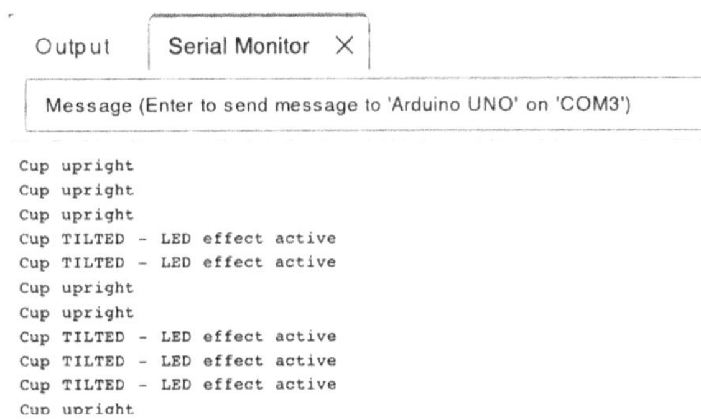

How the Code Works

The module outputs a digital HIGH when tilted. We read this with digitalRead() and print the status. If you have two Magic Light Cup modules, connecting their signal pins together creates the interactive pouring effect. For now, this experiment simply shows that even complex-looking effects are built from the same basic digital HIGH/LOW signals you have been using since Experiment 1.

Real-World Applications

- Interactive lighting toys
- Novelty LED products
- Tilt-responsive decorations
- Motion-activated displays
- Educational STEM kits

Level 2 - Sensor + Output Projects (56–90)

Experiment 56 | Button Controlled RGB LED

Sensor: Button Module + RGB LED

Difficulty: ★★ Intermediate

Objective: Change the RGB LED colour with each button press, cycling through Red, Green, Blue, and Off.

How It Works

An RGB LED contains three separate LEDs in one package - Red, Green, and Blue. By mixing these three colours at different brightness levels using PWM (Pulse Width Modulation), any colour can be produced. In this experiment each button press cycles through preset colours, demonstrating the most basic form of LED colour control.

Concepts Learned

- RGB LED control
- Colour cycling logic
- Button state machine
- PWM output basics

Components Required

Component	Qty
Arduino Uno	1
Button Module	1
RGB LED Module	1
Jumper Wires	6

Wiring

Component	Arduino Pin
Button S	D2
RGB R	D9
RGB G	D10
RGB B	D11
All +	5V
All -	GND

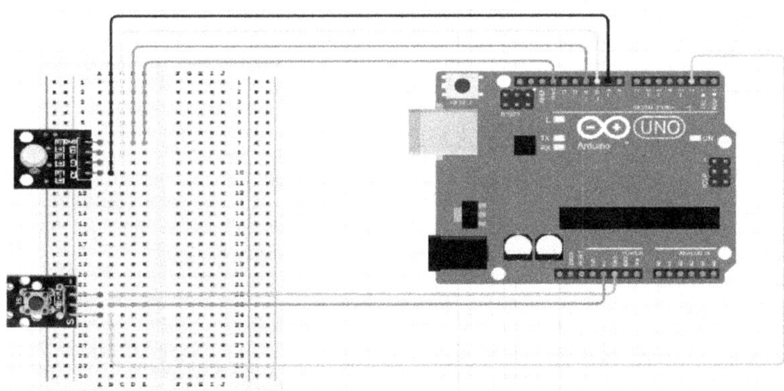

Arduino Code & Serial Monitor Output

```
const int btnPin = 2;
const int rPin = 9, gPin = 10, bPin = 11;
int mode = 0;
int lastState = HIGH;

void setColor(int r, int g, int b) {
  analogWrite(rPin, r);
  analogWrite(gPin, g);
  analogWrite(bPin, b);
}

void setup() {
  pinMode(btnPin, INPUT_PULLUP);
  Serial.begin(9600);
}

void loop() {
  int state = digitalRead(btnPin);
  if (state == LOW && lastState == HIGH) {
    mode = (mode + 1) % 4;
    if (mode == 0) { setColor(0,0,0);
Serial.println("OFF"); }
    if (mode == 1) { setColor(255,0,0);
Serial.println("RED"); }
    if (mode == 2) { setColor(0,255,0);
Serial.println("GREEN"); }
    if (mode == 3) { setColor(0,0,255);
Serial.println("BLUE"); }
    delay(200);
  }
  lastState = state;
}
```

Output | Serial Monitor ×

Message (Enter to send message to 'Arduino UNO' on 'COM3')

```
RED
GREEN
BLUE
OFF
RED
GREEN
BLUE
OFF
RED
GREEN
BLUE
OFF
RED
GREEN
BLUE
OFF
RED
GREEN
BLUE
---
```

How the Code Works

mode is a counter that cycles 0 → 1 → 2 → 3 → 0 using the modulo operator (%). Each mode value maps to a colour by calling setColor() with specific RGB values. setColor() uses analogWrite() which outputs a PWM signal - rapidly switching the pin on and off to simulate a voltage between 0 and 5V. 255 is full brightness, 0 is off. Edge detection on the button ensures one press = one colour change.

Real-World Applications

- Status indicator lights
- Interactive learning toys
- Smart home accent lights

Experiment 57 | Button Controlled Buzzer

Sensor: Button Module + Active Buzzer

Difficulty: ★ Beginner

Objective: Sound a buzzer while the button is held down, stop when released.

How It Works

This project directly links a digital input (button) to a digital output (buzzer). When the button is held, the buzzer sounds; when released, it stops. The active buzzer contains its own oscillator circuit - it makes a fixed tone whenever power is applied, so no PWM or frequency control is needed.

Concepts Learned

- Buzzer output control
- Momentary button-buzzer link
- Active buzzer operation
- Digital output

Components Required

Component	Qty
Arduino Uno	1
Button Module	1
Active Buzzer Module	1
Jumper Wires	5

Wiring

Component	Arduino Pin
Button S	D2
Buzzer S	D8
Both +	5V
Both -	GND

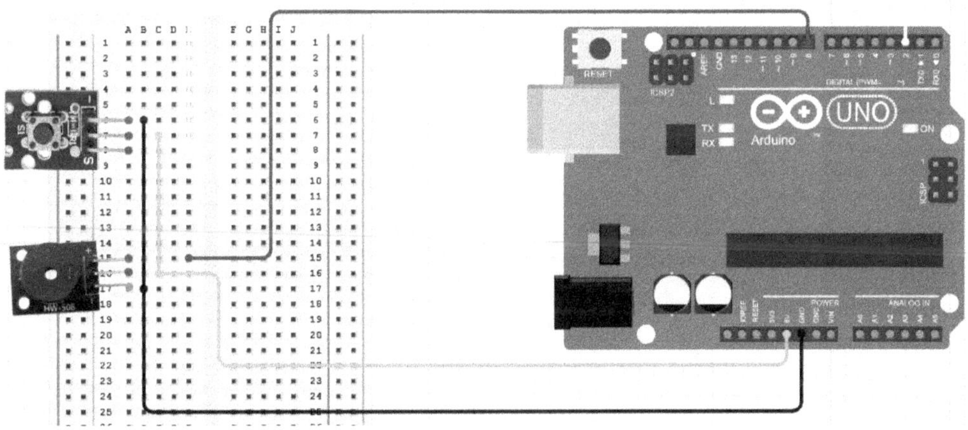

Arduino Code & Serial Monitor Output

```
const int btnPin = 2;
const int buzPin = 8;

void setup() {
  pinMode(btnPin, INPUT_PULLUP);
  pinMode(buzPin, OUTPUT);
}

void loop() {
  if (digitalRead(btnPin) == LOW) {
    digitalWrite(buzPin, HIGH);
  } else {
    digitalWrite(buzPin, LOW);
  }
```

Output | Serial Monitor ×

Message (Enter to send message to 'Arduino UNO' on 'COM3')

```
OFF
OFF
OFF
OFF
OFF
ON
ON
ON
ON
ON
ON
ON
OFF
OFF
```

```
}
```

How the Code Works

The loop() continuously reads the button state and writes it directly to the buzzer - if LOW (pressed) write HIGH to buzzer, otherwise write LOW. There is no debouncing needed here because we want continuous operation while held, not single events. This pattern of directly mapping input state to output state is called a pass-through and is the simplest possible sensor-to-output project.

Real-World Applications

- Doorbell systems
- Emergency call buttons
- Quiz buzzers
- Factory alert buttons
- Panic buttons

Experiment 58 | Touch Controlled Lamp

Sensor: Touch Sensor + RGB LED

Difficulty: ★ Beginner

Objective: Toggle an RGB LED on and off with each touch of the sensor.

How It Works

A touch-controlled lamp uses a latched state - each touch toggles the lamp between on and off. Unlike the button buzzer which is only on while held, this lamp stays on after you touch it and stays off after you touch it again. This requires storing the lamp state in a variable.

Concepts Learned

- Touch toggle logic
- State toggling
- LED on/off control
- Latched output

Components Required

Component	Qty
Arduino Uno	1
Metal Touch Sensor	1
RGB LED Module	1
Jumper Wires	5

Wiring

Component	Arduino Pin
`Touch S`	`D2`
`RGB R`	`D9`
`RGB G`	`D10`
`RGB B`	`D11`

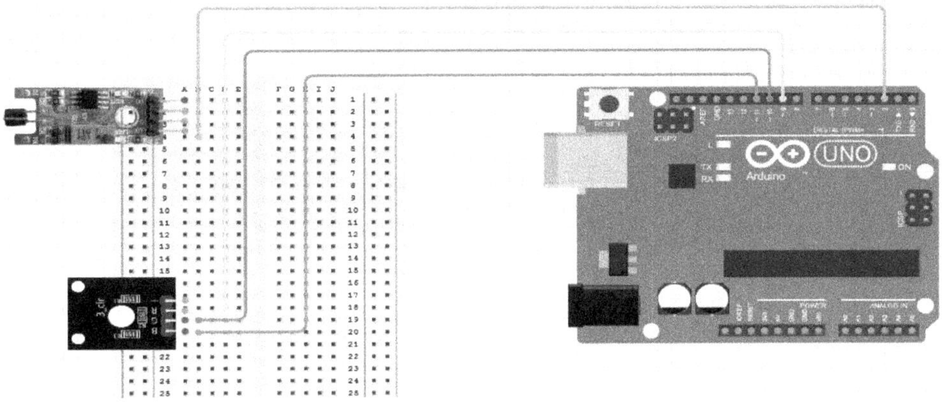

Arduino Code & Serial Monitor Output

```
const int touchPin = 2;
const int rPin=9, gPin=10, bPin=11;
bool lampOn = false;
int lastState = LOW;

void setup() {
  pinMode(touchPin, INPUT);
  Serial.begin(9600);
}

void loop() {
  int state = digitalRead(touchPin);
  if (state == HIGH && lastState == LOW) {
    lampOn = !lampOn;
    if (lampOn) { analogWrite(rPin,200);
analogWrite(gPin,180);
analogWrite(bPin,100);
Serial.println("Lamp ON"); }
    else        { analogWrite(rPin,0);
analogWrite(gPin,0);
analogWrite(bPin,0);
Serial.println("Lamp OFF"); }
    delay(150);
  }
  lastState = state;
}
```

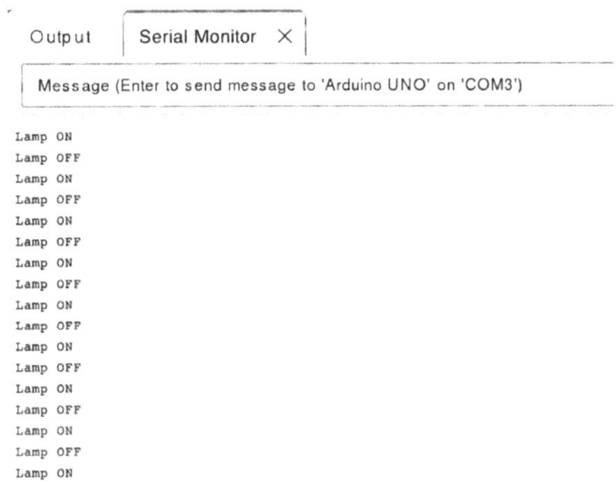

How the Code Works

lampOn is a boolean (true/false) variable that remembers whether the lamp is currently on. Edge detection on the touch sensor ensures one touch = one toggle. When lampOn is true, analogWrite sets warm white colour values (red=200, green=180, blue=100 approximates warm white). When false, all three channels are set to 0. constrain() prevents the brightness values from going outside the 0–255 valid range.

Real-World Applications

- Bedside touch lamps
- Cabinet lighting
- Touch night lights
- Smart furniture lighting
- Accessible switch lamps

Experiment 59 | Clap Activated LED

Sensor: Sound Sensor + RGB LED
Difficulty: ★★ Intermediate
Objective: Toggle an LED on and off with a clap.

How It Works

Sound-activated lighting detects a loud impulse (clap) and toggles an LED. This is the same impulse detection from Experiment 9, but now linked to an LED output. The combination creates a satisfying interaction - a single clap changes the room lighting. The 500ms delay after detection prevents the echoes of a clap from triggering multiple toggles.

Concepts Learned

- Sound threshold trigger
- LED toggle on sound
- Debounce for audio events
- State machine with sound

Components Required

Component	Qty
Arduino Uno	1
KY-038 Sound Sensor	1
RGB LED Module	1
Jumper Wires	5

Wiring

Component	Arduino Pin
Sound A0	A0
RGB R	D9
RGB G	D10
RGB B	D11

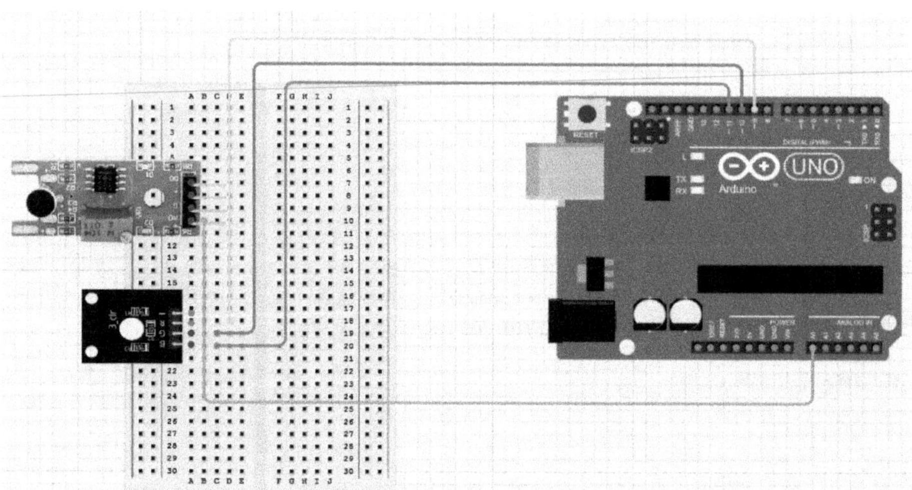

Arduino Code & Serial Monitor Output

```
const int soundPin = A0;
const int rPin=9, gPin=10, bPin=11;
const int threshold = 600;
bool ledOn = false;

void setup() { Serial.begin(9600); }

void loop() {
  if (analogRead(soundPin) > threshold) {
    ledOn = !ledOn;
    int v = ledOn ? 255 : 0;
    analogWrite(rPin, v);
analogWrite(gPin, v); analogWrite(bPin,
v);
    Serial.println(ledOn ? "LED ON" : "LED
OFF");
    delay(500);
  }
}
```

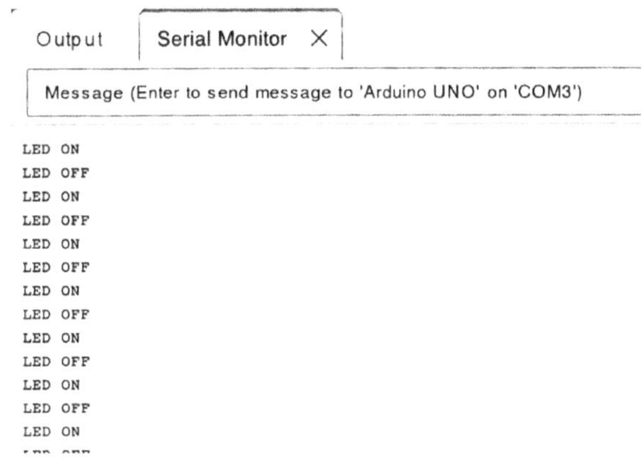

How the Code Works

ledOn is a boolean that tracks LED state. When the sound sensor reads above threshold, we flip ledOn with the ! (not) operator. We then calculate int v = ledOn ? 255 : 0 - if the LED should be on, v is 255 (full brightness); if off, v is 0. Then all three RGB channels are set to v simultaneously, creating white light when on. The 500ms delay is the anti-echo window.

Real-World Applications

- Clap-to-switch smart lights
- Hands-free light control
- Accessible lighting for disabled users
- Magic trick props
- Interactive art installations

Experiment 60 | Clap Activated Buzzer

Sensor: Sound Sensor + Active Buzzer
Difficulty: ★ Beginner
Objective: Sound a buzzer for 1 second each time a clap is detected.

How It Works

A clap-activated buzzer responds to each loud sound event with a fixed-duration beep. Unlike a continuous buzzer that stays on while the condition is true, this one always beeps for exactly 1 second regardless of how long the sound lasts. This is called a one-shot response and is common in alert systems.

Concepts Learned

- Sound event triggering
- Timed output response
- Feedback on audio event
- One-shot trigger

Components Required

Component	Qty
Arduino Uno	1
KY-038 Sound Sensor	1
Active Buzzer Module	1
Jumper Wires	4

Wiring

Component	Arduino Pin
`Sound A0`	`A0`
`Buzzer S`	`D8`

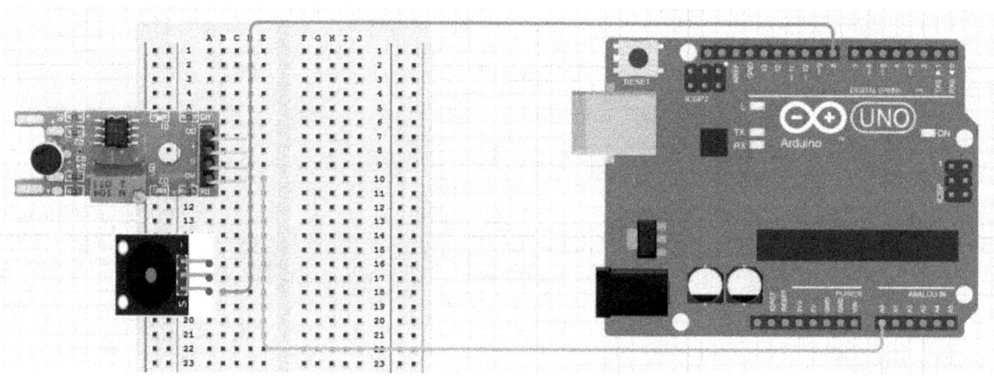

Arduino Code & Serial Monitor Output

```
const int soundPin = A0;
const int buzPin   = 8;
const int threshold = 600;

void setup() {
  pinMode(buzPin, OUTPUT);
  Serial.begin(9600);
}

void loop() {
  if (analogRead(soundPin) > threshold) {
    Serial.println("Clap! Buzzer ON");
    digitalWrite(buzPin, HIGH);
    delay(1000);
    digitalWrite(buzPin, LOW);
  }
}
```

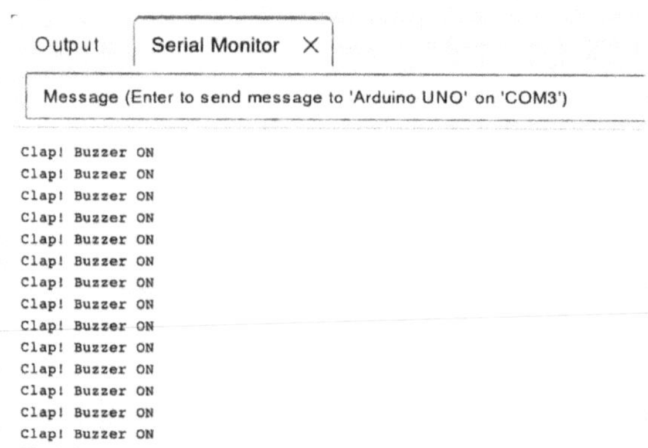

How the Code Works

When the sound exceeds the threshold, we immediately set the buzzer HIGH. Then delay(1000) pauses the entire program for 1 second - the buzzer stays on during this time. After the delay, the buzzer goes LOW. The entire response is contained in a single if block. Note that nothing else can happen during the 1-second delay, which is a limitation of this simple approach.

Real-World Applications

- Doorbell clap activation
- Noise alerts
- Sound-triggered alarms
- Game show buzzers
- Interactive sound feedback

Experiment 61 | Voice Activated RGB Light

Sensor: High-Sensitivity Voice Sensor + RGB LED
Difficulty: ★★ Intermediate
Objective: Change RGB LED colour each time a voice or loud sound is detected.

How It Works

Voice-reactive lighting changes colour in response to sound events. Each time the high-sensitivity sensor detects a sound, the colour advances one step in a cycle. The result is a light that responds visually to the rhythm of speech or music, creating an interactive ambient lighting effect.

Concepts Learned

- Voice event cycling
- Colour state machine
- High-sensitivity mic usage
- Sequential state changes

Components Required

Component	Qty
Arduino Uno	1
High-Sensitivity Voice Sensor	1
RGB LED Module	1
Jumper Wires	5

Wiring

Component	Arduino Pin
Voice D0	D2
RGB R	D9
RGB G	D10
RGB B	D11

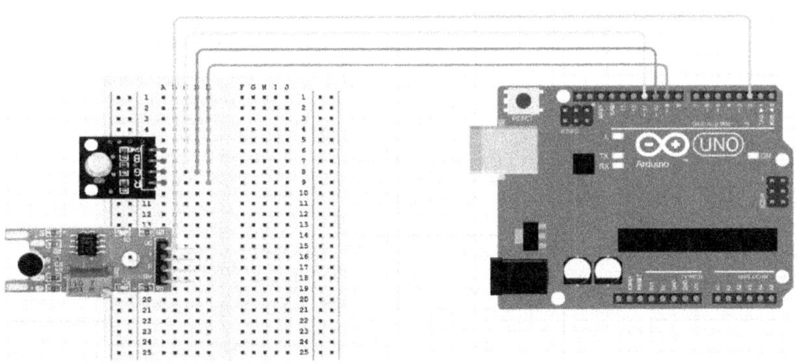

Arduino Code & Serial Monitor Output

```
const int voicePin=2, rPin=9, gPin=10,
bPin=11;
int colorMode = 0;
int lastState = HIGH;

void setup() { pinMode(voicePin, INPUT); }

void loop() {
  int s = digitalRead(voicePin);
  if (s == LOW && lastState == HIGH) {
    colorMode = (colorMode + 1) % 4;
    analogWrite(rPin, colorMode==1?255:0);
    analogWrite(gPin, colorMode==2?255:0);
    analogWrite(bPin, colorMode==3?255:0);
    delay(300);
  }
  lastState = s;
}
```

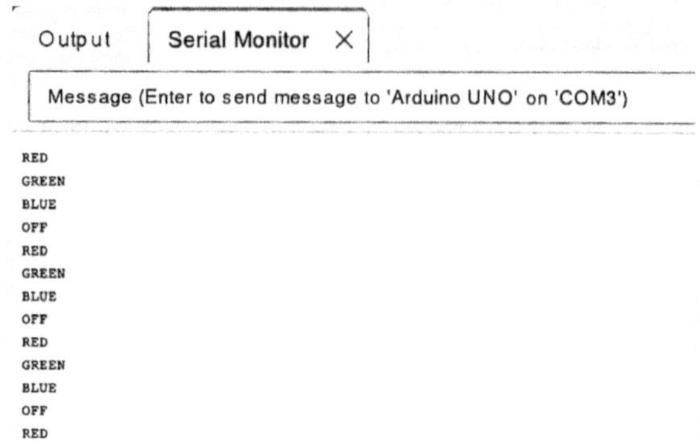

How the Code Works

colorMode cycles through 0, 1, 2, 3 using modulo. Modes 1, 2, and 3 set pure red, green, and blue respectively. Mode 0 turns the LED off. The ternary operators inside analogWrite set each channel: colorMode==1?255:0 means 'if colorMode is 1, use 255, otherwise use 0'. This creates one pure colour per mode. Edge detection on the voice pin ensures each sound event only advances the colour once.

Real-World Applications

- Voice-reactive party lights
- Hands-free room lighting
- Stage lighting FX
- Sound-to-colour art
- Smart speaker ambiance

Experiment 62 | Automatic Night Lamp

Sensor: LDR + RGB LED
Difficulty: ★ Beginner
Objective: Automatically turn on an LED lamp when it gets dark.

How It Works

An automatic night lamp turns on when ambient light drops below a threshold - exactly when you need it. It uses the inverse relationship between light level and lamp brightness: the darker the room, the brighter the lamp should be. This is the practical implementation of the Day/Night Detector from Level 1.

Concepts Learned

- Automatic light control
- Threshold-based output
- Sensor-driven automation
- Darkness detection

Components Required

Component	Qty
Arduino Uno	1

Component	Qty
Photo-Resistor Module	1
RGB LED Module	1
Jumper Wires	5

Wiring

Component	Arduino Pin
LDR S	A0
RGB R	D9
RGB G	D10
RGB B	D11

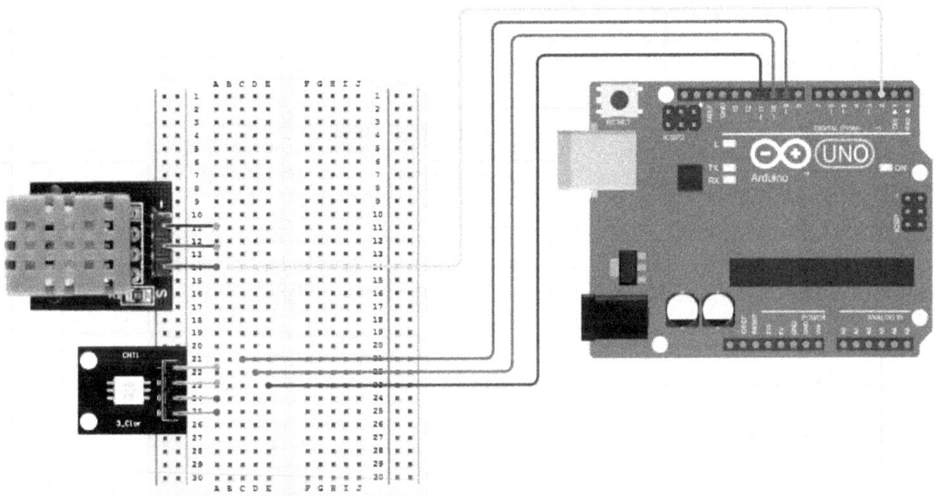

Arduino Code & Serial Monitor Output

```
const int ldrPin=A0, rPin=9, gPin=10,
bPin=11;
const int threshold = 400;

void setup() { Serial.begin(9600); }

void loop() {
  int light = analogRead(ldrPin);
  if (light < threshold) {
    analogWrite(rPin,200);
analogWrite(gPin,170);
analogWrite(bPin,80);
    Serial.println("Dark - Lamp ON");
  } else {
    analogWrite(rPin,0);
analogWrite(gPin,0); analogWrite(bPin,0);
    Serial.println("Bright - Lamp OFF");
  }
```

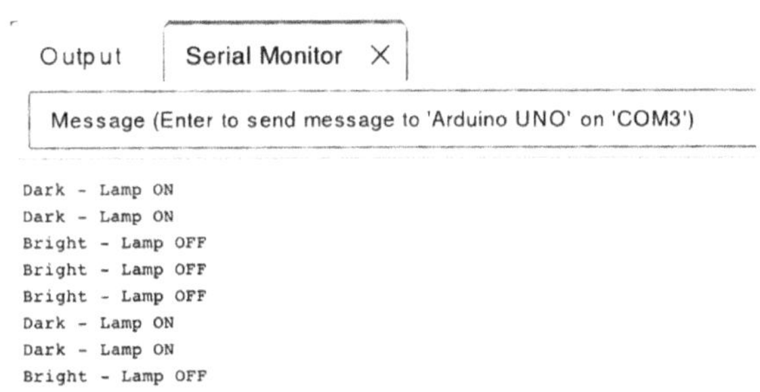

```
  delay(500);
}
```

How the Code Works

When light < threshold, we turn on the RGB LED with warm white values (red=200, green=170, blue=80 approximates incandescent warmth). When light is above the threshold the lamp turns off completely. The logic is clean and direct. In a real product you would add hysteresis - a slightly different threshold for turning on versus turning off - to prevent flickering at the boundary.

Real-World Applications

- Garden solar lights
- Hallway night lights
- Automatic street lamps
- Under-cabinet kitchen lighting
- Bedroom ambient lights

Experiment 63 | Dark Room Alarm

Sensor: LDR + Active Buzzer
Difficulty: ★ Beginner
Objective: Sound a buzzer alarm when the room becomes too dark.

How It Works

A dark room alarm is the complementary system to the night lamp - instead of providing light when it gets dark, it warns you when it gets too dark. This is useful in situations where darkness itself is the hazard, such as a power failure, a child entering a dark room, or a sensor detecting that protective covers have been removed.

Concepts Learned

- Threshold alarm
- Sensor-to-output mapping
- Darkness alert
- Safety system logic

Components Required

Component	Qty
Arduino Uno	1
Photo-Resistor Module	1
Active Buzzer Module	1
Jumper Wires	4

Wiring

Component	Arduino Pin
LDR S	A0
Buzzer S	D8

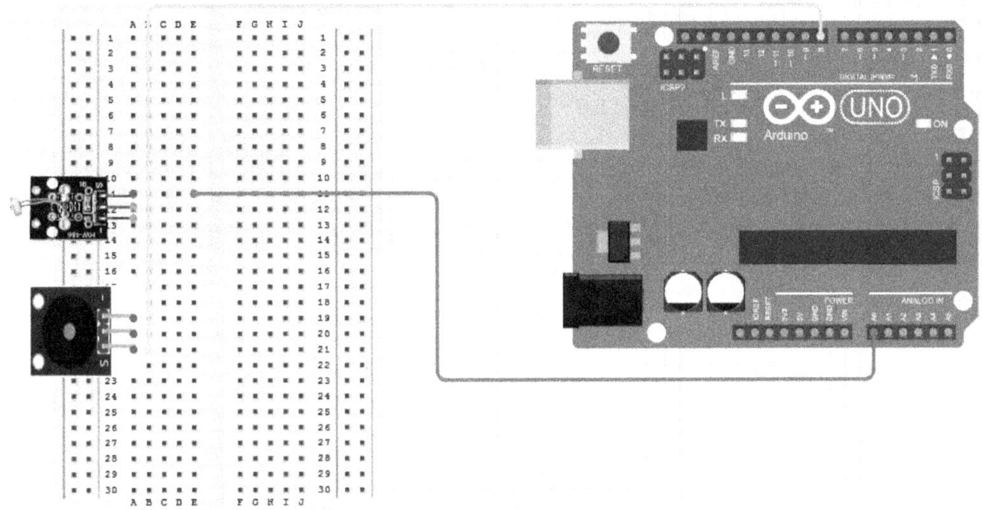

Arduino Code & Serial Monitor Output

```
const int ldrPin=A0, buzPin=8;
const int threshold = 300;

void setup() {
  pinMode(buzPin, OUTPUT);
  Serial.begin(9600);
}

void loop() {
  int light = analogRead(ldrPin);
  if (light < threshold) {
    digitalWrite(buzPin, HIGH);
    Serial.println("Too dark! ALARM");
  } else {
    digitalWrite(buzPin, LOW);
    Serial.println("Light OK");
  }
  delay(300);
}
```

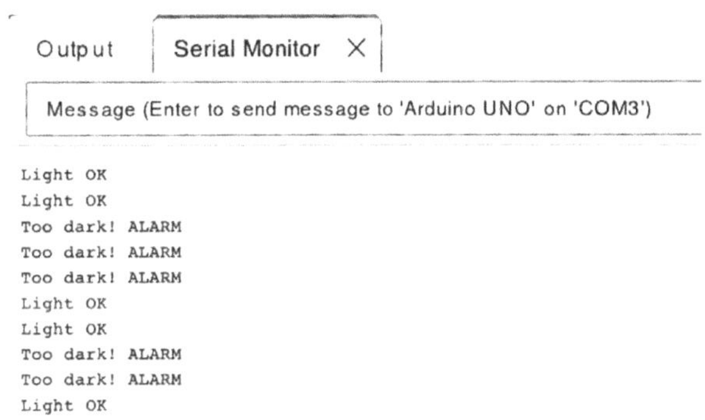

How the Code Works

The logic is a direct link from sensor to output. If light < threshold, buzzer goes HIGH and an alarm message prints. Otherwise the buzzer goes LOW and a safe message prints. The 300ms delay gives us about three checks per second. There is no latching here - the alarm stops automatically when light returns. For a latching alarm that stays on until reset, you would add a boolean variable similar to the touch lamp.

Real-World Applications

- Darkroom safety warning
- Child night alarm
- Tunnel entry warning
- Cellar safety systems
- Power-cut detection alerts

Experiment 64 | Light Controlled RGB Brightness

Sensor: LDR + RGB LED

Difficulty: ★★ Intermediate

Objective: Vary the brightness of an RGB LED inversely with ambient light - brighter in dark, dimmer in light.

How It Works

The map() function is one of the most useful tools in Arduino. It takes a number from one range and proportionally translates it to another range. Here we map the light reading (0–1023) to a brightness value (255–0) - note the reversed output range, which creates the inverse relationship: more light = less brightness.

Concepts Learned

- Analog output from analog input
- map() function
- Inverse relationship
- PWM brightness control

Components Required

Component	Qty
Arduino Uno	1
Photo-Resistor Module	1
RGB LED Module	1
Jumper Wires	5

Wiring

Component	Arduino Pin
`LDR S`	`A0`
`RGB R`	`D9`
`RGB G`	`D10`
`RGB B`	`D11`

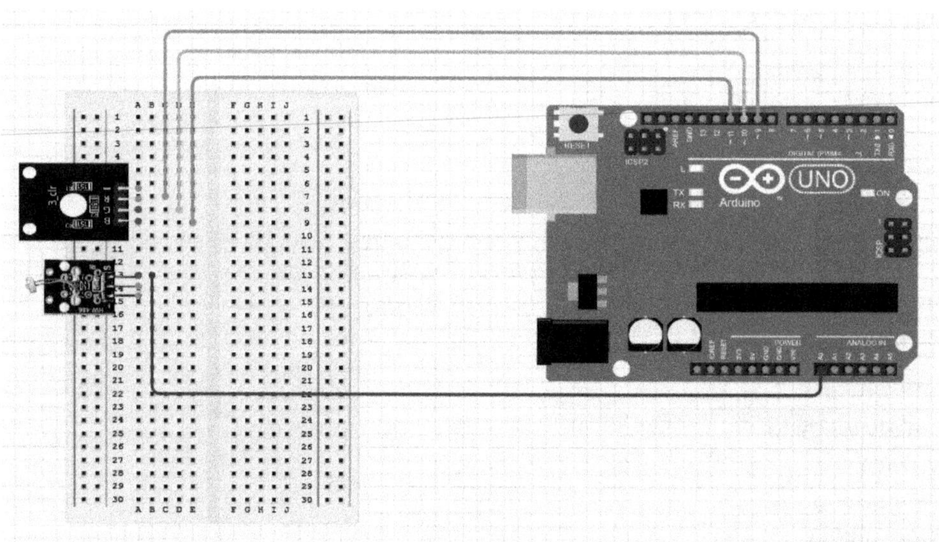

Arduino Code & Serial Monitor Output

```
const int ldrPin=A0, rPin=9, gPin=10,
bPin=11;

void setup() { Serial.begin(9600); }

void loop() {
  int light = analogRead(ldrPin);
  int bright = map(light, 0, 1023, 255,
0);  // inverse
  analogWrite(rPin, bright);
  analogWrite(gPin, bright);
  analogWrite(bPin, bright);
  Serial.print("Light: ");
Serial.print(light);
  Serial.print(" | Brightness: ");
Serial.println(bright);
  delay(100);
}
```

Output | Serial Monitor ×

Message (Enter to send message to 'Arduino UNO' on 'COM3')

```
Light: 1023 |  Brightness: 0
Light: 1018 |  Brightness: 1
Light: 1005 |  Brightness: 4
Light: 980  |  Brightness: 10
Light: 950  |  Brightness: 18
Light: 900  |  Brightness: 31
Light: 820  |  Brightness: 50
Light: 700  |  Brightness: 80
Light: 600  |  Brightness: 106
Light: 500  |  Brightness: 129
Light: 400  |  Brightness: 155
Light: 300  |  Brightness: 180
Light: 200  |  Brightness: 205
Light: 150  |  Brightness: 219
```

How the Code Works

map(light, 0, 1023, 255, 0) says: take the value light, which ranges from 0 to 1023, and map it to a new range from 255 down to 0. When light=0 (dark), brightness=255 (maximum). When light=1023 (bright), brightness=0 (off). All three RGB channels receive the same brightness value, creating white light at varying intensities. The Serial Monitor shows both values side by side so you can see the inverse relationship in real time.

Real-World Applications

- Adaptive screen brightness
- Car dashboard dimmer
- Smart office lighting
- Photography studio lights
- Energy-efficient lighting

Experiment 65 | Temperature Alarm

Sensor: DHT11 + Active Buzzer

Difficulty: ★★ Intermediate

Objective: Sound a buzzer when the temperature exceeds a set threshold.

How It Works

This project combines a temperature sensor with a buzzer to create a practical heat alarm. The DHT11 reads temperature every 2 seconds. If it exceeds the limit, the buzzer activates immediately. This is exactly how real overheating alarms work in server rooms, greenhouses, and electronics cooling systems.

Concepts Learned

- DHT11 reading + output
- Temperature threshold
- Alarm trigger from sensor
- Multi-component project

Components Required

Component	Qty
Arduino Uno	1

Component	Qty
DHT11 Sensor	1
Active Buzzer Module	1
Jumper Wires	5

Wiring

Component	Arduino Pin
DHT11 S	D2
Buzzer S	D8
Both +	5V
Both -	GND

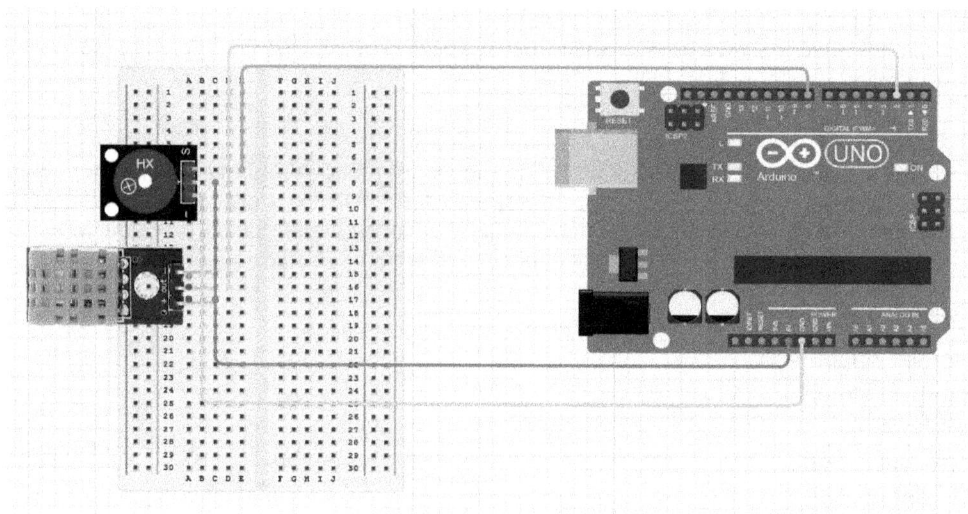

Arduino Code & Serial Monitor Output

```
#include <DHT.h>
DHT dht(2, DHT11);
const int buzPin = 8;
const float tempLimit = 30.0;

void setup() {
  dht.begin();
  pinMode(buzPin, OUTPUT);
  Serial.begin(9600);
}

void loop() {
  float t = dht.readTemperature();
  Serial.print("Temp: ");
Serial.println(t);
  if (t > tempLimit) {
    digitalWrite(buzPin, HIGH);
    Serial.println("TEMP ALARM!");
```

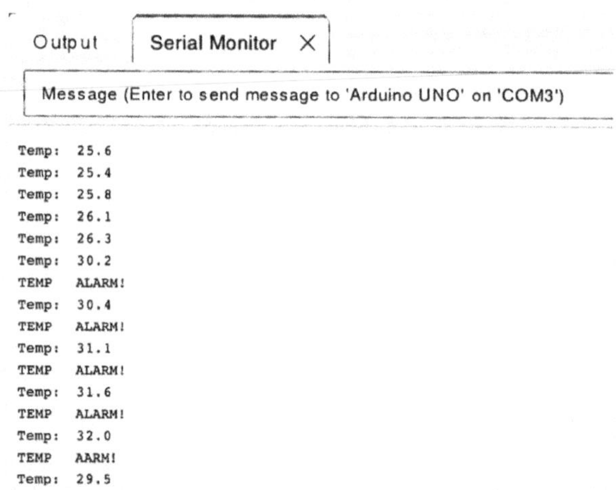

```
    } else {
      digitalWrite(buzPin, LOW);
    }
    delay(2000);
  }
```

How the Code Works

The DHT library is included and the sensor initialised as in earlier experiments. tempLimit = 30.0 is the alarm threshold in Celsius - adjust this to suit your environment. After reading the temperature, the if statement directly maps the condition (too hot) to an output (buzzer on). When temperature drops back below the limit, the buzzer turns off automatically on the next reading cycle.

Real-World Applications

- Overheating protection
- Server room temperature alarms
- Greenhouse heat alerts
- Baby room safety
- Industrial thermal warnings

Experiment 66 | Heat Warning Buzzer

Sensor: Analog Temperature Sensor + Active Buzzer
Difficulty: ★ Beginner
Objective: Sound a buzzer when the analog temperature sensor detects heat above a safe level.

How It Works

This experiment achieves the same goal as Experiment 65 but uses the simpler analog temperature sensor instead of the DHT11. No library is needed - just the voltage-to-temperature formula from Experiment 19. This shows that multiple solutions exist for the same problem, and sometimes the simpler sensor is the better choice.

Concepts Learned

- Analog temp reading + output
- Simple heat alarm
- No-library sensor use
- Voltage-to-temperature math

Components Required

Component	Qty
Arduino Uno	1
Analog Temperature Sensor	1
Active Buzzer Module	1
Jumper Wires	4

Wiring

Component	Arduino Pin
`Temp S`	`A0`
`Buzzer S`	`D8`

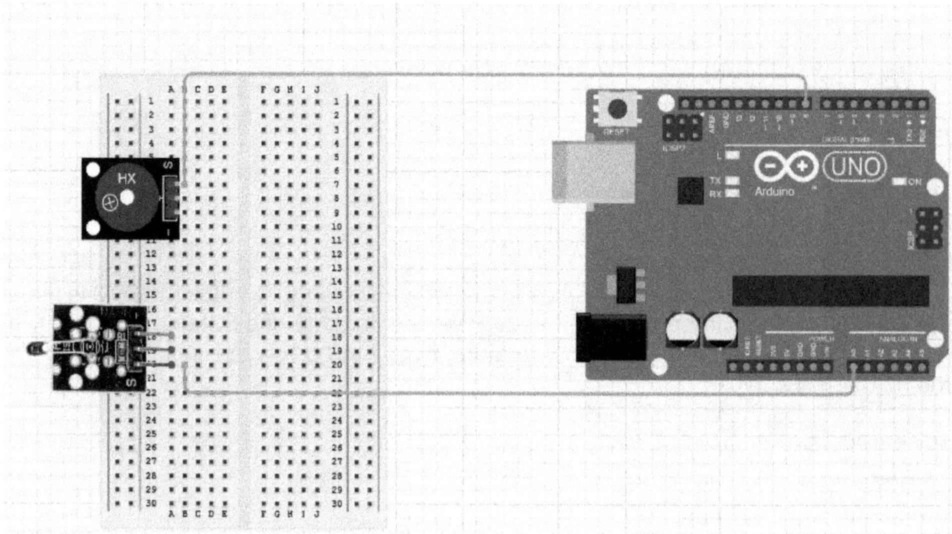

Arduino Code & Serial Monitor Output

```
const int tempPin=A0, buzPin=8;
const float limit = 35.0;

void setup() {
  pinMode(buzPin, OUTPUT);
  Serial.begin(9600);
}

void loop() {
  float v = analogRead(tempPin) * 5.0 /
1023.0;
  float t = (v - 0.5) * 100.0;
  Serial.print("Temp: ");
Serial.println(t);
  digitalWrite(buzPin, t > limit ? HIGH :
LOW);
  delay(1000);
}
```

Output | Serial Monitor ×

Message (Enter to send message to 'Arduino UNO' on 'COM3')

```
Temp: 26.42
Temp: 27.13
Temp: 28.08
Temp: 29.45
Temp: 31.02
Temp: 32.76
Temp: 34.21
Temp: 35.68
Temp: 37.24
Temp: 38.53
Temp: 39.81
Temp: 40.67
Temp: 41.29
Temp: 39.05
Temp: 37.12
Temp: 35.22
```

How the Code Works

The temperature calculation in one line combines the analogRead, voltage conversion, and temperature formula. The result is compared to limit = 35.0. The ternary operator on the final digitalWrite line is a compact way to write the on/off logic: t > limit ? HIGH : LOW means HIGH if too hot, LOW otherwise. Notice this approach is simpler than using the DHT11 for a pure temperature alarm.

Real-World Applications

- Engine overheat warning
- PCB temperature protection
- Battery heat guard
- Food storage alarms
- Laboratory safety

Experiment 67 | Humidity Indicator

Sensor: DHT11 + RGB LED

Difficulty: ★★ Intermediate

Objective: Use RGB LED colour to indicate humidity level: Blue (low), Green (ideal), Red (high).

How It Works

Using colour to represent data ranges is called data visualisation. Green for ideal, blue for dry, and red for too humid creates an immediate, intuitive display. You do not need to read numbers - a single glance at the LED colour tells you the room condition. This principle is used everywhere from traffic lights to hospital monitors.

Concepts Learned

- DHT11 + RGB output
- Humidity ranges
- Colour-coded status
- Multi-range if-else

Components Required

Component	Qty
Arduino Uno	1
DHT11 Sensor	1
RGB LED Module	1
Jumper Wires	6

Wiring

Component	Arduino Pin
DHT11 S	D2
RGB R	D9
RGB G	D10
RGB B	D11

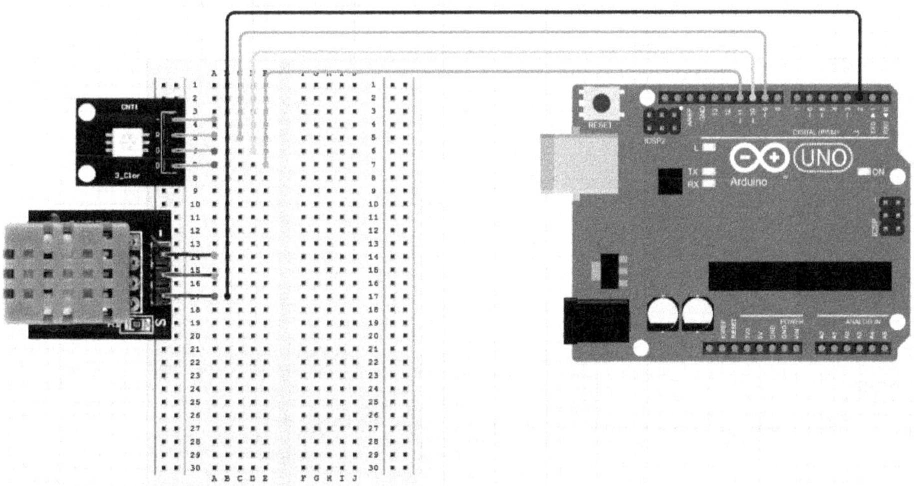

Arduino Code & Serial Monitor Output

```
#include <DHT.h>
DHT dht(2, DHT11);
const int rPin=9, gPin=10, bPin=11;

void setup() { dht.begin();
Serial.begin(9600); }

void loop() {
  float h = dht.readHumidity();
  Serial.print("Humidity: ");
Serial.println(h);
  if (h < 30) {
    analogWrite(rPin,0);
analogWrite(gPin,0);
analogWrite(bPin,255);
    Serial.println("DRY");
  } else if (h <= 60) {
    analogWrite(rPin,0);
analogWrite(gPin,255);
analogWrite(bPin,0);
    Serial.println("IDEAL");
  } else {
    analogWrite(rPin,255);
analogWrite(gPin,0); analogWrite(bPin,0);
    Serial.println("TOO HUMID");
  }
  delay(2000);
}
```

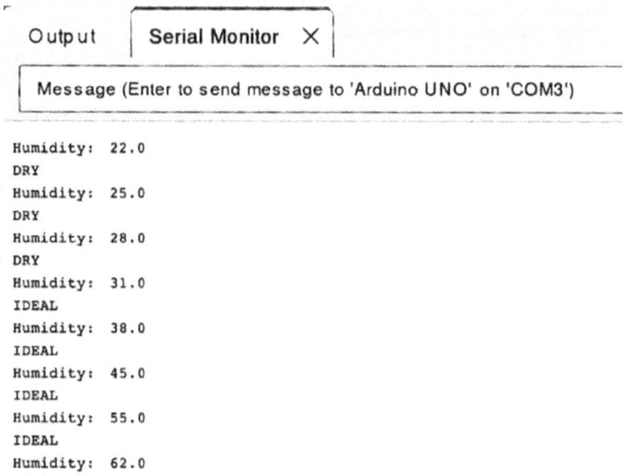

How the Code Works

Three if-else branches set distinct RGB values for each humidity range. Less than 30% is dry (blue), 30–60% is ideal (green), above 60% is too humid (red). Each branch sets all three RGB channels explicitly to avoid leftover colour from a previous state. The Serial Monitor shows both the numeric reading and the classification so you can see both representations simultaneously.

Real-World Applications

- Greenhouse humidity control
- Wine cellar indicator
- Museum artefact protection
- Baby room humidity display
- Server room monitoring

Experiment 68 | Flame Alarm System

Sensor: Flame Sensor + Active Buzzer

Difficulty: ★ Beginner

Objective: Trigger a buzzer alarm immediately when a flame is detected.

How It Works

The simplest possible fire alarm: if flame is detected, sound the buzzer. This direct sensor-to-alarm pipeline has no delay and no latching - the buzzer is on exactly as long as the flame is detected. In a real fire alarm this would be the core logic, surrounded by additional features like latching and manual reset.

Concepts Learned

- Flame to audio alarm
- Safety system integration
- Fast response triggering
- Latching alarm logic

Components Required

Component	Qty
Arduino Uno	1
Flame Sensor Module	1
Active Buzzer Module	1
Jumper Wires	5

Wiring

Component	Arduino Pin
Flame D0	D2
Buzzer S	D8
Both +	5V
Both -	GND

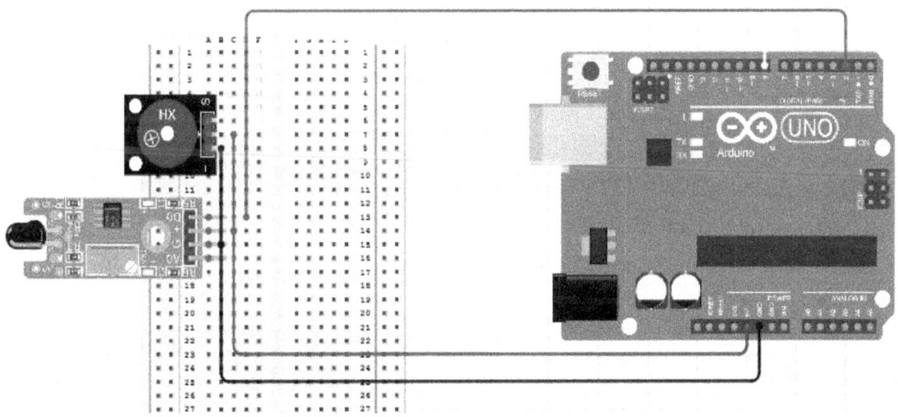

Arduino Code & Serial Monitor Output

```
const int flamePin=2, buzPin=8;

void setup() {
  pinMode(flamePin, INPUT);
  pinMode(buzPin, OUTPUT);
  Serial.begin(9600);
}

void loop() {
  if (digitalRead(flamePin) == LOW) {
    digitalWrite(buzPin, HIGH);
    Serial.println("FIRE ALARM!");
```

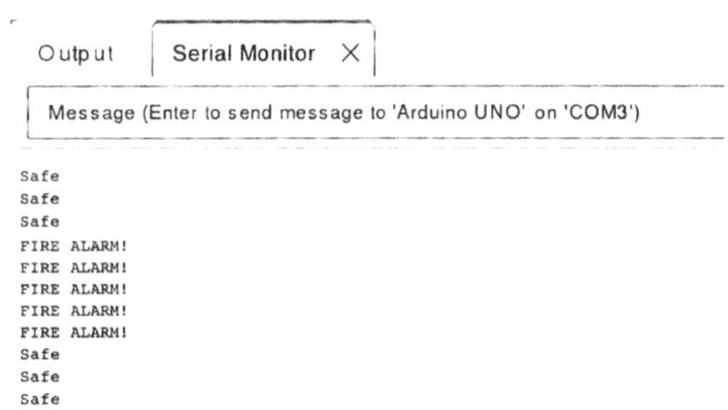

```
  } else {
    digitalWrite(buzPin, LOW);
    Serial.println("Safe");
  }
  delay(200);
}
```

How the Code Works

The logic is clean and direct: read flamePin, if LOW (flame present) set buzzer HIGH, otherwise LOW. The 200ms delay gives five checks per second. Notice both the buzzer and flame sensor need power and ground connections in addition to their signal pins. This experiment is a good template for any sensor-to-buzzer alarm - just replace the flame sensor with any digital sensor.

Real-World Applications

- Home fire alarms
- Kitchen safety systems
- Lab fire detection
- Campfire boundary alarms
- Industrial fire suppression triggers

Experiment 69 | Flame Activated Relay

Sensor: Flame Sensor + Relay

Difficulty: ★★ Intermediate

Objective: Activate a relay (which could control a pump or sprinkler) when a flame is detected.

How It Works

A relay is an electrically controlled switch. When you send a HIGH signal to the relay module, it closes an internal mechanical switch that can control a separate circuit - such as a 240V mains device. This is how Arduino controls real-world appliances. In a fire safety context, the relay could power a water pump or suppress a ventilation system.

Concepts Learned

- Relay switching basics
- Flame-to-relay pipeline
- High-power device control
- Safety relay wiring

Components Required

Component	Qty
Arduino Uno	1
Flame Sensor Module	1
Relay Module	1
Jumper Wires	5

Wiring

Component	Arduino Pin
Flame D0	D2
Relay S	D8

Component	Arduino Pin
Both +	5V
Both -	GND

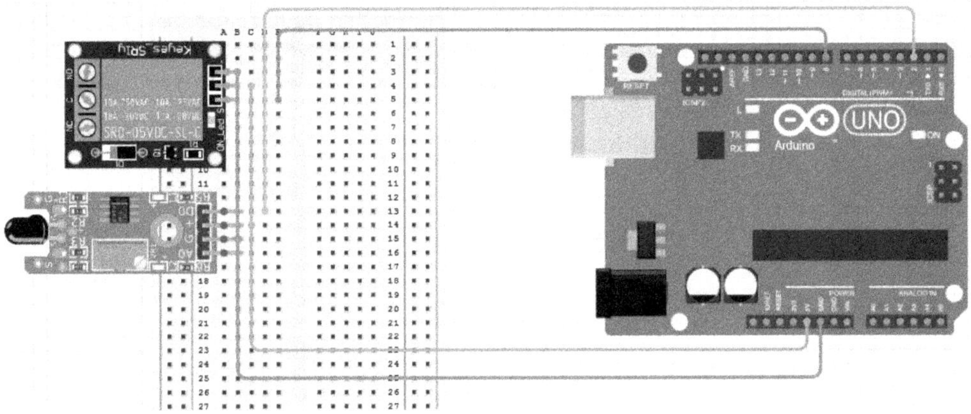

Arduino Code & Serial Monitor Output

```
const int flamePin=2, relayPin=8;

void setup() {
  pinMode(flamePin, INPUT);
  pinMode(relayPin, OUTPUT);
  Serial.begin(9600);
}

void loop() {
  if (digitalRead(flamePin) == LOW) {
    digitalWrite(relayPin, HIGH);  //
Activate pump/sprinkler
    Serial.println("FLAME! Relay ON");
  } else {
    digitalWrite(relayPin, LOW);
    Serial.println("No flame. Relay OFF");
  }
  delay(200);
}
```

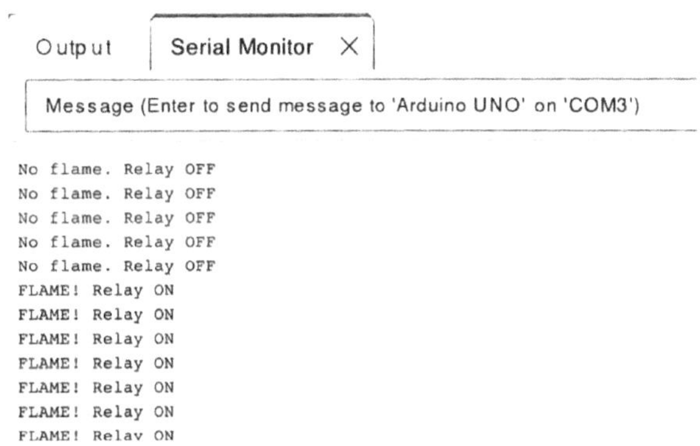

How the Code Works

The relay pin works identically to the buzzer pin - HIGH turns it on, LOW turns it off. The key difference is what the relay controls: connect a water pump, siren, or any DC/AC device across the relay's output terminals. The relay module isolates the Arduino from the high-voltage circuit for safety. Always treat the relay output side as potentially dangerous and follow electrical safety guidelines.

Real-World Applications

- Fire suppression systems
- Automatic sprinklers
- Water pump activation
- Fire safety relay boards
- Industrial fire control

Experiment 70 | Magnetic Door Alarm

Sensor: Reed Switch + Active Buzzer

Difficulty: ★ Beginner

Objective: Sound a buzzer alarm whenever a door (reed switch) is opened.

How It Works

The reed switch door sensor is mounted on a door frame, and a magnet is attached to the door. When the door is open, the magnet is far from the reed switch and the circuit is open - the switch reads HIGH. When the door closes, the magnet aligns with the switch and closes the circuit - reads LOW. The buzzer alarms whenever the switch reads HIGH (door open).

Concepts Learned

- Reed switch door sensor
- Buzzer on door open
- State change alarm
- Entry detection

Components Required

Component	Qty
Arduino Uno	1
Reed Switch Module	1
Active Buzzer Module	1
Magnet	1
Jumper Wires	5

Wiring

Component	Arduino Pin
Reed S	D2
Buzzer S	D8
Both +	5V
Both -	GND

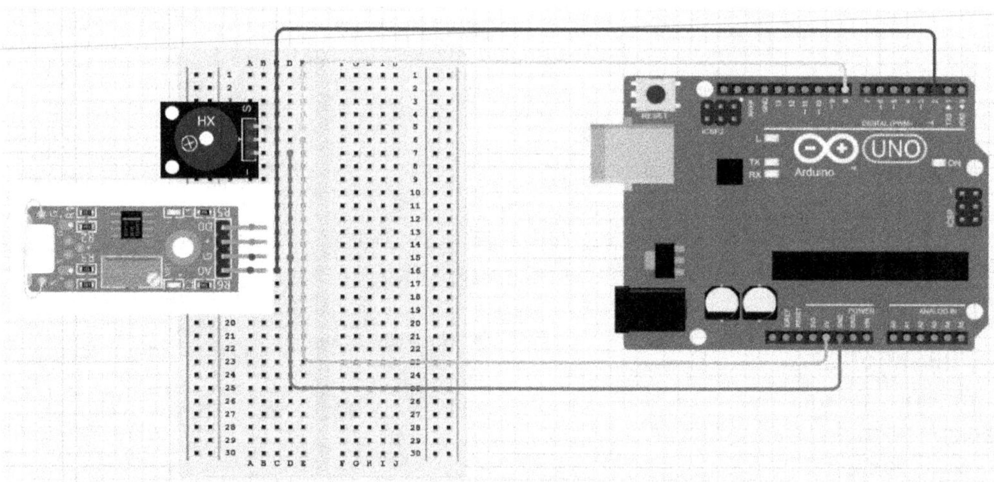

Arduino Code & Serial Monitor Output

```
const int reedPin=2, buzPin=8;

void setup() {
  pinMode(reedPin, INPUT_PULLUP);
  pinMode(buzPin, OUTPUT);
  Serial.begin(9600);
}

void loop() {
  if (digitalRead(reedPin) == HIGH) {
    digitalWrite(buzPin, HIGH);
    Serial.println("DOOR OPEN - ALARM!");
  } else {
    digitalWrite(buzPin, LOW);
    Serial.println("Door closed.");
  }
  delay(100);
}
```

```
Output    Serial Monitor ×
Message (Enter to send message to 'Arduino UNO' on 'COM3')

Door closed.
Door closed.
Door closed.
Door closed.
Door closed.
DOOR OPEN - ALARM!
DOOR OPEN - ALARM!
DOOR OPEN - ALARM!
DOOR OPEN - ALARM!
DOOR OPEN - ALARM!
DOOR OPEN - ALARM!
DOOR OPEN - ALARM!
DOOR OPEN - ALARM!
DOOR OPEN - ALARM!
DOOR OPEN - ALARM!
Door closed.
Door closed.
Door closed.
```

How the Code Works

The continuous alarm approach here means the buzzer sounds for as long as the door is open. When the door closes (LOW), the buzzer immediately stops. This is simpler than the edge-detection approach in Experiment 32 but uses more power. For a real alarm you might want edge detection (alarm only triggers once when opened) combined with a timer (alarm re-sounds if still open after N seconds).

Real-World Applications

- Home burglar alarm
- Shop entry chime
- Fridge door alert
- Safe door monitor
- Medicine cabinet alarm

Experiment 71 | Anti-Theft Shock Alarm

Sensor: Shock Sensor + Active Buzzer

Difficulty: ★ Beginner

Objective: Trigger an alarm when vibration or an impact is detected on a protected object.

How It Works

An anti-theft shock alarm detects the vibration caused by someone tampering with, lifting, or hitting a protected object. When shock is detected, the buzzer sounds for 3 seconds - long enough to alert people nearby but with an automatic reset so the system is ready for the next event. This is how basic car alarms and laptop security cables work.

Concepts Learned

- Vibration to alarm
- Shock event alarm trigger
- Physical security basics
- One-shot alarm with reset

Components Required

Component	Qty
Arduino Uno	1
Shock Switch Module	1
Active Buzzer Module	1
Jumper Wires	5

Wiring

Component	Arduino Pin
Shock S	D2
Buzzer S	D8
Both +	5V
Both -	GND

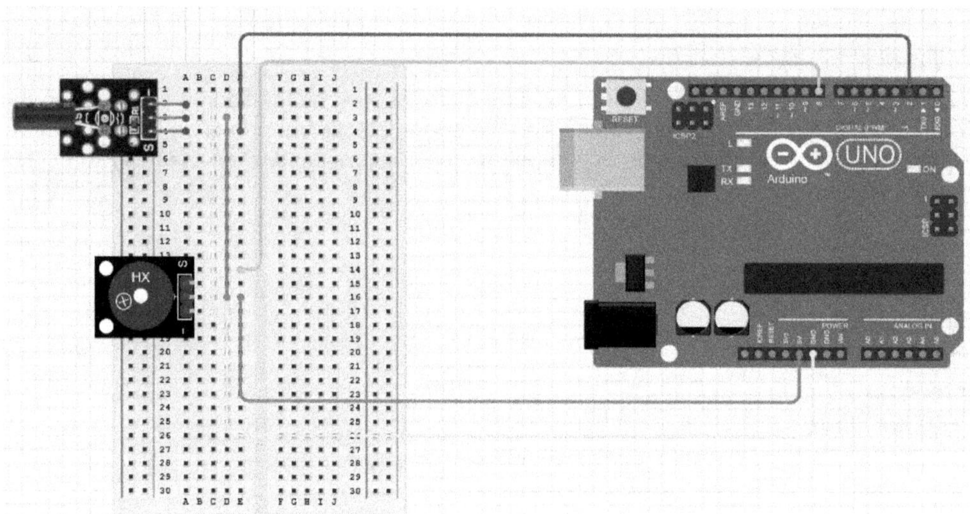

Arduino Code & Serial Monitor Output

```
const int shockPin=2, buzPin=8;

void setup() {
  pinMode(shockPin, INPUT_PULLUP);
  pinMode(buzPin, OUTPUT);
  Serial.begin(9600);
}

void loop() {
  if (digitalRead(shockPin) == LOW) {
    digitalWrite(buzPin, HIGH);
    Serial.println("VIBRATION ALARM!");
    delay(3000);
    digitalWrite(buzPin, LOW);
  }
}
```

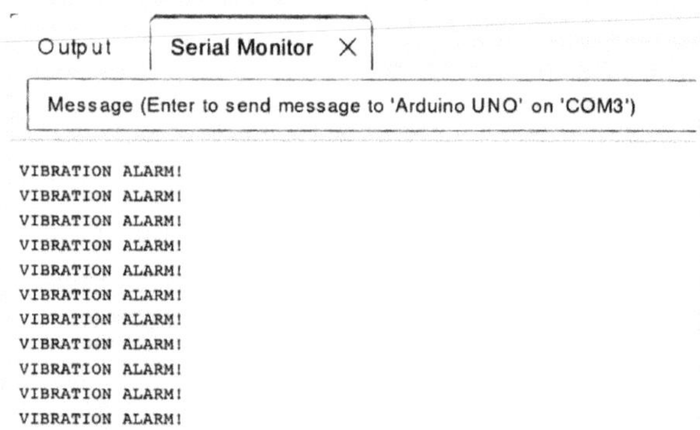

How the Code Works

When shockPin reads LOW (impact detected), the buzzer turns HIGH immediately. delay(3000) keeps it on for 3 seconds - nothing else runs during this time. After 3 seconds the buzzer turns LOW and alarm resets to false, ready for the next trigger. The 3-second fixed duration is a design choice: shorter might not alert anyone, longer might be annoying in a false-alarm scenario.

Real-World Applications

- Car anti-theft alarms
- Laptop theft deterrent
- Safe tampering detection
- Museum exhibit protection
- Package integrity monitoring

Experiment 72 | Tilt Warning System

Sensor: Tilt Sensor + Active Buzzer

Difficulty: ★ Beginner

Objective: Sound a warning buzzer when an object is tilted from its upright position.

How It Works

A tilt warning system monitors an object's orientation and immediately alerts if it moves from upright. Unlike the shock alarm which responds to impact, this responds to sustained tilt - useful for monitoring equipment that must remain level, such as server racks, sensitive instruments, or heavy machinery.

Concepts Learned

- Tilt detection + alarm
- Physical warning system
- Continuous alarm while tilted

Components Required

Component	Qty
Arduino Uno	1
Tilt Switch Module	1
Active Buzzer Module	1
Jumper Wires	5

Wiring

Component	Arduino Pin
`Tilt S`	D2
`Buzzer S`	D8

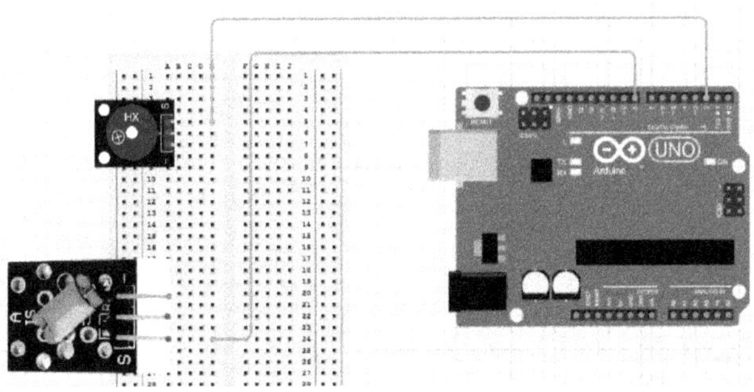

Arduino Code & Serial Monitor Output

```
const int tiltPin=2, buzPin=8;

void setup() {
  pinMode(tiltPin, INPUT_PULLUP);
  pinMode(buzPin, OUTPUT);
  Serial.begin(9600);
}

void loop() {
  bool tilted = (digitalRead(tiltPin) == LOW);
  digitalWrite(buzPin, tilted ? HIGH : LOW);
  Serial.println(tilted ? "WARNING: TILTED!" : "Upright");
  delay(200);
}
```

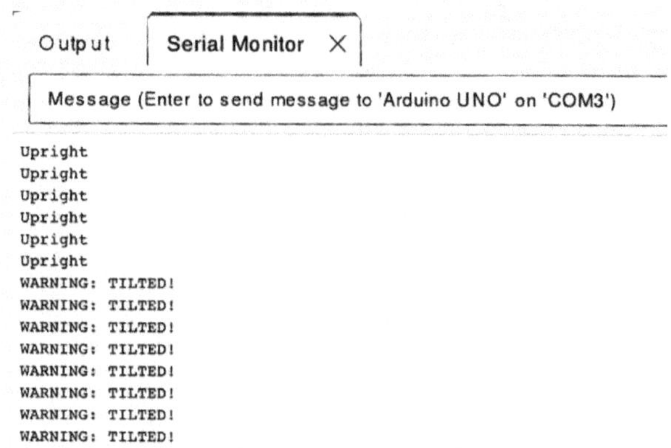

How the Code Works

The ternary operators condense both the buzzer and Serial output into single lines. tilted is calculated once and reused for both outputs, making the code efficient. Notice the buzzer mirrors the tilt state exactly: on when tilted, off when upright, with no delay or latching. This continuous response is appropriate here because tilt is a sustained condition, not a momentary event.

Real-World Applications

- Server rack tilt alerts
- Vehicle rollover warning
- Heavy machinery safety
- Medical equipment alarms
- Parcel handling protection

Experiment 73 | Smart Torch Detector

Sensor: LDR + Active Buzzer
Difficulty: ★ Beginner
Objective: Beep a buzzer when a sudden bright light (like a torch) is shone at the sensor.

How It Works

A torch (flashlight) or security spotlight produces a sudden, large increase in light level. By setting a threshold high enough to ignore normal daylight changes but low enough to catch a direct torch beam, we can detect deliberate illumination of the sensor. This is the principle behind light-barrier security systems.

Concepts Learned

- Bright flash detection
- Rising threshold detection
- Sudden change logic
- Light-triggered alerts

Components Required

Component	Qty
Arduino Uno	1
Photo-Resistor Module	1

Component	Qty
Active Buzzer Module	1
Jumper Wires	4

Wiring

Component	Arduino Pin
LDR S	A0
Buzzer S	D8

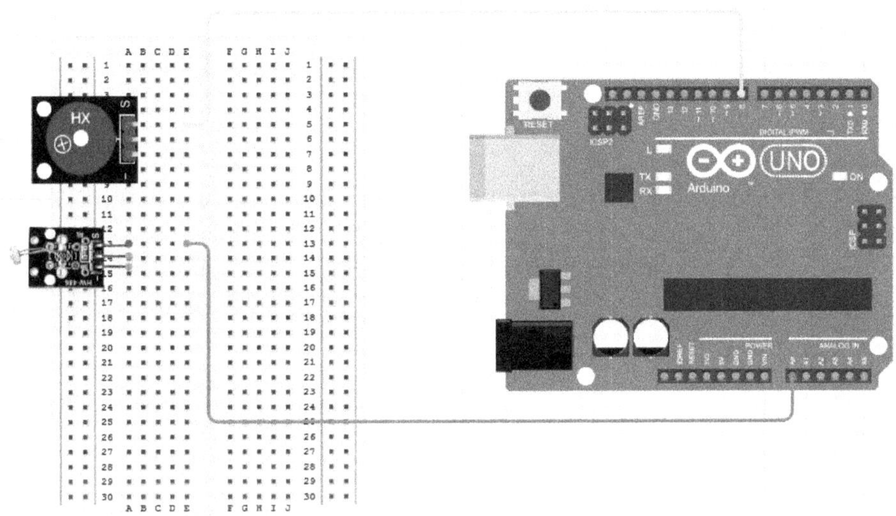

Arduino Code & Serial Monitor Output

```
const int ldrPin=A0, buzPin=8;
const int threshold = 700;

void setup() {
  pinMode(buzPin, OUTPUT);
  Serial.begin(9600);
}

void loop() {
  int light = analogRead(ldrPin);
  if (light > threshold) {
    digitalWrite(buzPin, HIGH);
    Serial.println("Bright light
detected!");
    delay(500);
    digitalWrite(buzPin, LOW);
  }
  delay(100);
}
```

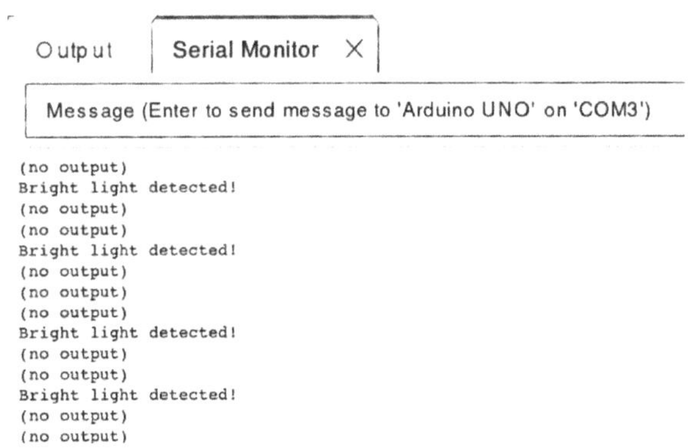

How the Code Works

The threshold = 700 is set high - it will only trigger on a direct, bright light source, not normal ambient changes. When a bright flash is detected, the buzzer beeps for 500ms and then resets. The 100ms delay at the end of loop() sets the sampling rate. Note this is a momentary detection - the light only needs to appear briefly to trigger the alarm.

Real-World Applications

- Security light beam alarm
- Camera flash detector
- Privacy protection alert
- Photocopier jam detection
- Light-based intruder detection

Experiment 74 | Laser Tripwire Alarm

Sensor: Laser Module + LDR + Active Buzzer
Difficulty: ★★ Intermediate
Objective: Trigger a buzzer alarm when the laser beam aimed at an LDR is broken.

How It Works

A laser tripwire creates an invisible barrier. The laser beam shines continuously onto the LDR. As long as the beam is intact, the LDR reads a high value - above beamThreshold. The moment someone walks through the beam, the LDR reading drops sharply because the laser is no longer hitting it. This drop triggers the alarm.

Concepts Learned

- Laser-LDR tripwire
- Beam break detection
- Multi-component integration
- Security system design

Components Required

Component	Qty
Arduino Uno	1
Laser Module	1
Photo-Resistor Module	1
Active Buzzer	1
Jumper Wires	6

Wiring

Component	Arduino Pin
`Laser S`	`D3`
`LDR S`	`A0`
`Buzzer S`	`D8`

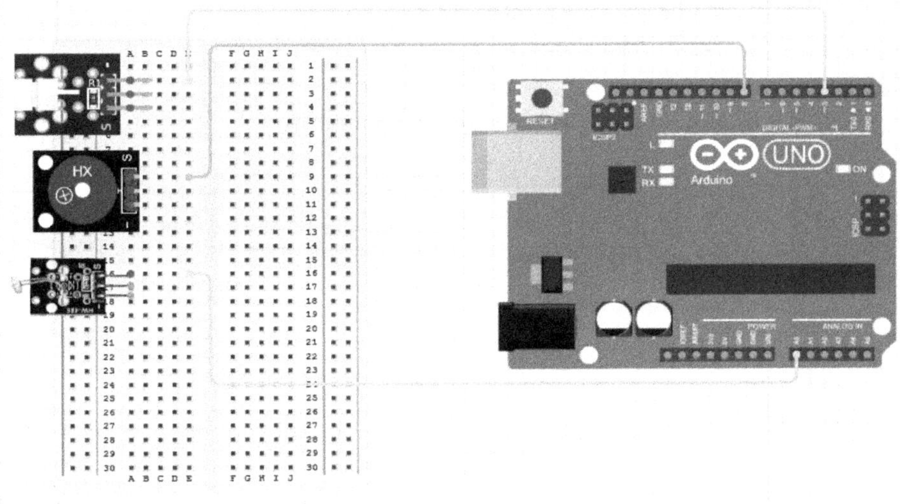

Arduino Code & Serial Monitor Output

```
const int laserPin=3, ldrPin=A0, buzPin=8;
const int beamThreshold = 600;

void setup() {
  pinMode(laserPin, OUTPUT);
  pinMode(buzPin, OUTPUT);
  digitalWrite(laserPin, HIGH);
  Serial.begin(9600);
}

void loop() {
  int ldrVal = analogRead(ldrPin);
  if (ldrVal < beamThreshold) {
    digitalWrite(buzPin, HIGH);
    Serial.println("TRIPWIRE BROKEN -
ALARM!");
  } else {
    digitalWrite(buzPin, LOW);
    Serial.println("Beam OK");
  }
  delay(100);
}
```

Output | Serial Monitor ×

Message (Enter to send message to 'Arduino UNO' on 'COM3')

```
Beam OK
Beam OK
Beam OK
Beam OK
Beam OK
TRIPWIRE BROKEN - ALARM!
TRIPWIRE BROKEN - ALARM!
TRIPWIRE BROKEN - ALARM!
TRIPWIRE BROKEN - ALARM!
TRIPWIRE BROKEN - ALARM!
TRIPWIRE BROKEN - ALARM!
Beam OK
Beam OK
```

How the Code Works

The laser is turned on in setup() and never turned off. In loop(), if ldrVal < beamThreshold the beam is broken and the buzzer sounds. If ldrVal >= beamThreshold the beam is intact and the buzzer is silent. Set beamThreshold about 100 points below your measured aligned reading to create a reliable trigger window. Too close to the aligned value causes false alarms from vibration; too low misses brief interruptions.

Real-World Applications

- Perimeter security systems
- Safe room protection
- Museum intrusion detection
- Package area alarms
- Escape room game mechanics

Experiment 75 | Obstacle Detection Alarm

Sensor: Obstacle Avoidance Sensor + Active Buzzer

Difficulty: ★ Beginner

Objective: Sound a buzzer alarm when an obstacle is detected nearby.

How It Works

This project adds a buzzer output to the obstacle detection from Experiments 37–38. The sensor constantly monitors for objects in its path. When detected, an immediate alarm sounds. This is the basic warning system used in reversing parking sensors, robot collision systems, and automated guided vehicles.

Concepts Learned

- Obstacle to alarm pipeline
- Continuous beep on detection
- Proximity-based response
- Simple robotics safety

Components Required

Component	Qty
Arduino Uno	1
Obstacle Avoidance Sensor	1
Active Buzzer Module	1
Jumper Wires	5

Wiring

Component	Arduino Pin
Obstacle OUT	D2
Buzzer S	D8

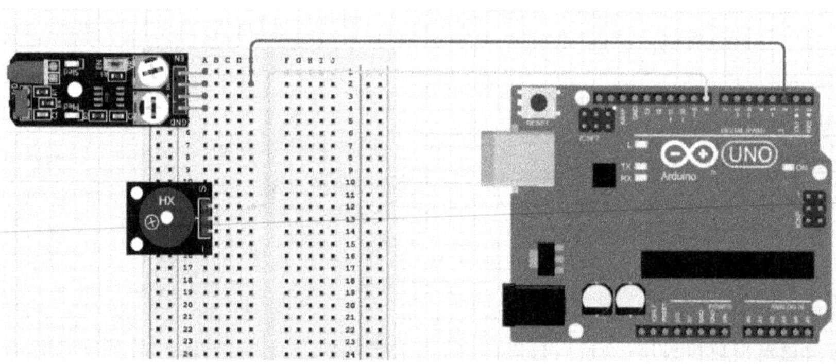

Arduino Code & Serial Monitor Output

```
const int obsPin=2, buzPin=8;

void setup() {
  pinMode(obsPin, INPUT);
  pinMode(buzPin, OUTPUT);
  Serial.begin(9600);
}
```

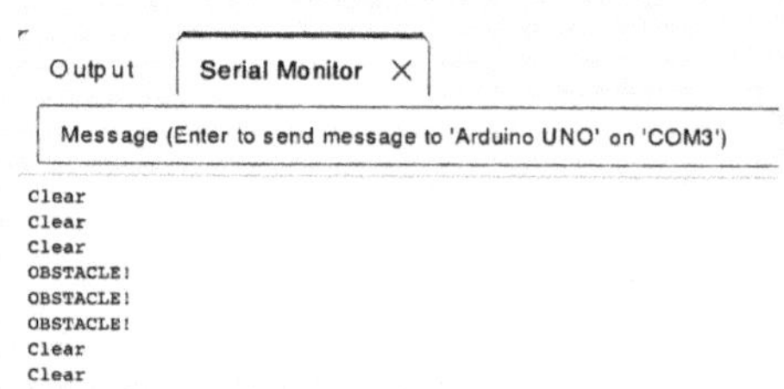

```
void loop() {
  bool detected = (digitalRead(obsPin) ==
LOW);
  digitalWrite(buzPin, detected ? HIGH :
LOW);
  Serial.println(detected ? "OBSTACLE!" :
"Clear");
  delay(200);
}
```

How the Code Works

detected is a boolean calculated from the sensor state. We pass detected directly to both the buzzer (using the ternary operator) and the Serial output. When detected is true, the buzzer is HIGH. This direct mapping means there is zero delay between detection and alarm. The 200ms loop delay sets the response time - reduce it for faster response, increase it to reduce false triggers from brief sensor fluctuations.

Real-World Applications

- Robot collision warning
- Reversing parking sensor
- Blind spot detection
- Warehouse safety
- Drone obstacle alarm

Experiment 76 | Smart Parking Indicator

Sensor: Obstacle Avoidance Sensor + RGB LED

Difficulty: ★★ Intermediate

Objective: Show Green (space free) or Red (space occupied) using an RGB LED based on obstacle detection.

How It Works

Colour-coded parking indicators are used in car parks and bicycle bays to show at a glance which spaces are free. Green means available, red means occupied. The obstacle sensor detects whether a vehicle or object is present in the space. This project shows how sensor data can be turned into immediately understandable visual information.

Concepts Learned

- Parking logic
- Colour-coded status
- Real-world sensor application
- Binary state to LED colour

Components Required

Component	Qty
Arduino Uno	1
Obstacle Avoidance Sensor	1
RGB LED Module	1
Jumper Wires	6

Wiring

Component	Arduino Pin
Obstacle OUT	D2

Component	Arduino Pin
RGB R	D9
RGB G	D10
RGB B	D11

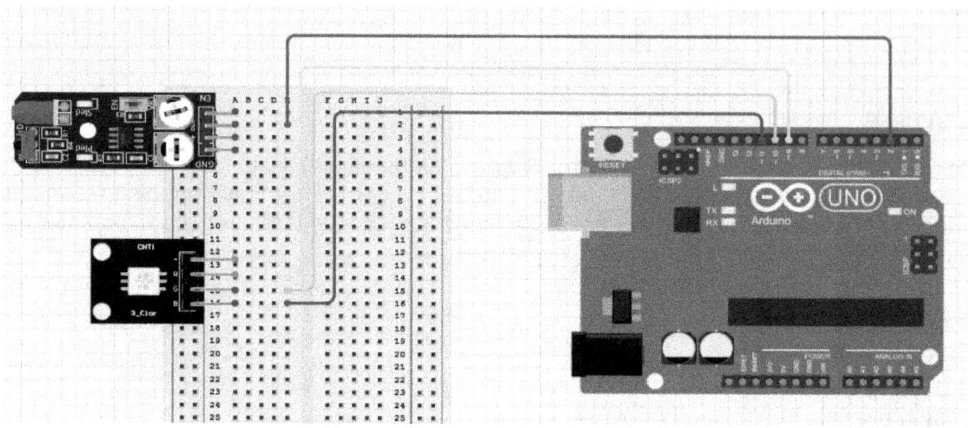

Arduino Code & Serial Monitor Output

```
const int obsPin=2, rPin=9, gPin=10,
bPin=11;

void setup() {
  pinMode(obsPin, INPUT);
  Serial.begin(9600);
}

void loop() {
  if (digitalRead(obsPin) == LOW) {
    analogWrite(rPin,255);
analogWrite(gPin,0); analogWrite(bPin,0);
    Serial.println("OCCUPIED");
  } else {
    analogWrite(rPin,0);
analogWrite(gPin,255);
analogWrite(bPin,0);
    Serial.println("FREE");
  }
  delay(300);
}
```

Output | Serial Monitor

Message (Enter to send message to 'Arduino UNO' on 'COM3')

```
FREE
FREE
FREE
OCCUPIED
OCCUPIED
OCCUPIED
FREE
FREE
FREE
FREE
OCCUPIED
OCCUPIED
OCCUPIED
FREE
```

How the Code Works

The logic is a simple if-else. If the sensor detects an obstacle (LOW), the LED turns red and OCCUPIED is printed. Otherwise green and FREE. Notice green uses channel 10 (gPin) and red uses channel 9 (rPin). Blue channel (bPin) is always 0. In a real parking system you would have one sensor and LED pair per space, all connected to a central controller.

Real-World Applications

- Car park space indicators
- Shopping trolley bay monitors
- Smart parking garages

- Bicycle stand monitors
- Locker availability display

Experiment 77 | Line Detection Indicator

Sensor: Tracking Sensor + RGB LED

Difficulty: ★ Beginner

Objective: Light up an RGB LED Red when a black line is detected, Green when on white surface.

How It Works

Connecting the tracking sensor output to an RGB LED creates a visual indicator for surface type. Red means black surface detected, green means white surface detected. This gives immediate visual confirmation of what the sensor sees, which is useful when building and testing a line-following robot.

Concepts Learned

- Surface detection to LED
- Status visualisation
- Real-time feedback
- Line-following robot basis

Components Required

Component	Qty
Arduino Uno	1
Tracking Sensor	1
RGB LED Module	1
Jumper Wires	6

Wiring

Component	Arduino Pin
`Tracking OUT`	D2
`RGB R`	D9
`RGB G`	D10
`RGB B`	D11

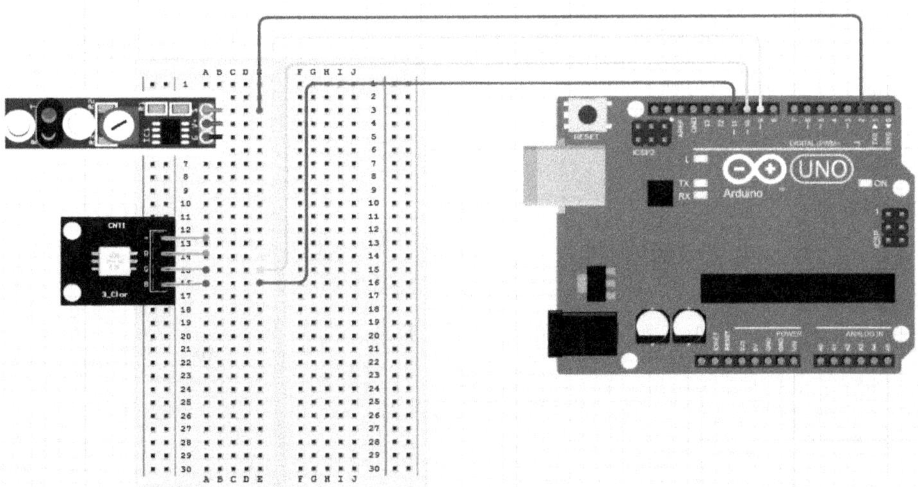

Arduino Code & Serial Monitor Output

```
const int trackPin=2, rPin=9, gPin=10,
bPin=11;

void setup() { pinMode(trackPin, INPUT); }

void loop() {
  if (digitalRead(trackPin) == LOW) {
    analogWrite(rPin,255);
analogWrite(gPin,0); analogWrite(bPin,0);
  } else {
    analogWrite(rPin,0);
analogWrite(gPin,255);
analogWrite(bPin,0);
  }
  delay(100);
}
```

```
No Serial Monitor output.

Object detected → RGB LED glows RED
No object → RGB LED glows GREEN
```

How the Code Works

The digitalRead result directly determines the LED colour with an if-else. This is one of the cleanest examples of sensor-to-output mapping in the book. The 100ms delay keeps the display responsive enough for a slowly moving robot test scenario. In a real robot this logic runs much faster - typically every 10–20ms - and the LED feedback is replaced by motor control commands.

Real-World Applications

- Line-follower robot feedback
- Label edge detection
- Barcode start/stop detection
- Conveyor alignment
- Printed mark reader

Experiment 78 | Joystick RGB Controller

Sensor: Joystick Module + RGB LED
Difficulty: ★★ Intermediate
Objective: Control the colour of an RGB LED using the X and Y axes of the joystick.

How It Works

Mapping a physical input range to a colour output range is a core interaction design pattern. Here the X axis of the joystick controls the red channel and the Y axis controls the green channel. As the joystick moves, the LED colour changes continuously. The blue channel is set as the inverse of red, creating complementary colour shifts.

Concepts Learned

- Joystick to colour mapping
- map() for two axes
- Dual-axis LED control
- Interactive input-output

Components Required

Component	Qty
Arduino Uno	1
Joystick Module	1

Component	Qty
RGB LED Module	1
Jumper Wires	7

Wiring

Component	Arduino Pin
Joystick VRX	A0
Joystick VRY	A1
RGB R	D9
RGB G	D10
RGB B	D11

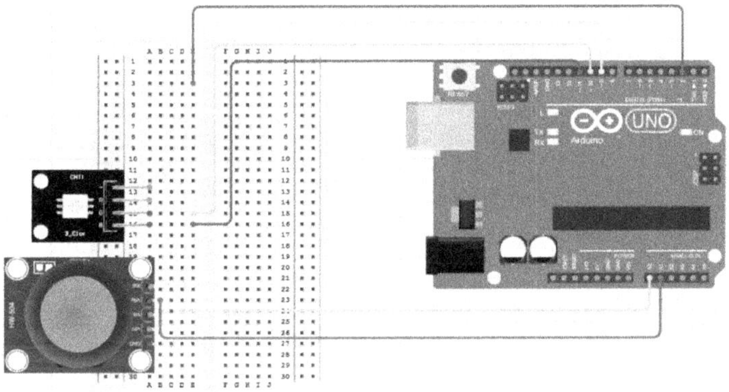

Arduino Code & Serial Monitor Output

```
const int xPin=A0, yPin=A1;
const int rPin=9, gPin=10, bPin=11;

void setup() { Serial.begin(9600); }

void loop() {
  int r = map(analogRead(xPin), 0, 1023,
0, 255);
  int g = map(analogRead(yPin), 0, 1023,
0, 255);
  int b = 255 - r;
  analogWrite(rPin, r);
  analogWrite(gPin, g);
  analogWrite(bPin, b);
  Serial.print("R:"); Serial.print(r);
  Serial.print(" G:"); Serial.print(g);
  Serial.print(" B:"); Serial.println(b);
  delay(50);
}
```

Message (Enter to send message to 'Arduino UNO' on 'COM3')

```
R:12 G:23 B:243
R:14 G:25 B:241
R:17 G:28 B:238
R:22 G:31 B:233
R:28 G:34 B:227
R:35 G:38 B:220
R:42 G:43 B:213
R:49 G:48 B:206
R:57 G:53 B:198
R:65 G:58 B:190
R:74 G:63 B:181
R:83 G:68 B:172
R:93 G:72 B:162
R:104 G:77 B:151
R:115 G:82 B:140
R:126 G:88 B:129
R:138 G:93 B:117
R:150 G:99 B:105
R:162 G:104 B:93
R:175 G:110 B:80
R:188 G:116 B:67
R:200 G:122 B:55
```

How the Code Works

map(analogRead(xPin), 0, 1023, 0, 255) reads the joystick X position and proportionally maps it to a brightness value between 0 and 255. The same happens for Y and the green channel. Blue is calculated as 255 - r which means when red is maximum, blue is zero and vice versa. This creates a warm-cool colour shift as you move the joystick left and right. The 50ms delay makes the response feel smooth.

Real-World Applications

- Interactive light art
- Colour mixing demo
- Stage lighting joystick
- Colour picker device
- Children's creative toy

Experiment 79 | Joystick Music Player

Sensor: Joystick Module + Passive Buzzer

Difficulty: ★★ Intermediate

Objective: Play different tones on a passive buzzer by moving the joystick in different directions.

How It Works

The passive buzzer can produce any frequency of sound because it has no built-in oscillator - the Arduino must generate the oscillating signal itself. The tone() function does this automatically: tone(pin, frequency) produces a square wave at the specified frequency on the output pin, which the buzzer converts to sound. noTone() stops the sound.

Concepts Learned

- Passive buzzer with tone()
- Joystick direction to tone
- tone() and noTone()
- Musical input mapping

Components Required

Component	Qty
Arduino Uno	1
Joystick Module	1
Passive Buzzer Module	1
Jumper Wires	5

Wiring

Component	Arduino Pin
`Joystick VRX`	`A0`
`Joystick VRY`	`A1`
`Buzzer S`	`D8`

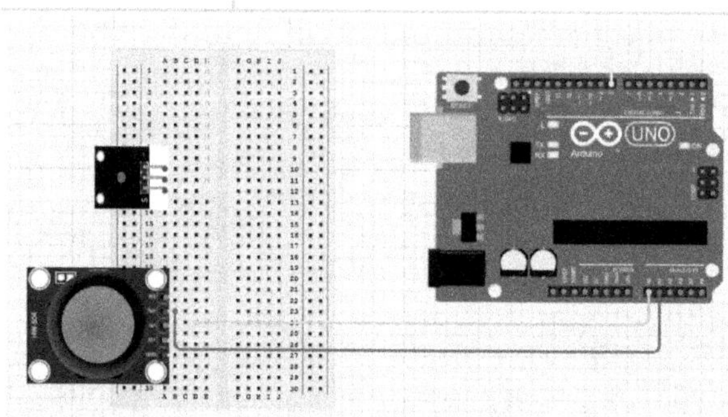

Arduino Code & Serial Monitor Output

```
const int xPin=A0, yPin=A1, buzPin=8;

void setup() {}

void loop() {
  int x = analogRead(xPin);
  int y = analogRead(yPin);
  if (x < 200){
   tone(buzPin, 262);
  } // C4 - Left
  else if (x > 800) { tone(buzPin,
330); } // E4 - Right
  else if (y < 200) { tone(buzPin,
392); } // G4 - Up
  else if (y > 800) { tone(buzPin,
523); } // C5 - Down
  else              { noTone(buzPin);
}
  delay(50);
}
```

```
No Serial Monitor output.

Joystick moved LEFT → Buzzer plays C4 (262
Hz)
Joystick moved RIGHT → Buzzer plays E4 (330
Hz)
Joystick moved UP → Buzzer plays G4 (392 Hz)
Joystick moved DOWN → Buzzer plays C5 (523
Hz)
Joystick centered → Buzzer OFF
```

How the Code Works

Four directional zones of the joystick are assigned musical notes: C4 (262Hz) for left, E4 (330Hz) for right, G4 (392Hz) for up, and C5 (523Hz) for down. These notes form a C major chord - pleasing to the ear. The centre position (512 ± 200) calls noTone() for silence. The 50ms delay sets the response speed. Try moving the joystick rhythmically to play simple melodies.

Real-World Applications

- Directional sound games
- Music teaching tools
- Sound-based navigation
- Interactive musical toys
- Directional audio feedback

Experiment 80 | Encoder Menu System

Sensor: Rotary Encoder
Difficulty: ★★ Intermediate
Objective: Navigate a simple menu by turning the encoder and selecting it with its push button.

How It Works

Rotary encoders are perfect for menu navigation because turning produces a clear directional signal and the click provides a confirm action. This is exactly how the control dial on most digital equipment works - car stereos, oscilloscopes, digital cameras, and ovens all use this interface pattern.

Concepts Learned

- Menu navigation concept
- Encoder for UI input
- Switch button select
- Circular menu index

Components Required

Component	Qty
Arduino Uno	1
Rotary Encoder Module	1
Jumper Wires	5

Wiring

Encoder Pin	Arduino Pin
CLK	D2
DT	D3
SW	D4
VCC	5V
GND	GND

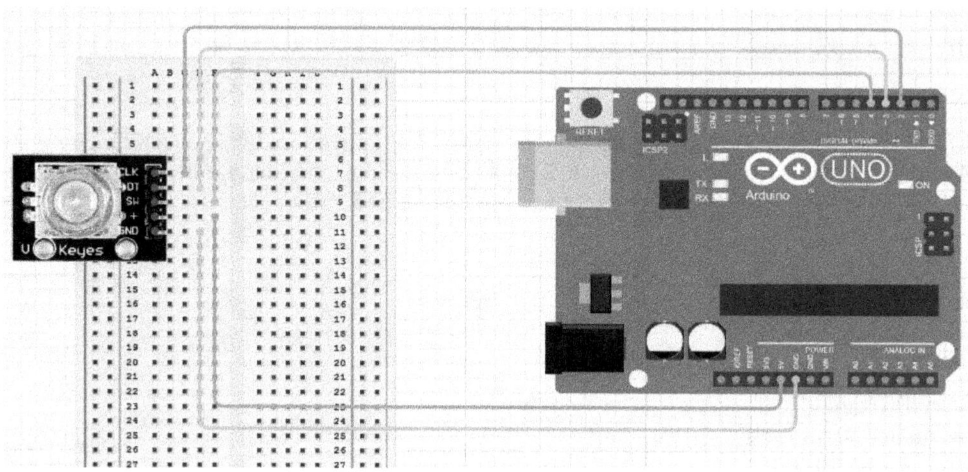

Arduino Code & Serial Monitor Output

```
const int clkPin=2, dtPin=3, swPin=4;
const char* menu[] =
{"Settings","Start","Stop","Info"};
const int menuLen = 4;
int selected = 0;
int lastClk;

void setup() {
  pinMode(clkPin,INPUT);
pinMode(dtPin,INPUT);
  pinMode(swPin, INPUT_PULLUP);
  Serial.begin(9600);
  lastClk = digitalRead(clkPin);
}

void loop() {
  int c = digitalRead(clkPin);
  if (c != lastClk && c == HIGH) {
```

```
Message (Enter to send message to 'Arduino Uno' on 'COM3')

Menu: Start
Menu: Stop
Menu: Info
Menu: Settings
Menu: Start
SELECTED: Start

Menu: Stop
Menu: Info
SELECTED: Info

Menu: Settings
Menu: Start
Menu: Stop
SELECTED: Stop

Menu: Info
Menu: Settings
SELECTED: Settings
```

```
    if (digitalRead(dtPin) != c) selected
= (selected+1) % menuLen;
    else                        selected
= (selected-1+menuLen) % menuLen;
    Serial.print("Menu: ");
Serial.println(menu[selected]);
  }
  lastClk = c;
  if (digitalRead(swPin) == LOW) {
    Serial.print("SELECTED: ");
Serial.println(menu[selected]);
    delay(300);
  }
}
```

How the Code Works

menu[] is an array of strings - the menu items. selected is the current position in the array. Turning the encoder moves selected up or down, with modulo wrapping it around at the ends. Pressing the switch (swPin == LOW) prints the selected item as a confirmation. The Serial Monitor shows the current selection as you scroll, then the final choice when you click.

Real-World Applications

- Device menu navigation
- Thermostat setting wheel
- Camera settings dial
- Industrial HMI input
- Music player track wheel

Experiment 81 | Encoder Controlled Brightness

Sensor: Rotary Encoder + RGB LED
Difficulty: ★★ Intermediate
Objective: Control the brightness of an LED by turning the rotary encoder clockwise/counter-clockwise.

How It Works

Connecting the rotary encoder's clockwise/counter-clockwise output to LED brightness creates a tactile brightness control. Turning right increases brightness, turning left decreases it. This is exactly how a physical dimmer switch works. The encoder position is not meaningful here - only the direction of each step matters.

Concepts Learned

- Encoder to PWM output
- Brightness mapping
- Clamping values (0–255)
- Analog output from digital input

Components Required

Component	Qty
Arduino Uno	1
Rotary Encoder Module	1
RGB LED Module	1
Jumper Wires	6

Wiring

Component	Arduino Pin
Encoder CLK	D2
Encoder DT	D3
RGB R	D9
RGB G	D10
RGB B	D11

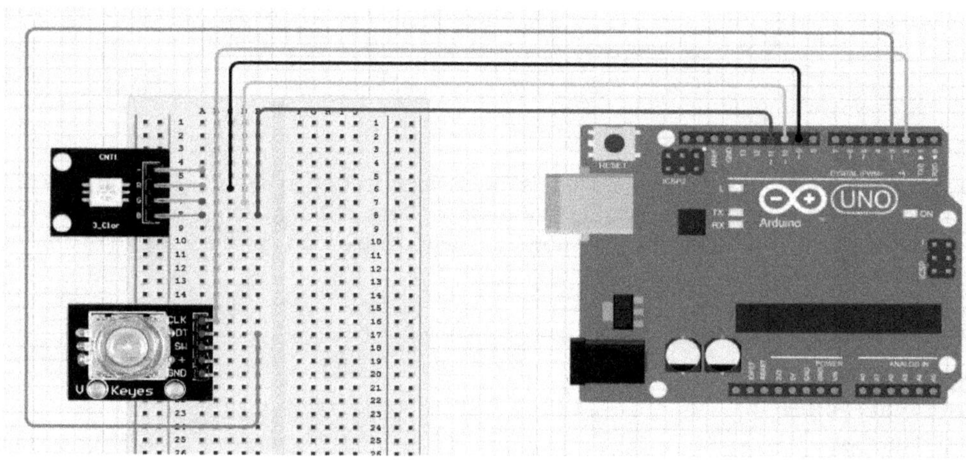

Arduino Code & Serial Monitor Output

```
const int clkPin=2, dtPin=3;
const int rPin=9, gPin=10, bPin=11;
int brightness = 128;
int lastClk;

void setup() {
  pinMode(clkPin,INPUT);
pinMode(dtPin,INPUT);
  lastClk = digitalRead(clkPin);
  Serial.begin(9600);
}

void loop() {
  int c = digitalRead(clkPin);
  if (c != lastClk && c == HIGH) {
    if (digitalRead(dtPin) != c)
brightness = min(255, brightness+10);
    else
brightness = max(0,   brightness-10);
    analogWrite(rPin, brightness);
    analogWrite(gPin, brightness);
    analogWrite(bPin, brightness);
    Serial.print("Brightness: ");
Serial.println(brightness);
  }
  lastClk = c;
}
```

```
Message (Enter to send message to 'Arduino Uno' on 'COM3')

Brightness: 138
Brightness: 148
Brightness: 158
Brightness: 168
Brightness: 178
Brightness: 198
Brightness: 208
Brightness: 218
Brightness: 228
Brightness: 238
Brightness: 248
Brightness: 255
Brightness: 255
Brightness: 245
Brightness: 225
Brightness: 215
Brightness: 205
Brightness: 195
Brightness: 185
Brightness: 175
Brightness: 165
Brightness: 155
Brightness: 145
Brightness: 135
Brightness: 125
Brightness: 115
Brightness: 105
Brightness: 95
Brightness: 85
Brightness: 75
Brightness: 65
```

How the Code Works

Each pulse from the encoder calls min(255, brightness+10) or max(0, brightness-10) depending on direction. min() and max() clamp the value so it never exceeds 255 or goes below 0. The clamped brightness value is then written to all three RGB channels simultaneously. The step size of 10 out of 255 gives 26 distinct brightness levels - smooth enough to feel continuous but coarse enough to reach full brightness in 26 clicks.

Real-World Applications

- Rotary dimmer switches
- Camera ISO dial
- Speaker volume knob
- Studio lighting control
- Medical device settings

Experiment 82 | IR Remote LED Control

Sensor: IR Receiver + RGB LED

Difficulty: ★★ Intermediate

Objective: Use specific buttons on a TV remote to turn an LED on and off.

How It Works

Once you know a specific IR button code (from Experiment 34), you can use it as a trigger for any action. This experiment uses the OK button to toggle an LED on and off. In a real smart home system, this same approach lets a TV remote control lights, fans, or any other device connected through an Arduino and relay.

Concepts Learned

- IR decode to action
- Specific button mapping
- LED toggle from remote
- Remote as input device

Components Required

Component	Qty
Arduino Uno	1
IR Receiver Module	1
RGB LED Module	1
TV Remote	1
Jumper Wires	6

Wiring

Component	Arduino Pin
`IR Receiver S`	`D2`
`RGB R`	`D9`
`RGB G`	`D10`
`RGB B`	`D11`

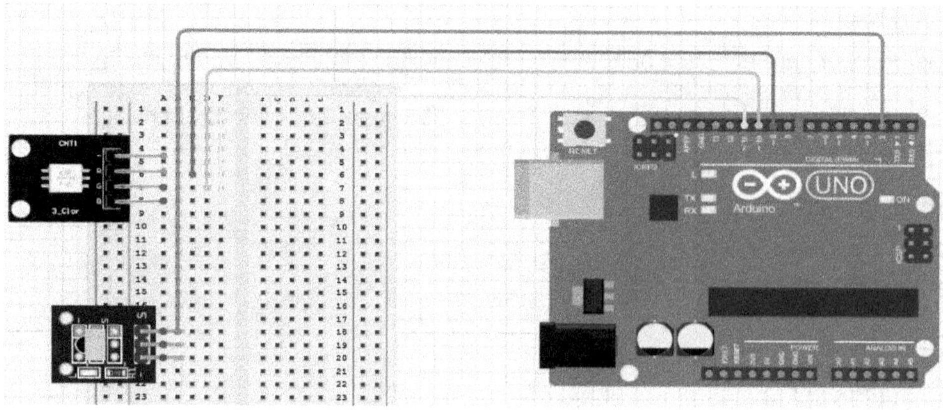

Arduino Code & Serial Monitor Output

```
#include <IRremote.h>
IRrecv irrecv(2);
decode_results res;
const int rPin=9,gPin=10,bPin=11;
bool ledOn = false;

void setup() {
  irrecv.enableIRIn();
  Serial.begin(9600);
}

void loop() {
  if (irrecv.decode(&res)) {
    if (res.value == 0xFF02FD) {   // OK
button - adjust to your remote
      ledOn = !ledOn;
      int v = ledOn ? 200 : 0;
      analogWrite(rPin,v);
analogWrite(gPin,v); analogWrite(bPin,v);
      Serial.println(ledOn ? "LED ON" :
"LED OFF");
    }
    irrecv.resume();
  }
}
```

```
Message (Enter to send message to 'Arduino Uno' on 'COM3')

LED ON
LED OFF
LED ON
LED OFF
LED ON
LED OFF
LED ON
LED OFF
LED ON
LED OFF
LED ON
LED OFF
LED ON
LED OFF
```

How the Code Works

The IR code 0xFF02FD is the OK button on a common NEC remote - yours will likely be different, so use Experiment 34 to find your own. When this specific code is received, ledOn is toggled and the LED brightness is set to 200 (slightly below maximum to avoid over-driving the LED). The key line is irrecv.resume() - without it, the receiver never listens again after the first button press.

Real-World Applications

- Smart TV accent lighting
- Remote-controlled lamps
- Home automation remotes
- Stage lighting remote
- IoT device IR control

Experiment 83 | IR Remote RGB Controller

Sensor: IR Receiver + RGB LED

Difficulty: ★★ Intermediate

Objective: Use different remote buttons to switch the RGB LED between colours.

How It Works

Mapping multiple remote buttons to different colours demonstrates the full power of IR remote control. Each button sends a unique code, and the Arduino responds with a different RGB colour. With 5 buttons mapped you already have a functional multi-colour remote-controlled light. Add more case entries to control more colours.

Concepts Learned

- Multi-button IR mapping
- Colour selection from remote
- Switch-case on IR codes
- RGB remote controller

Components Required

Component	Qty
Arduino Uno	1
IR Receiver Module	1
RGB LED Module	1
TV Remote	1
Jumper Wires	6

Wiring

Component	Arduino Pin
IR Receiver S	D2
RGB R	D9
RGB G	D10
RGB B	D11

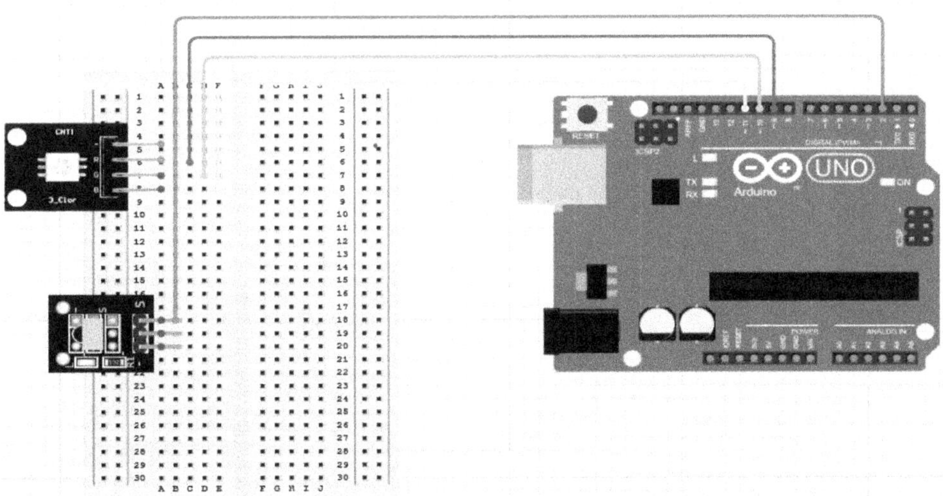

Arduino Code & Serial Monitor Output

```
#include <IRremote.h>
IRrecv irrecv(2);
decode_results res;
const int rPin=9,gPin=10,bPin=11;

void setRGB(int r,int g,int b){
analogWrite(rPin,r); analogWrite(gPin,g);
analogWrite(bPin,b); }

void setup() { irrecv.enableIRIn();
Serial.begin(9600); }

void loop() {
  if (irrecv.decode(&res)) {
    switch(res.value) {
      case 0xFF6897: setRGB(255,0,0);
Serial.println("RED");   break;
      case 0xFF9867: setRGB(0,255,0);
Serial.println("GREEN"); break;
      case 0xFFB04F: setRGB(0,0,255);
Serial.println("BLUE");  break;
      case 0xFF18E7: setRGB(255,255,0);
Serial.println("YELLOW");break;
      case 0xFF4AB5: setRGB(0,0,0);
Serial.println("OFF");   break;
    }
    irrecv.resume();
  }
}
```

```
Message (Enter to send message to 'Arduino Uno' on 'COM3')

RED
GREEN
BLUE
YELLOW
OFF
RED
GREEN
BLUE
YELLOW
OFF
YELLOW
BLUE
GREEN
RED
OFF
```

How the Code Works

The helper function setRGB() takes three parameters (r, g, b) and sets all three LED channels at once. This avoids repeating three analogWrite lines for every colour. The switch statement efficiently checks results.value against five known codes. The default case at the end handles any unrecognised button press - it simply ignores it. Replace the hex codes with your remote's actual codes from Experiment 34.

Real-World Applications

- Smart colour-changing bulbs
- Disco lighting control
- Aquarium colour control
- Mood lighting remote
- Stage RGB light remote

Experiment 84 | Remote Controlled Relay

Sensor: IR Receiver + Relay

Difficulty: ★★ Intermediate

Objective: Toggle a relay on and off using a TV remote button, enabling control of any mains device.

How It Works

This is the most practical home automation experiment in Level 2. An IR remote button toggles a relay, which can switch any electrical device on or off. The relay physically isolates the Arduino from the mains circuit. This means your Arduino controls a tiny signal, which controls the relay, which switches the actual power to the device.

Concepts Learned

- Relay as remote output
- IR to relay pipeline
- Remote-controlled switching
- Mains safety awareness

Components Required

Component	Qty
Arduino Uno	1
IR Receiver Module	1
Relay Module	1
TV Remote	1
Jumper Wires	5

Wiring

Component	Arduino Pin
IR Receiver S	D2
Relay S	D8

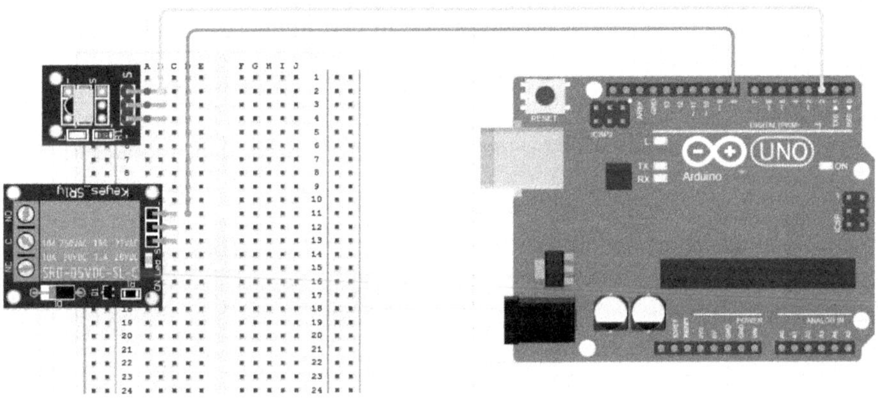

Arduino Code & Serial Monitor Output

```
#include <IRremote.h>
IRrecv irrecv(2);
decode_results res;
const int relayPin = 8;
bool relayOn = false;

void setup() {
  irrecv.enableIRIn();
  pinMode(relayPin, OUTPUT);
  Serial.begin(9600);
}

void loop() {
  if (irrecv.decode(&res)) {
    if (res.value == 0xFF02FD) {   // OK
button
```

Message (Enter to send message to 'Arduino Uno' on 'COM3')

```
Relay ON
Relay OFF
Relay ON
Relay OFF
Relay ON
Relay OFF
Relay ON
Relay OFF
Relay ON
Relay OFF
Relay ON
Relay OFF
Relay ON
Relay OFF
```

```
      relayOn = !relayOn;
      digitalWrite(relayPin, relayOn ?
HIGH : LOW);
      Serial.println(relayOn ? "Relay ON"
: "Relay OFF");
    }
    irrecv.resume();
  }
}
```

How the Code Works

relayOn is a boolean that tracks relay state. When the OK button code is received, relayOn flips and the relay is set accordingly. The relay stays in its state until the button is pressed again - this is latched behaviour. In a real installation you would connect your appliance (lamp, fan, etc.) across the relay's COM and NO (normally open) terminals. Always have a qualified electrician wire mains voltage connections.

Real-World Applications

- Remote appliance control
- Smart plug simulation
- TV-remote light switch
- Remote fan control
- Home automation prototype

Experiment 85 | Pulse Rate Alert System

Sensor: Heartbeat Sensor + Active Buzzer

Difficulty: ★★ Intermediate

Objective: Beep a buzzer each time a heartbeat pulse is detected, providing real-time audio feedback.

How It Works

Providing audio feedback for each heartbeat makes the pulse physically audible - you hear your own heartbeat as a beep. The buzzer gives an 80-millisecond beep for each detected pulse, which creates a satisfying heartbeat sound. This is exactly what hospital monitors do, though they use much more sophisticated signal processing.

Concepts Learned

- Heartbeat to audio feedback
- Pulse event to buzzer
- Bio-sensor integration
- Real-time response

Components Required

Component	Qty
Arduino Uno	1
Heartbeat Sensor	1
Active Buzzer Module	1
Jumper Wires	5

Wiring

Component	Arduino Pin
Heartbeat S	A0

Component	Arduino Pin
Buzzer S	D8

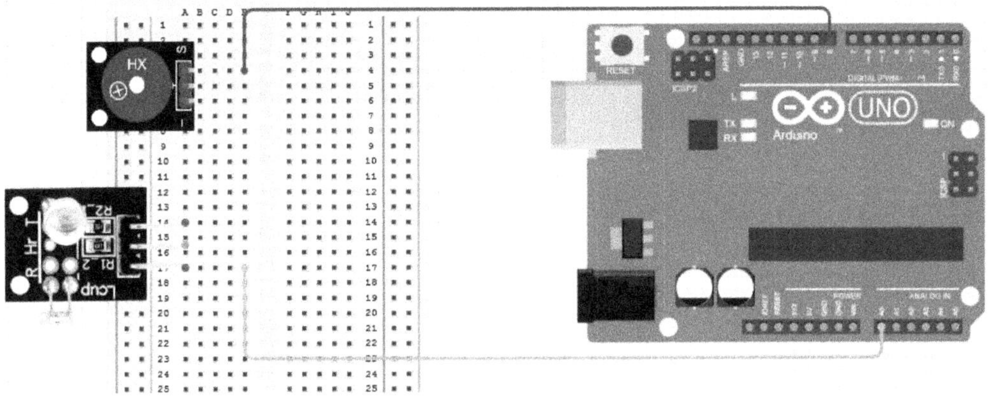

Arduino Code & Serial Monitor Output

```
const int pulsePin=A0, buzPin=8;
const int threshold = 550;
bool above = false;

void setup() {
  pinMode(buzPin, OUTPUT);
  Serial.begin(9600);
}

void loop() {
  int val = analogRead(pulsePin);
  if (val > threshold && !above) {
    digitalWrite(buzPin, HIGH);
    delay(80);
    digitalWrite(buzPin, LOW);
    Serial.println("BEAT");
    above = true;
  }
  if (val < threshold) above = false;
  delay(10);
}
```

Message (Enter to send message to 'Arduino Uno' on 'COM3')

```
BEAT
BEAT
BEAT
BEAT
BEAT
BEAT
BEAT
BEAT
BEAT
BEAT
BEAT
BEAT
BEAT
BEAT
BEAT
BEAT
BEAT
BEAT
```

How the Code Works

The above flag prevents multiple beeps from a single heartbeat peak. When the signal crosses the threshold for the first time (above goes false → true), the buzzer fires for 80ms and above is set to true. While the signal remains above threshold, above stays true and no further beeps occur. When the signal drops back below threshold, above resets to false, ready for the next beat.

Real-World Applications

- Heart rate audio monitors
- Medical alert systems
- Fitness pulse feedback
- Biofeedback therapy
- Pulse oximeter beeping

Experiment 86 | Touch Activated Relay

Sensor: Touch Sensor + Relay
Difficulty: ★★ Intermediate
Objective: Toggle a relay on and off with each touch of the metal touch sensor.

How It Works

Touch-controlled relays are used everywhere in modern smart home products. Instead of a mechanical switch you simply touch a metal pad to toggle a device. The touch sensor detects your finger's capacitance, the Arduino processes the toggle logic, and the relay switches the load. No moving parts, no wear, completely silent operation.

Concepts Learned

- Touch to relay control
- Toggle relay state
- Touch as smart switch
- Contactless switching

Components Required

Component	Qty
Arduino Uno	1
Metal Touch Sensor	1
Relay Module	1
Jumper Wires	5

Wiring

Component	Arduino Pin
`Touch S`	D2
`Relay S`	D8

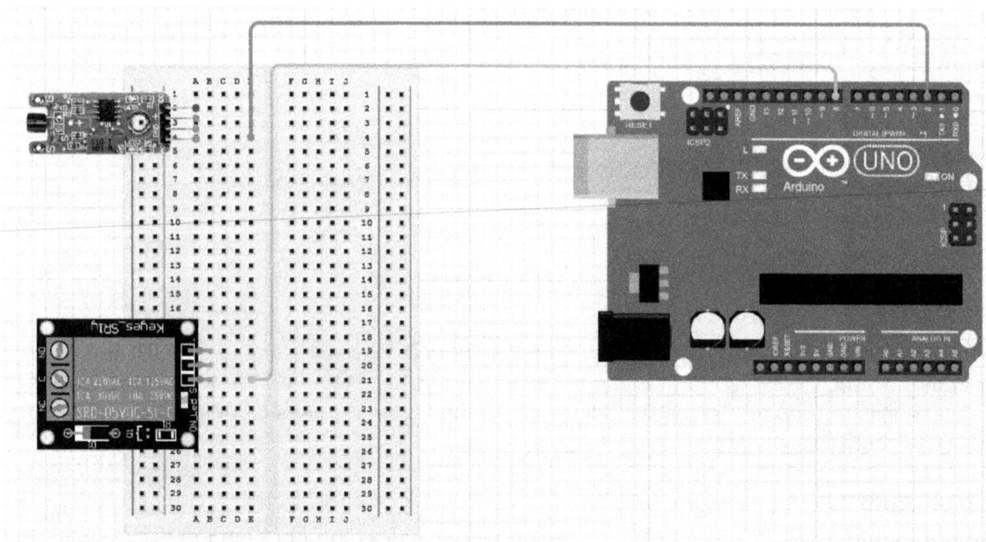

Arduino Code & Serial Monitor Output

```
const int touchPin=2, relayPin=8;
bool relayOn = false;
int lastState = LOW;

void setup() {
  pinMode(touchPin, INPUT);
  pinMode(relayPin, OUTPUT);
  Serial.begin(9600);
}

void loop() {
  int state = digitalRead(touchPin);
  if (state == HIGH && lastState == LOW) {
    relayOn = !relayOn;
    digitalWrite(relayPin, relayOn ? HIGH : LOW);
    Serial.println(relayOn ? "Relay ON" : "Relay OFF");
    delay(150);
  }
  lastState = state;
}
```

Message (Enter to send message to 'Arduino Uno' on 'COM3')

```
Relay ON
Relay OFF
Relay ON
Relay OFF
Relay ON
Relay OFF
Relay ON
Relay OFF
Relay ON
Relay OFF
Relay ON
Relay OFF
Relay ON
Relay OFF
```

How the Code Works

The pattern here is identical to the touch-controlled lamp from Experiment 58, except the output goes to a relay instead of an LED. relayOn tracks state, edge detection ensures one touch equals one toggle, and the 150ms delay prevents bouncing. This same logic works for any binary output - LED, buzzer, relay, or motor driver - just change the output pin and its controlling function.

Real-World Applications

- Touch-enabled smart switches
- Touchpad lamp control
- Accessible switches for disabled
- Bedside touch relay
- Touch keypad relay bank

Experiment 87 | Object Counter Display

Sensor: Photo Interrupter + Serial Monitor
Difficulty: ★★ Intermediate
Objective: Count and display objects passing through the beam, with a reset option via Serial.

How It Works

This experiment adds interactive reset functionality to the basic object counter. The counter keeps a running total, but typing R in the Serial Monitor input box and pressing Enter resets it to zero. This teaches bidirectional Serial communication - the Arduino can both send data to your computer and receive commands from it.

Concepts Learned

- Object count with display
- Serial input for reset
- Formatted output
- Production counter UI

Components Required

Component	Qty
Arduino Uno	1
Photo Interrupter Module	1
Jumper Wires	3

Wiring

Photo Interrupter Pin	Arduino Pin
OUT	D2
VCC	5V
GND	GND

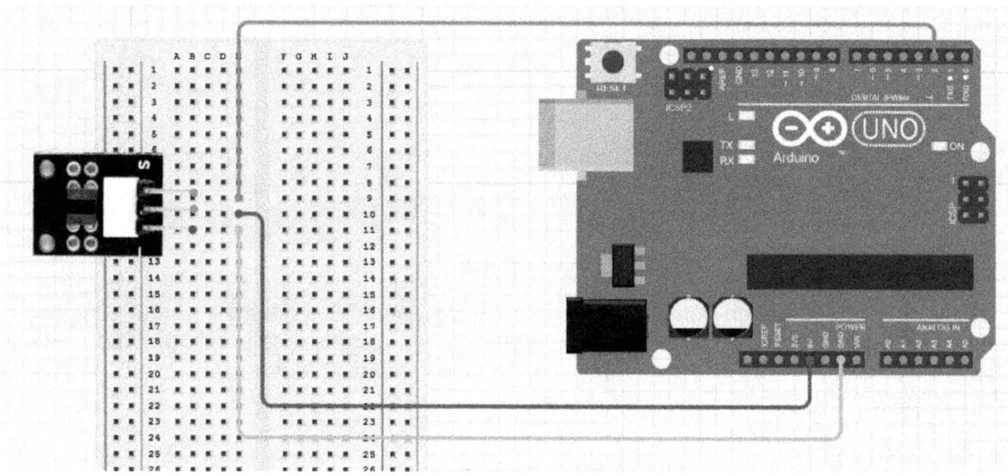

Arduino Code & Serial Monitor Output

```
const int irPin = 2;
int count = 0;
int lastState = HIGH;

void setup() {
  pinMode(irPin, INPUT);
  Serial.begin(9600);
  Serial.println("Object Counter Ready.
Send 'R' to reset.");
}

void loop() {
  int state = digitalRead(irPin);
  if (state == LOW && lastState == HIGH) {
    count++;
    Serial.print("Count: ");
Serial.println(count);
  }
  lastState = state;
  if (Serial.available() && Serial.read()
== 'R') {
```

```
Message (Enter to send message to 'Arduino Uno' on 'COM3')

Object Counter Ready. Send 'R' to reset.
Count: 1
Count: 2
Count: 3
Count: 4
Count: 5
Count: 6
Count: 7
Count: 8
Count: 9
Count: 10
Count: 11
Count: 12
R
Counter RESET
Count: 1
Count: 2
Count: 3
Count: 4
```

```
    count = 0;
    Serial.println("Counter RESET");
  }
  delay(30);
}
```

How the Code Works

Serial.available() returns the number of bytes waiting to be read from the Serial Monitor input. If this is greater than zero, Serial.read() reads one character. We compare it to the character 'R' - if they match, reset the counter. The main counting logic is edge detection as before. The prompt in setup() tells the user what command is available, which is good user interface design.

Real-World Applications

- Factory output counters
- Packaging line monitors
- Visitor counters
- Pill dispensing machines
- Parts quality checks

Experiment 88 | Conveyor Counter Simulation

Sensor: Photo Interrupter + RGB LED

Difficulty: ★★ Intermediate

Objective: Count items on a simulated conveyor and flash the LED every 5 items as a batch signal.

How It Works

Batch counting is fundamental to manufacturing and logistics. Instead of just counting individual items, a batch counter signals when a specific quantity has been reached. Here every 5 items triggers a flash on the green LED to indicate a complete batch. The modulo operator (%) is the key - it returns the remainder of a division, and any multiple of 5 has remainder 0.

Concepts Learned

- Batch counting logic
- Modulo operator
- Batch complete signal
- Industrial automation basics

Components Required

Component	Qty
Arduino Uno	1
Photo Interrupter Module	1
RGB LED Module	1
Jumper Wires	6

Wiring

Component	Arduino Pin
IR OUT	D2
RGB R	D9
RGB G	D10

Component	Arduino Pin
RGB B	D11

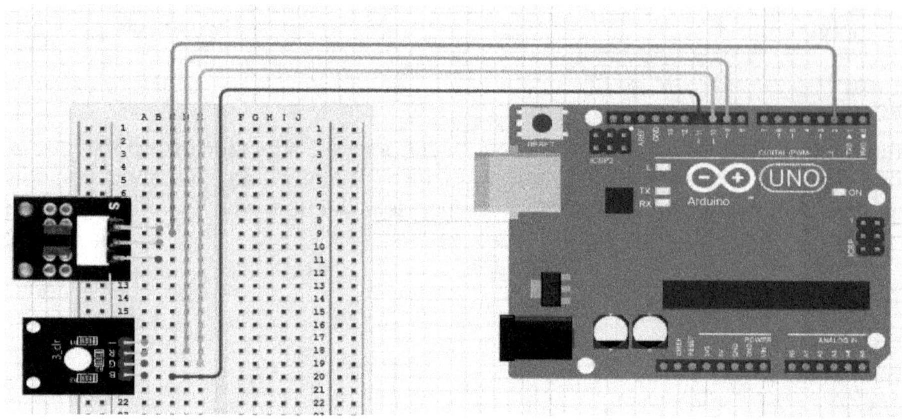

Arduino Code & Serial Monitor Output

```
const int irPin=2, rPin=9, gPin=10,
bPin=11;
int count=0;
int lastState=HIGH;

void flashGreen() {
  for(int i=0;i<3;i++){
    analogWrite(gPin,255); delay(100);
    analogWrite(gPin,0);   delay(100);
  }
}

void setup() { pinMode(irPin,INPUT);
Serial.begin(9600); }

void loop() {
  int s = digitalRead(irPin);
  if (s==LOW && lastState==HIGH) {
    count++;
    Serial.print("Item: ");
Serial.println(count);
    if (count % 5 == 0) {
      Serial.println("--- Batch of 5
complete ---");
      flashGreen();
    }
  }
  lastState = s;
  delay(30);
}
```

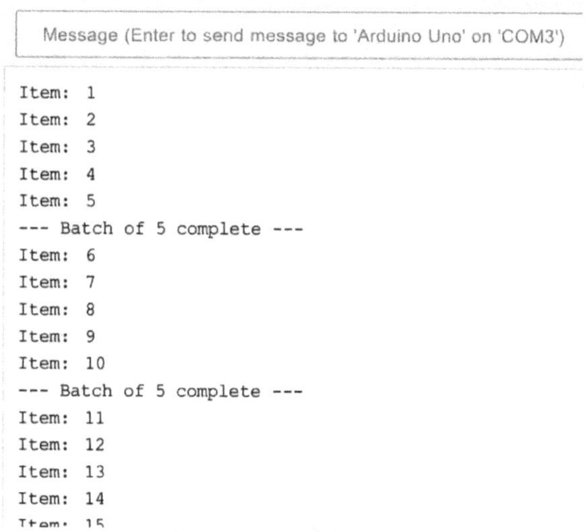

How the Code Works

After incrementing count, we check count % 5 == 0. The % operator returns 0 whenever count is exactly divisible by 5 - at 5, 10, 15, 20, and so on. When this is true, flashGreen() runs, which loops 3 times flashing the LED rapidly to signal batch completion. The for loop inside flashGreen controls the number of flashes. Try changing the batch size from 5 to any number by changing the modulo value.

Real-World Applications

- Assembly line batch signalling
- Box fill monitoring
- Bottling line counting
- Warehouse packing lines
- Production target tracking

Experiment 89 | Smart Room Light Indicator

Sensor: LDR + Sound Sensor + RGB LED

Difficulty: ★★ Intermediate

Objective: Combine light and sound sensors to control an RGB LED: light only on when dark AND quiet.

How It Works

Combining multiple sensors with AND logic creates a smarter, more specific trigger condition. The night light only activates when it is both dark AND quiet - perfect for a bedroom. If you have the light on (not dark) or if there is noise (not quiet), the light stays off. This prevents the light from activating during the day or when someone is moving around.

Concepts Learned

- Multi-sensor logic
- AND condition
- Environment-aware automation
- Combined sensor decisions

Components Required

Component	Qty
Arduino Uno	1
Photo-Resistor Module	1
KY-038 Sound Sensor	1
RGB LED Module	1
Jumper Wires	7

Wiring

Component	Arduino Pin
LDR S	A0
Sound A0	A1
RGB R	D9
RGB G	D10
RGB B	D11

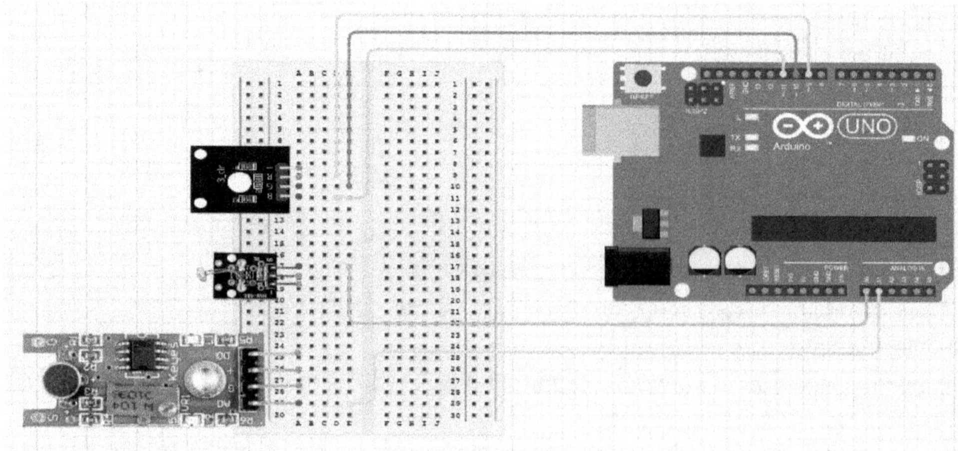

Arduino Code & Serial Monitor Output

```
const int ldrPin=A0, sndPin=A1;
const int rPin=9, gPin=10, bPin=11;
const int darkThresh=400, quietThresh=200;

void setup() { Serial.begin(9600); }

void loop() {
  int light = analogRead(ldrPin);
  int sound = analogRead(sndPin);
  bool dark   = (light < darkThresh);
  bool quiet  = (sound < quietThresh);
  if (dark && quiet) {
    analogWrite(rPin,180);
analogWrite(gPin,150);
analogWrite(bPin,80);
    Serial.println("Dark + Quiet: Night
light ON");
  } else {
    analogWrite(rPin,0);
analogWrite(gPin,0); analogWrite(bPin,0);
    Serial.println("Light off");
  }
  delay(500);
}
```

```
Message (Enter to send message to 'Arduino Uno' on 'COM3')

Light off
Light off
Light off
Dark + Quiet: Night light ON
Dark + Quiet: Night light ON
Dark + Quiet: Night light ON
Light off
Light off
Dark + Quiet: Night light ON
Dark + Quiet: Night light ON
Light off
Light off
Light off
Dark + Quiet: Night light ON
Dark + Quiet: Night light ON
Dark + Quiet: Night light ON
```

How the Code Works

Two boolean variables, dark and quiet, are calculated from the respective sensor readings. The combined condition dark & quiet (AND) is only true when both are true simultaneously. If either condition is false, the LED turns off. This AND logic pattern is fundamental to building nuanced automated systems. Try changing it to dark || noisy (OR) to see how the behaviour changes.

Real-World Applications

- Smart night lights
- Baby room auto light
- Energy-saving office lights
- Automated study lamp
- Smart bedroom ambient light

Experiment 90 | Sensor Testing Console

Sensor: All Sensors (Sequential Test)
Difficulty: ★★ Intermediate
Objective: Read from 5 key sensors simultaneously and display all readings in a formatted console.

How It Works

A sensor console reads multiple sensors and displays all their values in a structured format simultaneously. This is the pattern used in industrial monitoring systems, data loggers, and IoT dashboards. Seeing all values at once lets you understand relationships between sensors - for example, how a door opening affects temperature, or how noise affects light readings.

Concepts Learned

- Multi-sensor reading
- Formatted Serial output
- System integration
- Sensor dashboard concept

Components Required

Component	Qty
Arduino Uno	1
Button Module	1
LDR Module	1
DHT11 Sensor	1
Sound Sensor	1
Jumper Wires	8

Wiring

Component	Arduino Pin
Button S	D2
LDR S	A0
DHT11 S	D3
Sound A0	A1

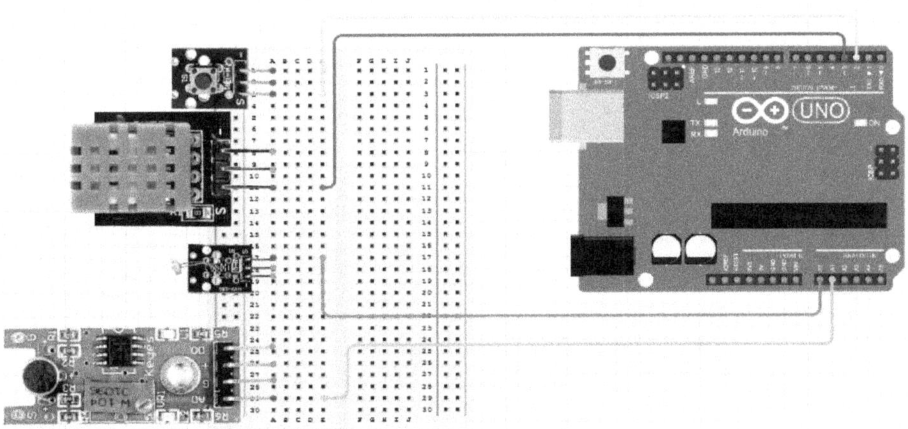

Arduino Code & Serial Monitor Output

```
#include <DHT.h>
DHT dht(3, DHT11);
const int btnPin=2, ldrPin=A0, sndPin=A1;

void setup() {
  pinMode(btnPin, INPUT_PULLUP);
  dht.begin();
  Serial.begin(9600);
}

void loop() {
  bool btn   = (digitalRead(btnPin) ==
LOW);
  int  light = analogRead(ldrPin);
  int  sound = analogRead(sndPin);
  float temp = dht.readTemperature();
  float hum  = dht.readHumidity();
  Serial.println("======= SENSOR CONSOLE
=======");
  Serial.print("Button : ");
Serial.println(btn ? "PRESSED" :
"Released");
  Serial.print("Light  : ");
Serial.println(light);
  Serial.print("Sound  : ");
Serial.println(sound);
  Serial.print("Temp   : ");
Serial.print(temp);  Serial.println(" C");
  Serial.print("Humid  : ");
Serial.print(hum);   Serial.println(" %");
  delay(2000);
}
```

```
Message (Enter to send message to 'Arduino Uno' on 'COM3')

======= SENSOR CONSOLE =======
Button : Released
Light  : 623
Sound  : 312
Temp   : 28.30 C
Humid  : 61.00 %

======= SENSOR CONSOLE =======
Button : PRESSED
Light  : 598
```

How the Code Works

Each sensor is read into its own clearly named variable. The formatted output uses a consistent style with labels and units, making it easy to read. The 2-second delay between readings is a design choice - fast enough to catch changes, slow enough to read comfortably. Notice how including the DHT11 forces a 2-second minimum delay for the whole system because of that sensor's limitations.

Real-World Applications

- IoT sensor dashboards
- Lab monitoring systems
- Environmental testing
- Sensor validation rigs
- Educational demo boards

Level 3 - Real World Projects (91–101)

Experiment 91 | Digital Door Monitor

Sensor: Reed Switch + Active Buzzer + RGB LED

Difficulty: ★★★ Pro

Objective: Build a complete door monitoring system that shows door status with colour and sounds an alarm if left open for more than 10 seconds.

How It Works

A complete door monitor tracks both current state and duration. An open door for a few seconds is normal; an open door for 10 seconds might be a security issue. This project uses the reed switch to detect door state, the RGB LED to show it visually (green=closed, red=open), and a timer to trigger the buzzer alarm if the door stays open too long.

Concepts Learned

- State machines
- Timed alarm logic
- Multi-output integration
- Door security system design

Components Required

Component	Qty
Arduino Uno	1
Reed Switch Module	1
Active Buzzer Module	1
RGB LED Module	1
Magnet	1
Jumper Wires	7

Wiring

Component	Arduino Pin
Reed S	D2
Buzzer S	D8
RGB R	D9
RGB G	D10
RGB B	D11

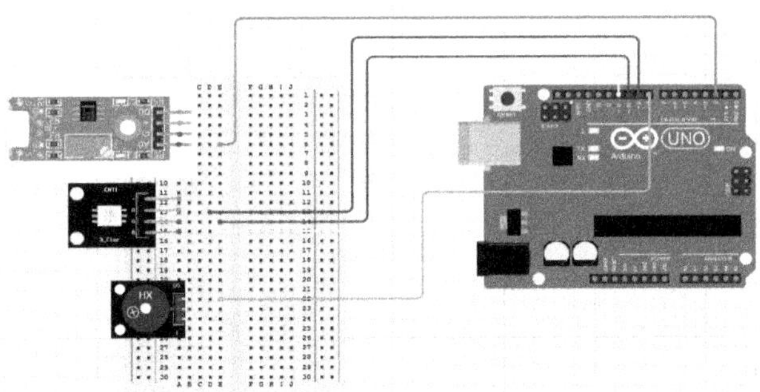

Arduino Code & Serial Monitor Output

```
const int reedPin=2, buzPin=8;
const int rPin=9, gPin=10, bPin=11;
unsigned long openTime = 0;
bool doorOpen = false;

void setup() {
  pinMode(reedPin, INPUT_PULLUP);
  pinMode(buzPin, OUTPUT);
  Serial.begin(9600);
}

void loop() {
  bool isOpen = (digitalRead(reedPin) ==
HIGH);
  if (isOpen && !doorOpen) {
    openTime = millis();
    doorOpen = true;
    Serial.println("Door OPENED");
  }
  if (!isOpen && doorOpen) {
    doorOpen = false;
    digitalWrite(buzPin, LOW);
    Serial.println("Door closed");
  }
  if (doorOpen) {
    analogWrite(rPin,255);
analogWrite(gPin,0); analogWrite(bPin,0);
    if (millis() - openTime > 10000) {
      digitalWrite(buzPin, HIGH);
      Serial.println("ALARM: Door open too
long!");
    }
  } else {
    analogWrite(rPin,0);
analogWrite(gPin,255);
analogWrite(bPin,0);
  }
  delay(200);
}
```

```
Message (Enter to send message to 'Arduino Uno' on 'COM3')

Door OPENED
Door OPENED
ALARM: Door open too long!
ALARM: Door open too long!
ALARM: Door open too long!
ALARM: Door open too long!
ALARM: Door open too long!
ALARM: Door open too long!
ALARM: Door open too long!
ALARM: Door open too long!
Door closed
Door OPENED
ALARM: Door open too long!
ALARM: Door open too long!
```

How the Code Works

When the door first opens, openTime captures the current millisecond timestamp with millis(). As long as the door remains open, we check millis() - openTime on every loop iteration. When this difference exceeds 10000 (10 seconds), the buzzer activates. When the door closes, doorOpen resets to false, the buzzer silences, and the LED returns to green - ready for the next event.

Real-World Applications

- Home security
- Office access control
- Cold storage door monitoring
- Server room door alarm
- Safe room entry detection

Experiment 92 | Home Intrusion Alarm

Sensor: Shock Sensor + IR Obstacle + Active Buzzer + RGB LED
Difficulty: ★★★ Pro
Objective: Build a multi-sensor alarm triggered by either vibration or motion proximity.

How It Works

Using two sensors increases the detection reliability of an alarm system. The shock sensor catches someone trying to break through a wall or window. The obstacle sensor catches someone approaching. Either trigger alone can cause false alarms, but requiring only one of the two to be true (OR logic) means the system is sensitive without being overly specific.

Concepts Learned

- Multi-sensor alarm
- OR logic triggers
- Alarm latch with reset
- Dual-input safety system

Components Required

Component	Qty
Arduino Uno	1
Shock Sensor Module	1
Obstacle Avoidance Sensor	1
Active Buzzer Module	1
RGB LED Module	1
Jumper Wires	8

Wiring

Component	Arduino Pin
`Shock S`	`D2`
`Obstacle OUT`	`D3`
`Buzzer S`	`D8`
`RGB R`	`D9`
`RGB G`	`D10`
`RGB B`	`D11`

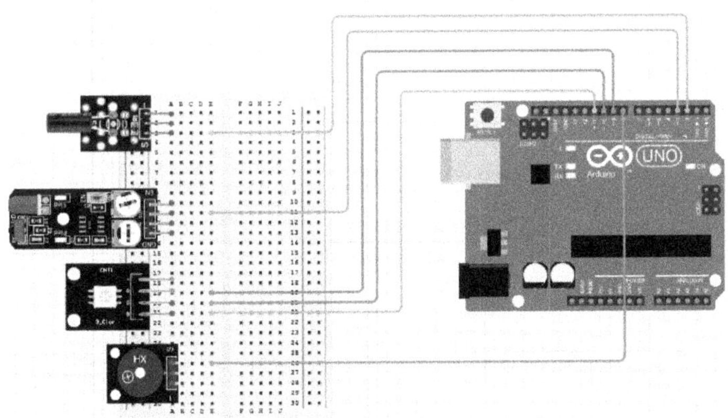

Arduino Code & Serial Monitor Output

```
const int shockPin=2, obsPin=3, buzPin=8;
const int rPin=9, gPin=10, bPin=11;
bool alarm = false;

void setup() {
  pinMode(shockPin, INPUT_PULLUP);
  pinMode(obsPin, INPUT);
  pinMode(buzPin, OUTPUT);
  Serial.begin(9600);
}

void loop() {
  bool vibration  = (digitalRead(shockPin)
== LOW);
  bool proximity  = (digitalRead(obsPin)
== LOW);
  if (vibration || proximity) alarm =
true;
  if (alarm) {
    digitalWrite(buzPin, HIGH);
    analogWrite(rPin,255);
analogWrite(gPin,0); analogWrite(bPin,0);
    Serial.println(vibration?"Vibration
intrusion!":"Motion intrusion!");
    delay(5000);
    alarm = false;
    digitalWrite(buzPin, LOW);
  } else {
    analogWrite(rPin,0);
analogWrite(gPin,255);
analogWrite(bPin,0);
  }
  delay(100);
}
```

Message (Enter to send message to 'Arduino Uno' on 'COM3')

```
Vibration intrusion!
Vibration intrusion!
Motion intrusion!
Vibration intrusion!
Vibration intrusion!
Motion intrusion!
Motion intrusion!
Vibration intrusion!
Motion intrusion!
Vibration intrusion!
Motion intrusion!
Vibration intrusion!
Vibration intrusion!
Motion intrusion!
```

How the Code Works

vibration and proximity are booleans calculated from their respective sensors. The condition vibration || proximity (OR) triggers the alarm when either is true. Once the alarm is set to true, the buzzer sounds and the LED turns red for 5 seconds - regardless of what the sensors read during that time. After 5 seconds, the alarm resets to false and the system returns to normal, ready for the next intrusion.

Real-World Applications

- Home burglar alarms
- Shop security systems
- Vehicle perimeter alarm
- Shed intrusion detection
- Remote cabin protection

Experiment 93 | Classroom Noise Monitor

Sensor: KY-038 Sound Sensor + RGB LED

Difficulty: ★★ Intermediate

Objective: Build a classroom noise monitor that displays noise level via colour: Green (quiet), Yellow (moderate), Red (too loud).

How It Works

A classroom noise monitor gives real-time visual feedback on noise level without singling out individuals. The three-zone colour coding (green=quiet, yellow=moderate, red=loud) communicates the situation instantly to everyone in the room. This type of ambient display is used in open-plan offices, libraries, and call centres.

Concepts Learned

- Multi-zone threshold
- Colour-coded status display
- Real-time sound monitoring
- Environmental feedback system

Components Required

Component	Qty
Arduino Uno	1
KY-038 Sound Sensor	1
RGB LED Module	1
Jumper Wires	6

Wiring

Component	Arduino Pin
Sound A0	A0
RGB R	D9
RGB G	D10
RGB B	D11

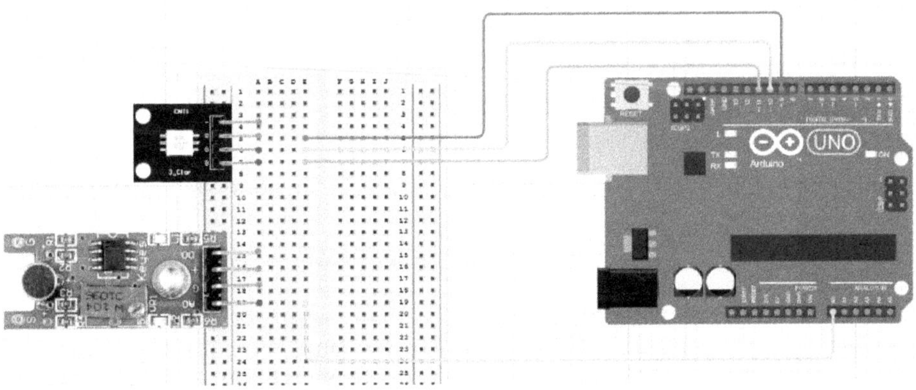

Arduino Code & Serial Monitor Output

```
const int sndPin=A0, rPin=9, gPin=10,
bPin=11;

void setup() { Serial.begin(9600); }

void loop() {
  int sound = analogRead(sndPin);
  Serial.print("Noise: ");
Serial.print(sound); Serial.print(" -->
");
```

```
Message (Enter to send message to 'Arduino Uno' on 'COM3')

Noise: 82  --> QUIET
Noise: 94  --> QUIET
Noise: 118  --> QUIET
Noise: 143  --> QUIET
Noise: 176  --> MODERATE
Noise: 221  --> MODERATE
Noise: 287  --> MODERATE
Noise: 356  --> MODERATE
Noise: 412  --> TOO LOUD!
Noise: 523  --> TOO LOUD!
Noise: 612  --> TOO LOUD!
Noise: 478  --> TOO LOUD!
```

```
  if (sound < 150) {
    analogWrite(rPin,0);
analogWrite(gPin,255);
analogWrite(bPin,0);
    Serial.println("QUIET");
  } else if (sound < 400) {
    analogWrite(rPin,255);
analogWrite(gPin,200);
analogWrite(bPin,0);
    Serial.println("MODERATE");
  } else {
    analogWrite(rPin,255);
analogWrite(gPin,0); analogWrite(bPin,0);
    Serial.println("TOO LOUD!");
  }
  delay(200);
}
```

How the Code Works

Three noise zones are defined with two thresholds: below 150 is quiet (green), 150–400 is moderate (yellow), above 400 is too loud (red). Yellow requires mixing red and green channels (255 and 200 respectively) because yellow is not a pure LED colour. Each zone explicitly sets all three channels to prevent colour mixing from previous states. Adjust the thresholds to match your specific environment.

Real-World Applications

- School noise monitors
- Library quiet alerts
- Office open-plan noise control
- Hospital ward monitors
- Call centre floor management

Experiment 94 | Smart Study Lamp

Sensor: LDR + Touch Sensor + RGB LED

Difficulty: ★★★ Pro

Objective: Build a study lamp that auto-adjusts brightness based on ambient light and can be toggled on/off by touch.

How It Works

The smart lamp combines two independent control mechanisms: automatic brightness based on ambient light, and manual on/off via touch. The touch control takes priority - if the lamp is off, it stays off regardless of how dark the room is. When on, brightness adjusts automatically. This combination of automation and manual override is called supervisory control.

Concepts Learned

- Auto-brightness with override
- Touch toggle state
- Inverse brightness logic
- Smart automation + manual control

Components Required

Component	Qty
Arduino Uno	1

Component	Qty
Photo-Resistor Module	1
Metal Touch Sensor	1
RGB LED Module	1
Jumper Wires	7

Wiring

Component	Arduino Pin
LDR S	A0
Touch S	D2
RGB R	D9
RGB G	D10
RGB B	D11

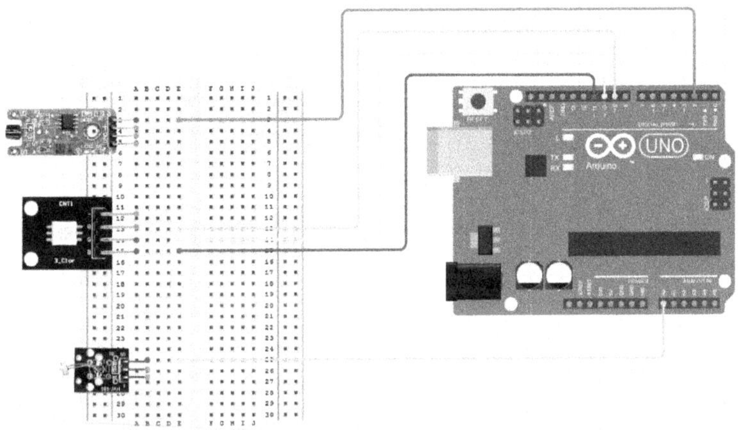

Arduino Code & Serial Monitor Output

```
const int ldrPin=A0, touchPin=2;
const int rPin=9, gPin=10, bPin=11;
bool lampOn = true;
int lastTouch = LOW;

void setup() {
  pinMode(touchPin, INPUT);
  Serial.begin(9600);
}

void loop() {
  int t = digitalRead(touchPin);
  if (t == HIGH && lastTouch == LOW) {
    lampOn = !lampOn;
    if (!lampOn) { analogWrite(rPin,0);
analogWrite(gPin,0); analogWrite(bPin,0);
}
    delay(150);
  }
```

```
Message (Enter to send message to 'Arduino Uno' on 'COM3')

Brightness: 142
Brightness: 143
Brightness: 144
Brightness: 143
Brightness: 142
Brightness: 140
Brightness: 139
Brightness: 138
Brightness: 137
Brightness: 136
Brightness: 135
Brightness: 135
Brightness: 134
Brightness: 133
Brightness: 132
Brightness: 132
Brightness: 131
Brightness: 130
Brightness: 129
Brightness: 128
Brightness: 127
Brightness: 127
Brightness: 126
Brightness: 125
Brightness: 124
Brightness: 124
Brightness: 123
Brightness: 122
Brightness: 121
```

```
    lastTouch = t;
    if (lampOn) {
      int light = analogRead(ldrPin);
      int bright = map(light, 0, 1023, 255,
  30);
      bright = constrain(bright, 30, 255);
      analogWrite(rPin, bright);
  analogWrite(gPin, bright*0.9);
  analogWrite(bPin, bright*0.5);
      Serial.print("Brightness: ");
  Serial.println(bright);
    }
    delay(100);
  }
```

How the Code Works

The touch toggle runs first in loop(), setting lampOn true or false. The brightness control only runs inside the if(lampOn) block - it is skipped entirely when the lamp is off. Inside, map() with constrain() converts light level to brightness and clamps it between 30 (dim but visible) and 255 (maximum). Multiplying the green and blue channels by 0.9 and 0.5 respectively shifts the colour toward warm white.

Real-World Applications

- Smart desk lamps
- Study room automation
- Office energy saving
- Accessible bedroom lamps
- Child study area lighting

Experiment 95 | Smart Weather Station

Sensor: DHT11 + LDR

Difficulty: ★★★ Pro

Objective: Read temperature, humidity, and light level to display a complete weather station report.

How It Works

A weather station combines multiple environmental sensors and interprets the combined data to generate a meaningful forecast. Temperature and humidity together are more informative than either alone - hot and humid feels different from hot and dry, and requires different responses. Adding light level provides context about time of day and cloud cover.

Concepts Learned

- Multi-sensor data fusion
- Weather parameter logging
- Formatted report output
- Environmental monitoring system

Components Required

Component	Qty
Arduino Uno	1
DHT11 Sensor	1
Photo-Resistor Module	1

Component	Qty
Jumper Wires	5

Wiring

Component	Arduino Pin
DHT11 S	D2
LDR S	A0
Both +	5V
Both -	GND

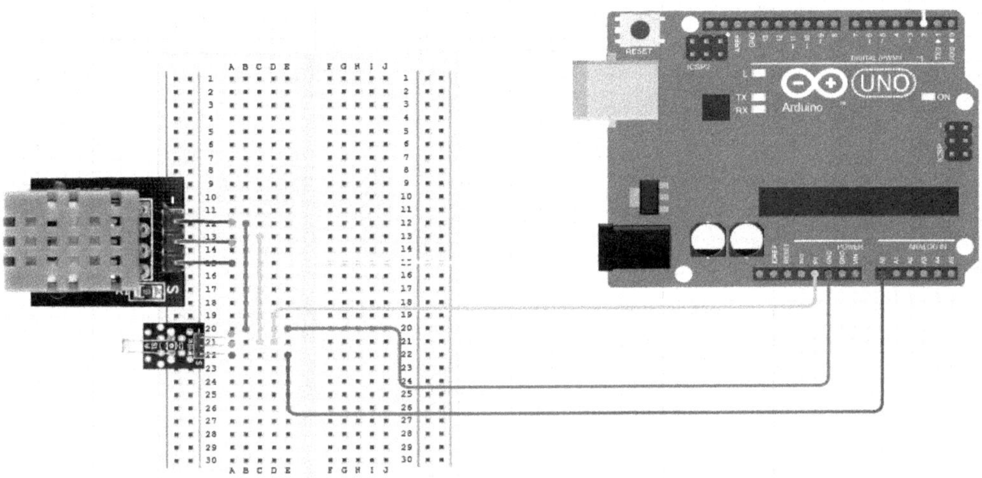

Arduino Code & Serial Monitor Output

```
#include <DHT.h>
DHT dht(2, DHT11);
const int ldrPin = A0;

void setup() {
  dht.begin();
  Serial.begin(9600);
}

void loop() {
  float t = dht.readTemperature();
  float h = dht.readHumidity();
  int   l = analogRead(ldrPin);
  String light = l > 600 ? "Bright" : l >
300 ? "Moderate" : "Dark";
  Serial.println("===== WEATHER STATION
=====");
  Serial.print("Temperature : ");
Serial.print(t); Serial.println(" C");
  Serial.print("Humidity    : ");
Serial.print(h); Serial.println(" %");
```

Message (Enter to send message to 'Arduino Uno' on 'COM3')

```
===== WEATHER STATION =====
Temperature : 29.60 C
Humidity    : 78.00 %
Light Level : 723 (Bright)
Forecast: HOT & HUMID

===== WEATHER STATION =====
Temperature : 24.90 C
Humidity    : 65.00 %
Light Level : 450 (Moderate)
Forecast: COMFORTABLE
```

```
  Serial.print("Light Level : ");
Serial.print(l); Serial.print(" (");
Serial.print(light); Serial.println(")");
  if (t > 28 && h > 70)
Serial.println("Forecast: HOT & HUMID");
  else if (t < 18)
Serial.println("Forecast: COLD");
  else if (h > 80)
Serial.println("Forecast: HUMID/RAIN");
  else
Serial.println("Forecast: COMFORTABLE");
  delay(3000);
}
```

How the Code Works

Three sensors are read in sequence at the start of loop(). The String type is used for the light label - a convenient way to store text that changes based on conditions. The forecast logic at the bottom checks conditions in priority order: hot and humid first (most serious), then just cold, then just humid, then comfortable. All values are printed in a formatted console-style report every 3 seconds.

Real-World Applications

- Home weather stations
- Agricultural monitoring
- School science projects
- IoT environmental nodes
- Greenhouse climate control

Experiment 96 | Fire Safety System

Sensor: Flame Sensor + DHT11 + Active Buzzer + RGB LED

Difficulty: ★★★ Pro

Objective: Build a complete fire safety system that triggers on flame detection OR high temperature.

How It Works

A robust fire safety system uses redundant detection - both a flame sensor AND a temperature sensor. Either one alone might give false alarms (a bright light triggering the flame sensor; hot weather triggering the temperature sensor). But both detecting a problem simultaneously is much more reliable. The OR logic here is intentional: either detection alone is enough to trigger the alarm, because in a real fire you want to respond fast.

Concepts Learned

- Multi-sensor fire detection
- OR safety logic
- Multi-output alarm system
- Redundant sensor safety

Components Required

Component	Qty
Arduino Uno	1
Flame Sensor Module	1
DHT11 Sensor	1

Component	Qty
Active Buzzer Module	1
RGB LED Module	1
Jumper Wires	8

Wiring

Component	Arduino Pin
Flame D0	D2
DHT11 S	D3
Buzzer S	D8
RGB R	D9
RGB G	D10
RGB B	D11

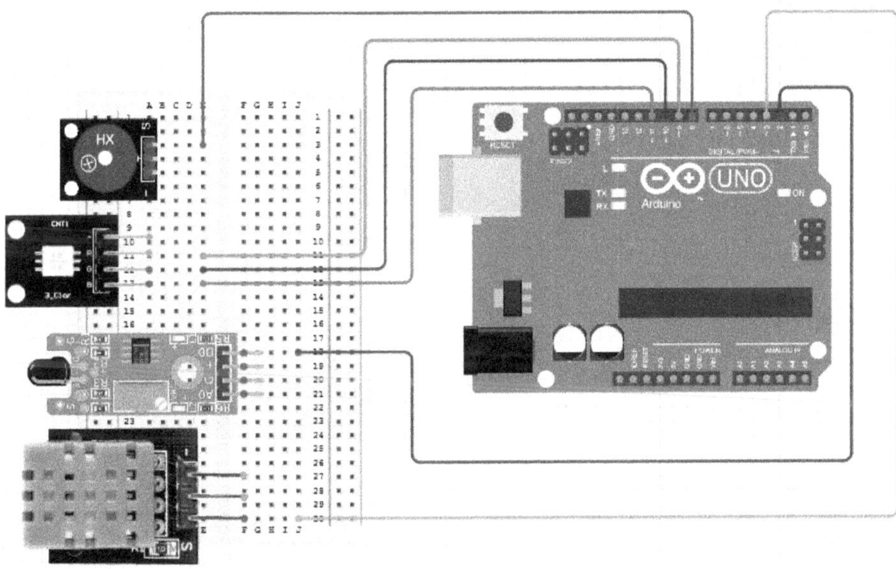

Arduino Code & Serial Monitor Output

```
#include <DHT.h>
DHT dht(3, DHT11);
const int flamePin=2, buzPin=8;
const int rPin=9, gPin=10, bPin=11;

void setup() {
  pinMode(flamePin, INPUT);
  pinMode(buzPin, OUTPUT);
  dht.begin();
  Serial.begin(9600);
}

void loop() {
  bool flame = (digitalRead(flamePin) ==
LOW);
  float temp  = dht.readTemperature();
  bool  hot   = (temp > 40.0);
  Serial.print("Temp: ");
Serial.print(temp);
  Serial.print(" | Flame: ");
Serial.println(flame ? "YES" : "NO");
  if (flame || hot) {
    digitalWrite(buzPin, HIGH);
    analogWrite(rPin,255);
analogWrite(gPin,0); analogWrite(bPin,0);
    Serial.println("FIRE SAFETY ALERT!");
  } else {
    digitalWrite(buzPin, LOW);
    analogWrite(rPin,0);
analogWrite(gPin,255);
analogWrite(bPin,0);
    Serial.println("System: SAFE");
  }
  delay(1000);
}
```

```
Message (Enter to send message to 'Arduino Uno' on 'COM3')

Temp: 29.40 | Flame: NO
System: SAFE
Temp: 30.10 | Flame: NO
System: SAFE
Temp: 31.00 | Flame: NO
System: SAFE
Temp: 32.20 | Flame: NO
System: SAFE
Temp: 33.60 | Flame: NO
System: SAFE
Temp: 34.80 | Flame: NO
System: SAFE
Temp: 41.20 | Flame: NO
FIRE SAFETY ALERT!
Temp: 42.30 | Flame: NO
FIRE SAFETY ALERT!
Temp: 43.10 | Flame: NO
```

How the Code Works

flame and hot are booleans from different sensors. The || (OR) operator means the alarm triggers if either is true. Both indicators are checked and printed in every loop even when no alarm is active - this continuous monitoring gives you a live readout of the system status. When the alarm triggers, all outputs (buzzer and LED) activate together. When both sensors return to safe values, everything resets automatically.

Real-World Applications

- Home fire safety systems
- Kitchen monitoring
- Laboratory safety
- Industrial fire detection
- Server room protection

Experiment 97 | Visitor Detection System

Sensor: IR Obstacle Sensor + Photo Interrupter + Active Buzzer

Difficulty: ★★★ Pro

Objective: Count visitors entering through a door using the photo interrupter beam, and chime the buzzer on entry.

How It Works

A visitor detection system counts entries and provides audio feedback - a double-beep chime rather than a plain buzz, which sounds welcoming rather than alarming. The photo interrupter beam across a doorway counts each crossing. The custom chime() function generates a specific two-beep pattern to make the system feel polished.

Concepts Learned

- Visitor counter system
- Entry detection + chime
- Count with welcome sound
- Dual-sensor architecture

Components Required

Component	Qty
Arduino Uno	1
Photo Interrupter Module	1
Active Buzzer Module	1
Jumper Wires	5

Wiring

Component	Arduino Pin
Photo Interrupter OUT	D2
Buzzer S	D8

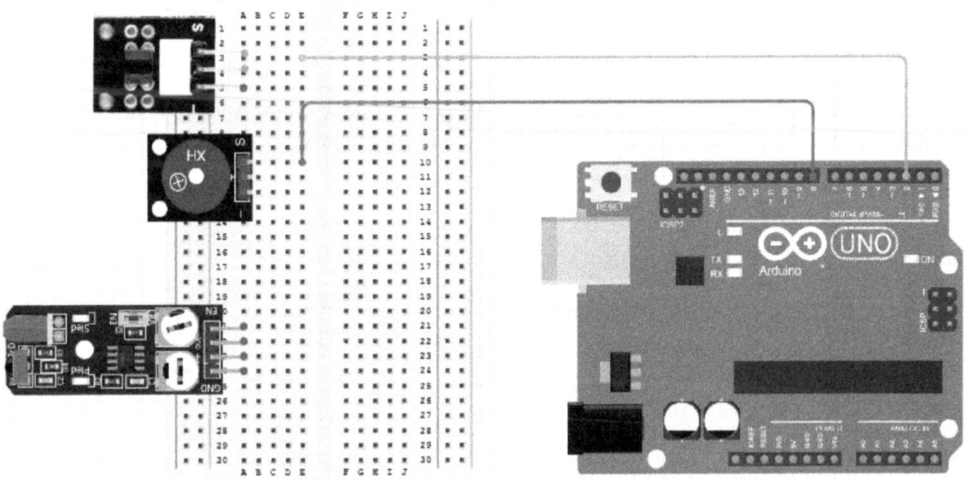

Arduino Code & Serial Monitor Output

```
const int irPin=2, buzPin=8;
int visitors = 0;
int lastState = HIGH;

void chime() {
  digitalWrite(buzPin, HIGH); delay(150);
  digitalWrite(buzPin, LOW);  delay(100);
  digitalWrite(buzPin, HIGH); delay(100);
  digitalWrite(buzPin, LOW);
}

void setup() {
  pinMode(irPin, INPUT);
  pinMode(buzPin, OUTPUT);
  Serial.begin(9600);
}

void loop() {
  int s = digitalRead(irPin);
  if (s == LOW && lastState == HIGH) {
    visitors++;
    chime();
    Serial.print("Visitor #");
Serial.println(visitors);
  }
  lastState = s;
  delay(50);
}
```

```
Message (Enter to send message to 'Arduino Uno' on 'COM3')

Visitor #1
Visitor #2
Visitor #3
Visitor #4
Visitor #5
Visitor #6
Visitor #7
Visitor #8
Visitor #9
Visitor #10
Visitor #11
Visitor #12
Visitor #13
Visitor #14
Visitor #15
Visitor #16
Visitor #17
Visitor #18
Visitor #19
```

How the Code Works

The chime() function uses four sequential digitalWrite and delay calls to create a two-beep pattern. Calling a function like this keeps loop() clean and readable. Edge detection counts each beam break as one visitor. The counter grows indefinitely until the Arduino is reset. In a real shop installation you would also add a second sensor to detect exits, subtracting from the count when someone leaves.

Real-World Applications

- Shop entry counters
- Museum visitor tracking
- Crowd management
- Event attendance logging
- Library entry systems

Experiment 98 | Smart Environment Monitor

Sensor: DHT11 + LDR + Sound Sensor + RGB LED

Difficulty: ★★★ Pro

Objective: Monitor temperature, humidity, light, and noise. Use RGB LED to show overall environment status.

How It Works

A smart environment monitor scores the environment by counting how many parameters are outside their ideal range. Zero issues = optimal (green). One issue = warning (yellow). Two or more issues = poor conditions (red). This scoring approach is more informative than a single threshold because it captures the overall quality of the environment, not just one factor.

Concepts Learned

- Multi-parameter monitoring
- Weighted environment score
- Status LED from multiple inputs
- IoT data aggregation

Components Required

Component	Qty
Arduino Uno	1
DHT11 Sensor	1
Photo-Resistor Module	1
Sound Sensor	1
RGB LED Module	1
Jumper Wires	8

Wiring

Component	Arduino Pin
DHT11 S	D2
LDR S	A0
Sound A0	A1
RGB R	D9
RGB G	D10
RGB B	D11

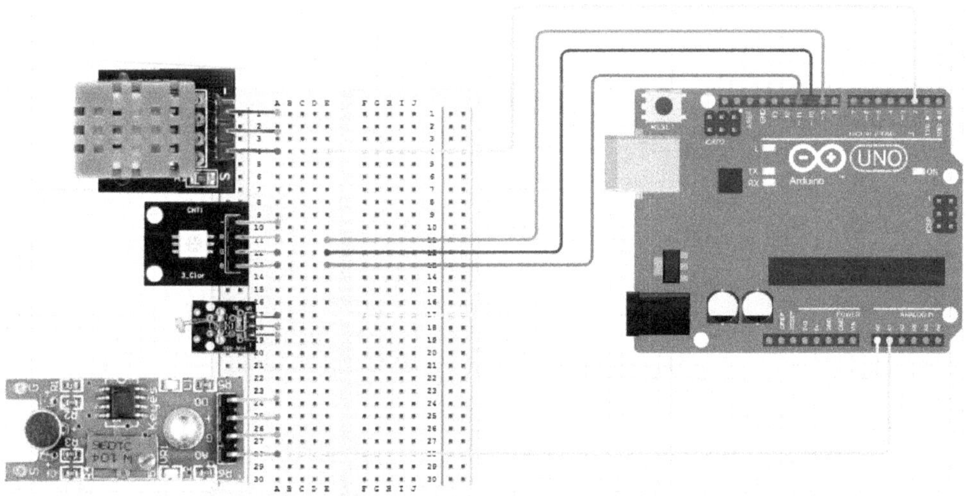

Arduino Code & Serial Monitor Output

```
#include <DHT.h>
DHT dht(2, DHT11);
const int ldrPin=A0, sndPin=A1;
const int rPin=9, gPin=10, bPin=11;

void setup() { dht.begin();
Serial.begin(9600); }

void loop() {
  float t = dht.readTemperature();
  float h = dht.readHumidity();
  int light = analogRead(ldrPin);
  int noise = analogRead(sndPin);
  int issues = 0;
  if (t > 30 || t < 15) issues++;
  if (h > 70 || h < 25)  issues++;
  if (light < 200)        issues++;
  if (noise > 400)        issues++;

Serial.print("T:");Serial.print(t);Serial.
print(" H:");Serial.print(h);
  Serial.print("
L:");Serial.print(light);Serial.print("
N:");Serial.println(noise);
  if (issues == 0) { analogWrite(rPin,0);
analogWrite(gPin,255);
analogWrite(bPin,0);
Serial.println("OPTIMAL"); }
  else if (issues == 1) {
analogWrite(rPin,255);
analogWrite(gPin,200);
analogWrite(bPin,0);
Serial.println("WARNING"); }
  else { analogWrite(rPin,255);
analogWrite(gPin,0); analogWrite(bPin,0);
Serial.println("POOR"); }
  delay(3000);
}
```

Message (Enter to send message to 'Arduino Uno' on 'COM3')

```
T:24.10 H:52.00 L:623 N:212
OPTIMAL
T:31.40 H:65.00 L:540 N:198
WARNING
T:32.70 H:75.00 L:480 N:305
WARNING
T:33.10 H:80.00 L:310 N:256
POOR
T:14.80 H:40.00 L:180 N:150
POOR
T:22.30 H:20.00 L:410 N:180
WARNING
```

How the Code Works

Each if statement checks one parameter and increments issues if it is out of range. After checking all four sensors, the total issues score drives the LED colour and status label. This additive scoring pattern scales well - add a fifth sensor (CO2, UV, etc.) by adding another if block and the rest of the logic works unchanged.

Real-World Applications

- Smart building management
- Office comfort systems
- Healthcare facility monitoring
- School classroom sensors
- IoT environmental dashboards

Experiment 99 | Home Automation Control Panel

Sensor: Joystick + Button + IR Remote + Relay + RGB LED

Difficulty: ★★★ Pro

Objective: Build a control panel that uses button, joystick, and IR remote to control multiple outputs.

How It Works

A control panel integrates multiple input methods - button, joystick click, and IR remote - each controlling a different output. The button toggles a relay (device power), the joystick click cycles LED colours (ambiance), and the IR remote's OK button turns everything off (all-off command). This separation of input responsibilities to specific outputs is how real control panels are designed.

Concepts Learned

- Multi-input control system
- Priority-based input handling
- Relay and LED outputs
- Home automation prototype

Components Required

Component	Qty
Arduino Uno	1
Button Module	1
Joystick Module	1
IR Receiver Module	1
Relay Module	1
RGB LED Module	1
Jumper Wires	10

Wiring

Component	Arduino Pin
`Button S`	`D4`
`Joystick SW`	`D5`
`IR Receiver S`	`D2`
`Relay S`	`D8`
`RGB R`	`D9`
`RGB G`	`D10`
`RGB B`	`D11`

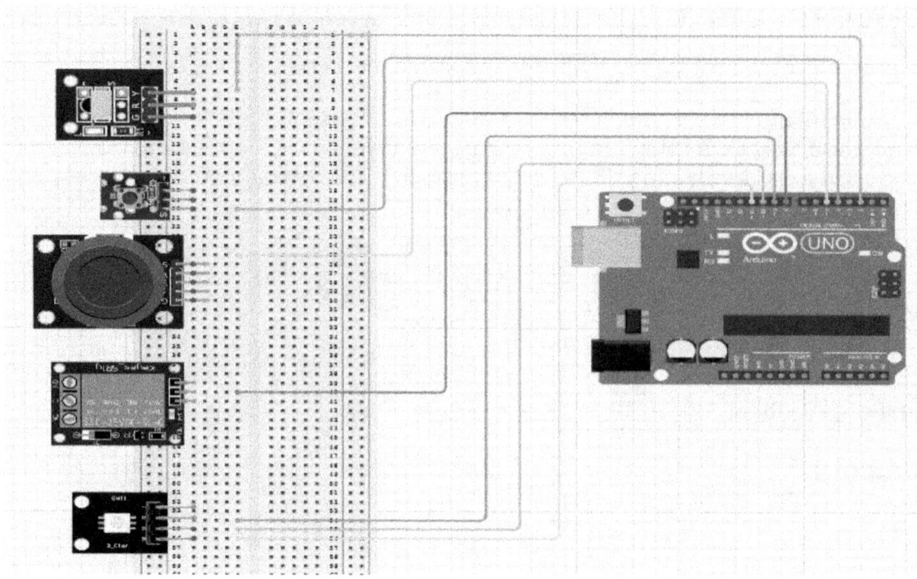

Arduino Code & Serial Monitor Output

```
#include <IRremote.h>
IRrecv irrecv(2);
decode_results irRes;
const int btnPin=4, jswPin=5, relayPin=8;
const int rPin=9, gPin=10, bPin=11;
bool relayState=false;
int  colorMode=0;

void setRGB(int r,int g,int
b){analogWrite(rPin,r);analogWrite(gPin,g)
;analogWrite(bPin,b);}

void setup() {
  pinMode(btnPin,INPUT_PULLUP);
pinMode(jswPin,INPUT_PULLUP);
  pinMode(relayPin,OUTPUT);
irrecv.enableIRIn(); Serial.begin(9600);
}

void loop() {
  // Button toggles relay
  if (digitalRead(btnPin)==LOW) {
    relayState=!relayState;
digitalWrite(relayPin,relayState);
    Serial.println(relayState?"Relay
ON":"Relay OFF"); delay(300);
  }
  // Joystick click cycles colour
  if (digitalRead(jswPin)==LOW) {
    colorMode=(colorMode+1)%3;
    if(colorMode==0) setRGB(255,0,0);
    if(colorMode==1) setRGB(0,255,0);
    if(colorMode==2) setRGB(0,0,255);
    delay(300);
  }
  // IR remote all-off
```

Message (Enter to send message to 'Arduino Uno' on 'COM3')

```
Relay ON
Relay OFF
Relay ON
Relay OFF
Relay ON
Relay OFF
Relay ON
Relay OFF
Relay ON
ALL OFF
Relay ON
Relay OFF
Relay ON
```

```
    if (irrecv.decode(&irRes)) {
      if(irRes.value==0xFF02FD){
  setRGB(0,0,0); digitalWrite(relayPin,LOW);
  Serial.println("ALL OFF"); }
      irrecv.resume();
    }
  }
```

How the Code Works

Each input is checked independently in sequence within loop(). The button block toggles relayState. The joystick click block cycles colorMode through 3 colours. The IR remote block checks for the OK code and runs an all-off command. Because each section only runs when its specific trigger fires, all three work simultaneously without interfering. This independent handling pattern is the foundation of multi-input control systems.

Real-World Applications

- Home automation hubs
- Smart room control panels
- Office device control
- Hotel room automation
- Educational automation demo

Experiment 100 | Smart Home Status Panel

Sensor: DHT11 + LDR + Reed Switch + Sound Sensor

Difficulty: ★★★ Pro

Objective: Display a complete smart home status report covering temperature, humidity, light level, door status, and noise level.

How It Works

The smart home status panel collects data from four sensors spanning the key parameters of a comfortable, secure home: temperature, humidity, door security, light level, and noise. All readings are formatted into a visual table in the Serial Monitor with borders and labels. This is the closest thing to a real smart home dashboard this kit can produce.

Concepts Learned

- Complete home monitoring
- Data from 4+ sensors
- Status panel formatting
- Decision-based status messages

Components Required

Component	Qty
Arduino Uno	1
DHT11 Sensor	1
Photo-Resistor Module	1
Reed Switch Module	1
Sound Sensor	1
Jumper Wires	8

Wiring

Component	Arduino Pin
DHT11 S	D2
Reed S	D3
LDR S	A0
Sound A0	A1

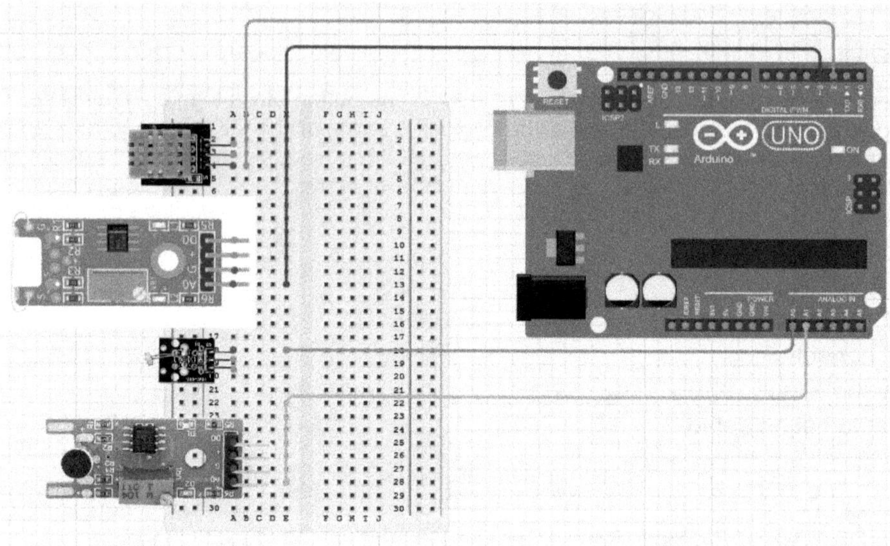

Arduino Code & Serial Monitor Output

```
#include <DHT.h>
DHT dht(2, DHT11);
const int reedPin=3, ldrPin=A0, sndPin=A1;

void setup() {
  dht.begin();
  pinMode(reedPin, INPUT_PULLUP);
  Serial.begin(9600);
}

void loop() {
  float t = dht.readTemperature();
  float h = dht.readHumidity();
  bool  doorOpen = (digitalRead(reedPin)
== HIGH);
  int   light    = analogRead(ldrPin);
  int   noise    = analogRead(sndPin);
  Serial.println("+====== SMART HOME
STATUS ======+");
  Serial.print("| Temperature  : ");
Serial.print(t);       Serial.println("
C");
  Serial.print("| Humidity     : ");
Serial.print(h);       Serial.println("
%");
  Serial.print("| Door         : ");
Serial.println(doorOpen ? "OPEN" :
"Closed");
```

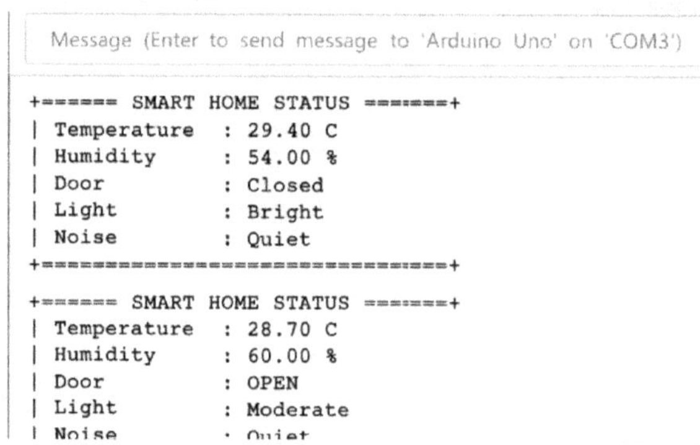

```
Message (Enter to send message to 'Arduino Uno' on 'COM3')

+====== SMART HOME STATUS =======+
| Temperature   : 29.40 C
| Humidity      : 54.00 %
| Door          : Closed
| Light         : Bright
| Noise         : Quiet
+================================+
+====== SMART HOME STATUS =======+
| Temperature   : 28.70 C
| Humidity      : 60.00 %
| Door          : OPEN
| Light         : Moderate
| Noise         : Quiet
```

```
  Serial.print("| Light        : ");
Serial.println(light>600?"Bright":light>30
0?"Moderate":"Dark");
  Serial.print("| Noise        : ");
Serial.println(noise>400?"LOUD":"Quiet");

Serial.println("+========================
=======+");
  delay(5000);
}
```

How the Code Works

Each sensor is read and stored in a named variable. Door state from the reed switch is a boolean. Light is converted from a number to a descriptive String using nested ternary operators - light>600?'Bright':light>300?'Moderate':'Dark'. Noise is a simple threshold comparison. The formatted output uses + for string concatenation, building each display line from labels and values. The 5-second delay between updates keeps the display readable.

Real-World Applications

- Smart home dashboards
- Building management systems
- Security status displays
- Energy management panels
- Rental property monitoring

Experiment 101 | Sensor Monitoring Station

Sensor: All 37 Sensors (Mega Project)

Difficulty: ★★★ Pro

Objective: Build the ultimate sensor monitoring station reading from all major sensor categories simultaneously and printing a complete status report.

How It Works

The monitoring station brings together the major sensor categories from the entire kit into one unified system: environmental (temperature, humidity), optical (light), acoustic (sound), security (reed switch, shock), safety (flame), and user input (button). A simple scoring system determines the overall status, and the RGB LED shows it at a glance while the buzzer responds to emergencies.

Concepts Learned

- System architecture
- Library management
- Multi-sensor reading
- Complete IoT data aggregation
- Structured Serial output

Components Required

Component	Qty
Arduino Uno	1
DHT11 Sensor	1
Photo-Resistor Module	1
KY-038 Sound Sensor	1
Flame Sensor Module	1

Component	Qty
Reed Switch Module	1
Shock Switch Module	1
Button Module	1
Active Buzzer Module	1
RGB LED Module	1
Jumper Wires	15

Wiring

Component	Arduino Pin
DHT11 S	D2
Reed S	D3
Button S	D4
Flame D0	D5
Shock S	D6
Buzzer S	D8
RGB R	D9
RGB G	D10
RGB B	D11
LDR S	A0
Sound A0	A1

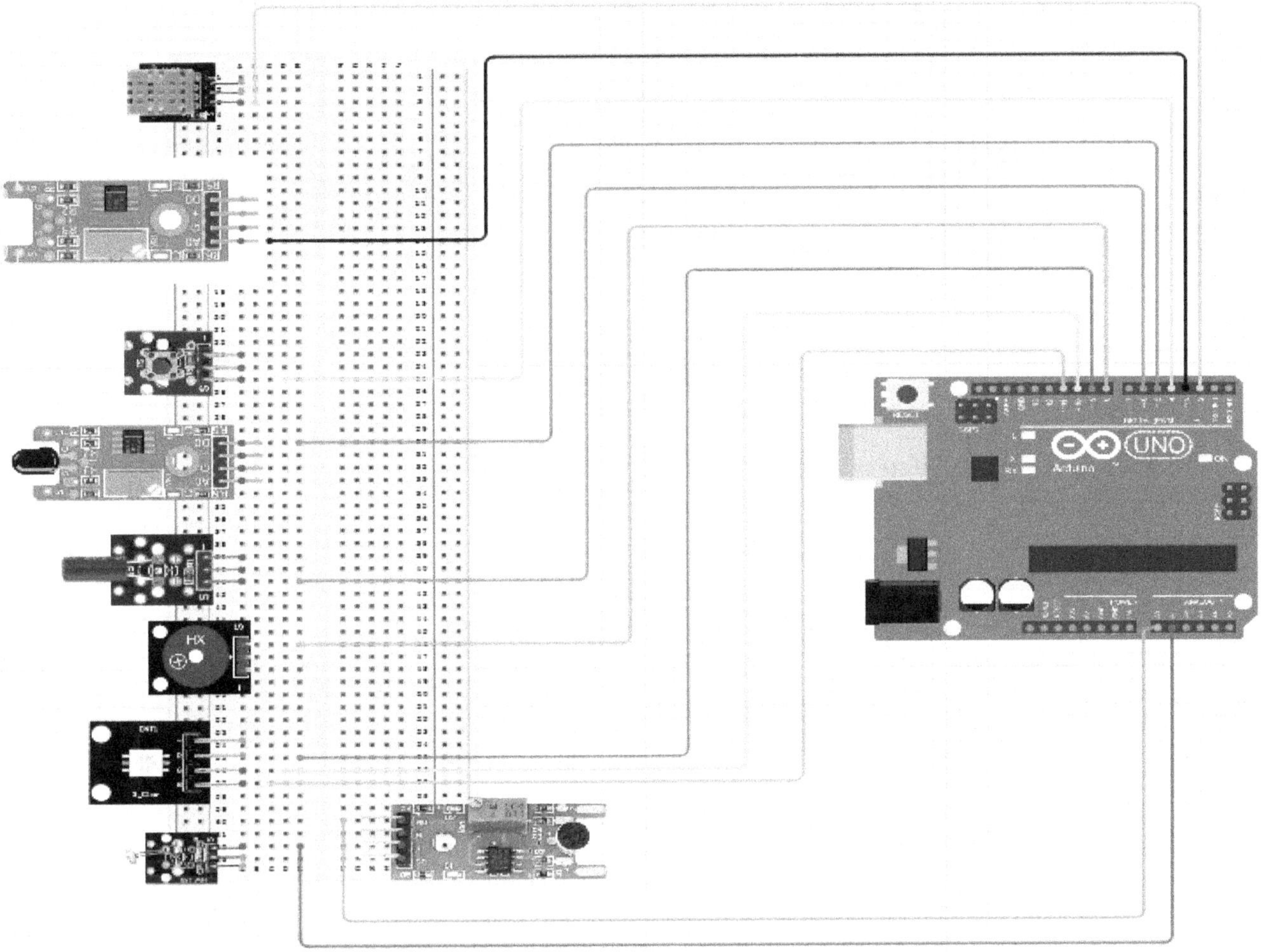

Arduino Code & Serial Monitor Output

```
#include <DHT.h>
DHT dht(2, DHT11);
const int reedPin=3, btnPin=4, flamePin=5,
shockPin=6;
const int buzPin=8, rPin=9, gPin=10,
bPin=11;
const int ldrPin=A0, sndPin=A1;

void setup() {
  dht.begin();
  pinMode(reedPin,INPUT_PULLUP);
pinMode(btnPin,INPUT_PULLUP);
  pinMode(flamePin,INPUT);
pinMode(shockPin,INPUT_PULLUP);
  pinMode(buzPin,OUTPUT);
  Serial.begin(9600);
  Serial.println("SENSOR MONITORING
STATION READY");
}

void loop() {
  float t    = dht.readTemperature();
```

Message (Enter to send message to 'Arduino Uno' on 'COM3')

```
SENSOR MONITORING STATION READY

+======= MONITORING STATION ========+
| Temp       :  28.40 C
| Humidity   :  56.00 %
| Light      :  520
| Sound      :  210
| Door       :  Closed
| Button     :  Released
| Flame      :  None
| Vibration  :  None
| Status     :  NORMAL
+===================================+

+======= MONITORING STATION ========+
| Temp       :  29.80 C
| Humidity   :  63.00 %
| Light      :  150
| Sound      :  430
| Door       :  OPEN
| Button     :  PRESSED
| Flame      :  None
| Vibration  :  None
| Status     :  NORMAL
+===================================+
```

```
  float h    = dht.readHumidity();
  int   light = analogRead(ldrPin);
  int   sound = analogRead(sndPin);
  bool  door  = (digitalRead(reedPin) ==
HIGH);
  bool  btn   = (digitalRead(btnPin)  ==
LOW);
  bool  flame = (digitalRead(flamePin)==
LOW);
  bool  shock = (digitalRead(shockPin)==
LOW);
  // Emergency outputs
  bool emergency = flame || (t > 40);
  digitalWrite(buzPin, emergency ? HIGH :
LOW);
  if (emergency) { analogWrite(rPin,255);
analogWrite(gPin,0); analogWrite(bPin,0);
}
  else if (door) { analogWrite(rPin,255);
analogWrite(gPin,100);
analogWrite(bPin,0); }
  else           { analogWrite(rPin,0);
analogWrite(gPin,255);
analogWrite(bPin,0); }
  Serial.println("+======= MONITORING
STATION ========+");
  Serial.print("| Temp      : ");
Serial.print(t);     Serial.println(" C");
  Serial.print("| Humidity  : ");
Serial.print(h);     Serial.println(" %");
  Serial.print("| Light     : ");
Serial.println(light);
  Serial.print("| Sound     : ");
Serial.println(sound);
  Serial.print("| Door      : ");
Serial.println(door  ? "OPEN"     :
"Closed");
  Serial.print("| Button    : ");
Serial.println(btn   ? "PRESSED"  :
"Released");
  Serial.print("| Flame     : ");
Serial.println(flame ? "DETECTED" :
"None");
  Serial.print("| Vibration : ");
Serial.println(shock ? "DETECTED" :
"None");
  Serial.print("| Status    : ");
Serial.println(emergency ? "EMERGENCY!" :
"NORMAL");

Serial.println("+=========================
==========+");
  delay(3000);
}
```

How the Code Works

Each sensor is read into a clearly named boolean or numeric variable. The emergency condition combines the two most critical triggers: flame OR extremely high temperature (>40°C). Emergency status drives both the buzzer and LED red. A door open condition shows amber (red+orange mix). All other normal conditions show green. The formatted report at the end prints every variable with a clear label. This is the complete practical application of everything learned in the book.

Real-World Applications

- Full IoT monitoring nodes
- Smart home hubs
- Industrial sensor arrays
- Environmental research stations
- Arduino education kits

Glossary

Key terms and concepts used throughout this book.

`Analog`	A signal that varies continuously between values, like a dimmer switch. Arduino analog pins read 0–1023.
`analogRead()`	Arduino function that reads a voltage from an analog pin and returns a number from 0 to 1023.
`analogWrite()`	Arduino function that outputs a PWM signal to simulate a voltage between 0V and 5V.
`Baud Rate`	The speed of serial communication, measured in bits per second. Most experiments use 9600 baud.
`Boolean`	A variable that holds only two values: true or false.
`Breadboard`	A plastic board with holes for inserting components, used to build circuits without soldering.
`Capacitance`	The ability of an object to store electrical charge. Touch sensors detect your finger's natural capacitance.
`Debounce`	A short delay added after a button press to prevent a single physical press from being read multiple times.
`delay()`	Arduino function that pauses the program for a specified number of milliseconds.
`Digital`	A signal that is either ON (HIGH, 5V) or OFF (LOW, 0V). Like a light switch.
`digitalRead()`	Arduino function that reads a digital pin and returns HIGH or LOW.
`digitalWrite()`	Arduino function that sets a digital pin to HIGH (5V) or LOW (0V).
`Edge Detection`	Code that detects the exact moment a signal changes state, rather than its current state.
`float`	A variable type that stores decimal numbers, such as 23.5 or 0.75.
`GND`	Ground - the 0V reference point in a circuit. All sensors need a GND connection.
`Hall Effect`	A phenomenon where a magnetic field creates a voltage across a conductor. Used in Hall sensors.
`HIGH`	A digital signal at 5V - the ON state.
`if / else`	A conditional statement that runs different code depending on whether a condition is true or false.
`INPUT`	A pinMode setting that configures a pin to receive signals from a sensor.
`INPUT_PULLUP`	A pinMode setting that enables an internal resistor to keep a pin stable at HIGH when nothing is connected.
`int`	A variable type that stores whole numbers, such as 42 or -7.

`Interrupt`	A mechanism that immediately pauses the main code to run a specific function when a pin changes state.
`IR (Infrared)`	Invisible light just beyond red in the spectrum. Used by remote controls and proximity sensors.
`KDP`	Kindle Direct Publishing - Amazon's self-publishing platform for print and digital books.
`Library`	Extra software you install in the Arduino IDE to add support for specific sensors or features.
`loop()`	The main Arduino function that runs repeatedly, forever, after setup() completes.
`LOW`	A digital signal at 0V - the OFF state.
`map()`	Arduino function that proportionally converts a number from one range to another.
`millis()`	Arduino function that returns the number of milliseconds since the board was powered on.
`Modulo (%)`	A mathematical operator that returns the remainder after division. Used for cycling and batch counting.
`OneWire`	A communication protocol that sends data over a single wire. Used by the DS18B20 sensor.
`OUTPUT`	A pinMode setting that configures a pin to send signals to a component like an LED or buzzer.
`pinMode()`	Arduino function that sets a pin as either INPUT or OUTPUT.
`PWM`	Pulse Width Modulation - rapidly switching a pin on and off to simulate a voltage between 0V and 5V.
`Relay`	An electrically controlled switch that allows a low-voltage Arduino signal to switch a high-voltage device.
`Resistor`	An electronic component that limits electrical current. The DS18B20 needs a 4.7kΩ pull-up resistor.
`Serial Monitor`	A window in the Arduino IDE that displays text messages sent from the Arduino board.
`Serial.begin()`	Opens serial communication between Arduino and your computer at a specified baud rate.
`Serial.print()`	Sends text or a number to the Serial Monitor without adding a new line.
`Serial.println()`	Sends text or a number to the Serial Monitor followed by a new line.
`setup()`	The Arduino function that runs once at startup. Used for initialising pins and sensors.
`threshold`	A value used as a boundary - readings above or below trigger a different response.
`tone()`	Arduino function that generates a sound frequency on a passive buzzer pin.
`unsigned long`	A variable type for storing large positive numbers, used with millis() for timing.
`Variable`	A named storage location in code that holds a value which can change during the program.
`VCC / 5V`	The positive power supply pin on the Arduino - provides 5 volts to power sensors.
`void`	Indicates a function that does not return a value. setup() and loop() are both void functions.
`volatile`	A keyword that tells the compiler a variable can be changed by an interrupt function.

What's Next?

Congratulations on completing the Arduino Experiments! You have gone from reading a button state to building a multi-sensor smart home monitoring station. That is a genuine achievement.

Here are some ideas for where to go next:

> **Add a display** - Connect an I2C LCD screen (16x2) or OLED display to show sensor readings without needing a computer.
>
> **Go wireless** - Add a Bluetooth module (HC-05) or Wi-Fi module (ESP8266) to send sensor data to your phone.

Log your data - Connect an SD card module to save readings to a file - real data logging.
Build a robot - Combine the obstacle, tracking, and motor driver modules to build a fully autonomous robot.
Try ESP32 - Upgrade to an ESP32 board - it has built-in Wi-Fi, Bluetooth, and more processing power.

About This Book

This book was written specifically for the popular 37 sensor Arduino kit. Every experiment was designed to work out of the box with the components included in the kit. No additional purchases are required beyond the kit itself and an Arduino Uno board.

Enjoyed this book?

Please leave a review on Amazon. Reviews help other beginners discover the book and make a real difference for independent authors. Even a few sentences is greatly appreciated.

Thank you for reading.

Arduino Experiments - Beginner to Pro
First Edition

For enquiries or feedback, contact the author's parents via the publisher's website.

www.ingramcontent.com/pod-product-compliance
Lightning Source LLC
LaVergne TN
LVHW060037210926
848481LV00013B/3885